Moral Soundings

Moral Soundings

Readings on the Crisis of Values in Contemporary Life

Edited by
Dwight Furrow

ROWMAN & LITTLEFIELD PUBLISHERS, INC.
Lanham • Boulder • New York • Toronto • Oxford

ROWMAN & LITTLEFIELD PUBLISHERS, INC.

Published in the United States of America
by Rowman & Littlefield Publishers, Inc.
A wholly owned subsidiary of The Rowman & Littlefield Publishing Group, Inc.
4501 Forbes Boulevard, Suite 200, Lanham, Maryland 20706
www.rowmanlittlefield.com

PO Box 317
Oxford
OX2 9RU, UK

British Library Cataloguing in Publication Information Available

Library of Congress Cataloging-in-Publication Data

Moral surroundings : readings on the crisis of values in contemporary
life / Dwight Furrow.
    p. cm.
  Includes bibliographical references and index.
  ISBN 0-7425-3369-7 (hardcover : alk. paper) — ISBN 0-7425-3370-0
(pbk. : alk. paper)
  1. Ethics. I. Furrow, Dwight.
BJ1012.M63525 2004
170—dc22

2003024596

Printed in the United States of America

∞™ The paper used in this publication meets the minimum requirements of
American National Standard for Information Sciences—Permanence of Paper
for Printed Library Materials, ANSI/NISO Z39.48-1992.

Acknowledgments

I would like to thank Michael Kuttnauer (San Diego Mesa College) and George Harris (College of William and Mary) who read and commented on portions of this manuscript, and Nina Rosenstand (San Diego Mesa College) for her conversation and encouragement. As always, I am indebted to my wife, Lynn, for her unflagging support and helpful comments on the manuscript.

Contents

Preface

The state of our moral health is a topic of constant public discussion and an issue that deeply divides Americans. Whether one celebrates our liberation from the repressive social norms of the past or laments the loss of the old moral certainties, the question of our moral trajectory percolates beneath the surface of most of our social and political controversies. However, in college textbooks, although contemporary moral issues are discussed as exemplifications of theory in a variety of disciplines, there is little discussion of the underlying conceptual framework that drives this public debate on moral values, which often diverges from academic and disciplinary concerns.

The purpose of this book is threefold. First, I want to show that there is a common denominator to many of our current disagreements. That common denominator is a disagreement over the meaning and value of personal autonomy. Second, I want to help the reader think through the urgent issues that confront contemporary society by highlighting various dimensions of personal autonomy and the way in which disagreements about moral values implicate this important concept. Third, I want to contribute to resolving these disagreements by suggesting further developments in our idea of autonomy.

In order to accomplish these goals, I have chosen, for the most part, articles from public interest journals written by authors who are active participants in this public debate about values. The contributors are highly regarded experts in their academic fields who are proficient at writing for a general audience. Although one might complain that this kind of writing is polemical, often rhetorical, and ideologically biased, it is important for readers to grasp the ideas that are the source of these polemics if they are to understand current public controversies. Furthermore, because of their provenance, the essays are written in an accessible, engaging style that requires no background in a particular discipline on the part of the reader, and the personal quality of this writing lends intimacy and details of life experience to the presentation of the issues.

A book of this sort, of course, cannot replace theoretical texts that expose students to the standards, methods, and concepts used in the various disciplines concerned with questions of moral value. It is intended as a supplement that connects theory in philosophy, the humanities, and the social sciences to public debates and personal reflections on perhaps the central personal dilemma of our time—striking the proper balance between personal autonomy and other values.

Dwight Furrow
San Diego
October 2003

Introduction: What Crisis? Whose Values?

Do we look forward to a future of increasing wealth, security, and satisfaction or a future of uncertainty and disenchantment in a world profaned by humanity's darkest desires? Even a casual observer of our conflicted culture might be genuinely confused about the answer to this question. If we are fortune's favorite, it is because our wealth has increased exponentially over the last century. Although the poorest among us confront grinding poverty and few prospects, most Americans lead lives that even the most wealthy inhabitants of the late nineteenth century could not have imagined. Average Americans enjoy excellent health care, a nutritious and varied diet, spacious and comfortable living accommodations, as much education as one has time for, the opportunity to travel, nonstop entertainment, and a market system that eventually makes available the latest technological inventions at reasonable prices. Women and people of color, although still fighting discrimination, have nevertheless made significant strides in the battle for equality. Democracy and freedom continue to spread, though slowly and unevenly, and American cultural products dominate the world, setting the agenda in almost all areas of human endeavor.

Of course, all is not well with the world. The threat of war, mayhem, and economic uncertainty mar even the most optimistic visions of the near future. Globalization and unregulated markets have produced inequalities and suffering as they uproot traditional ways of life throughout the world; and our wealth producing machine may have unleashed forces that will destroy our environment if left unchecked. However, according to this rosy scenario, greater prosperity, increasingly refined technology, and the indefatigable American spirit can solve these problems. If the past is prelude to the future, markets will adapt, friends of freedom will unite, and prosperity and freedom will strengthen despite the obstacles.

However, there is another side to the story as troubling as the rosy picture is comforting. The terrorist attacks on September 11, 2001, exposed our vulnerability to global instability, perhaps permanently undermining Americans' sunny optimism and self-confidence. The demands of increased security force us to reevaluate the nature and importance of civil liberties and freedoms we had previously taken for granted, and our military response has provoked widespread opposition to U.S. global dominance. Furthermore, the attacks and their aftermath have brought home the hard truth that millions of people throughout the world question our values and way of life, resisting the modernization processes and liberties, which are often assumed to be the markers of human progress. In light of these events, although few will endorse the wholesale rejection of Western liberal democracy, many will advocate a reevaluation of its elements including our foreign policy, our moral responsibilities toward the rest of the world, the sovereignty of ethnic and religious minorities, consumerism, and the ethics of warfare.

Yet, even before September 11, according to a wide range of social indicators, our sense of meaning and purpose was crumbling as we failed at ordinary moral tasks such as keeping families together or trusting our neighbors. If our future is bleak, it is because nearly half of our marriages end in divorce and over 30 percent of newborn children are born to unmarried mothers.[1] According to many social psychologists, these children of broken families will, more likely than not, lack the skills and character required to lead flourishing lives. If our future is bleak, it is because 70 percent of high school students admit to cheating on an exam and 47 percent admit to stealing from a store in the previous year, according to a 1998 survey by the Josephson Institute for Ethics.[2] Although crime rates have dropped from the stunningly high rates of a decade ago, prison populations have grown sixfold since 1960, and we remain one of the most violent societies on earth. According to the Satcher Report, domestic violence, rape, and violence against homosexuals show substantial increases.[3]

Young, unformed minds incapable of sorting reality from fantasy consume images of corruption, degradation, and mayhem that an unfettered media pour into our homes. Psychologists report that cases of depression have increased tenfold over the last half-century, suicide rates among teenagers continue to soar, while the percentage of people who report being happy and satisfied with their lives has declined.[4] Some sociologists lament weakening social connections based on recent surveys that apparently show we are increasingly less likely to join civic associations, entertain friends, or feel we can trust others.[5] In the United States, pockets of poverty and an increasing gap between the wealthy and the destitute that persists despite economic growth exacerbate these social ills, while the issues of abortion and racism continue to plague us from both sides of a yawning political divide dashing facile hopes for social peace. Throughout the world, massive poverty, social dislocation, and deplorable health care embarrass a civilization that values liberty and equality.

Which vision of our future is correct? Is civilization withering or are these troubling social pathologies and affronts to our way of life mere superficial wounds that will soon succumb to our technical and productive genius? Do we need moral rearmament? Will a fairer, more equitable distribution of wealth resolve these problems, or can we depend on our productivity, technology, and creativity to sustain a sense of moral purpose? Increasingly, the state of our moral health worries and divides Americans. In a yearly Gallup poll, respondents consistently list a decline in morality as the second most important issue facing this country today.

To make matters worse, new technologies raise troubling moral questions that heighten our anxiety, for they threaten to permanently change the way we think about our relationships and ourselves. Computer and network technologies already make it possible to work, play, and be educated in the isolation of our homes. How do we develop trust and a sense of community when new technologies diminish the face-to-face interactions that sustain trust and communal norms? As we develop new modes of surveillance that track our habits, preferences, and activities, the privacy that is central to our sense of individuality and freedom is under assault. In a society where information is the most valuable commodity, how far should we go to protect ourselves from unwanted intrusions on our private space? Gene therapy promises to push back the frontiers of aging and mortality; but how will our understanding of what has value and significance be changed when death is a less constant, insidious companion? Proponents of genetic engineering promise us the ability to choose the characteristics of our offspring, but do parents have the right to exercise such control over their offspring without their consent? Do we have the knowledge and capacity for judgment that such awesome choices require? Lurking in the background of our concern for the future is the possibility that technology may have already unleashed destructive processes that will degrade our environment for centuries.

Because the impact of these technologies is likely to permanently transform what it means to be human, we bear an enormous burden of responsibility to make good choices. Yet, we may have to do so without guidance from traditional institutions and ideals. The religious traditions and moral principles that frame our judgments about value were formed and have been tested under vastly different historical conditions when individuals had fewer choices, change occurred more slowly, and life presented fewer ambiguities. Our traditional moral sources may or may not be up to the task of providing guidance in a world so significantly transformed.

Thus, it is no wonder that Americans worry about morality. We are most adept at producing wealth and technological marvels, but less successful at providing a moral framework that exists comfortably with our prosperity, rapid innovation, and individual freedoms. Happiness appears as elusive as ever. Of course, we are unlikely to give up our pursuit of wealth and technology and should not do so, since they have significantly reduced human suffering. Only the blinkered or insensitive wish a return to the past when most human beings lived with crushing poverty, rampant disease, and political tyranny. Widely distributed material wealth and individual liberty are good things. However, as the social pathologies listed above indicate, material wealth and freedom may not be enough to guarantee happiness or a secure, civilized future.

Have the remarkable social and economic changes of the past one hundred years resulted in what the historian Gertrude Himmelfarb has called the "de-moralization of society?" If we live in a spiritual and moral vacuum, what thoughts and activities should fill it? What changes should we make in the way we see our values and ourselves that will enable wealth and freedom to produce happiness? Or are these worries about moral decline exaggerated by nostalgic yearnings for a past no longer available or relevant to the aspirations of contemporary citizens?

The answers to these questions are unlikely to be simple or easy to discover. If our experiment in liberal democracy has taught us anything, it is that left to their own devices human beings will develop life plans that diverge in a variety of incompatible directions. From traditional moralists to new-age libertines, from techno-geeks to neo-Luddites, from radical environmentalists to shopping mall mavens and everything in between, our culture is home to a seemingly infinite variety of conceptions of how to live— and thus an infinite variety of responses to our moral condition. The same facts that lead some people to claim that only a return to conservative religious practices and traditional values will stem the tide of corruption and degradation lead others to insist that contemporary society is the crucible in which new, more progressive, enlightened values are forming to replace the exhausted, oppressive norms of the past. How can we sort through the conflicting preferences and ideologies to gain some clarity regarding the condition of our culture?

Fortunately, many of these controversies tend to converge around a single concept, consideration of which can help us think through the complexities of these issues. Despite the diverse moral commitments of Americans, disagreements over the nature and importance of autonomy are fundamental to our domestic debates as well as to the clash between Western culture and its critics. For many Americans, their deepest desire is to be autonomous—to be in control of their own lives, to make their own decisions about what is right and wrong and what has value and what does not without excessive external influence or control. Yet, this extraordinary power in the hands of individuals is the source of our most salient fears as we worry about whether individuals will make good decisions when their actions affect others. Thus, in debates over the legal regulation of social norms in areas of reproductive choice, gay rights, marriage, gun control, smoking and health related regulations, the debate is in part about to what degree government institutions should regulate behavior that many think ought to be matters of personal decision. On distributive justice issues such as affirmative action, welfare, and tax policies, and on issues such as environmental regulation, privacy, and security concerns, the disagreement is often over to what degree private resources can be compelled to serve desirable social ends. In all cases, the disagreement in part rests on perceptions regarding how large the sphere of personal autonomy is and what the boundaries of that sphere should be.

Our form of life originated in the desire for autonomy. The Puritans chafing under the dictates of the Church of England, the colonists throwing tea into Boston harbor in protest over being taxed, the slaves risking life and limb to escape to the north via the underground railroad all felt this desire. Whether we seek political autonomy or personal autonomy, the idea that a substantial portion of our lives ought to be under our own collective or individual control is basic to our democratic ideals and individual freedoms. Both political autonomy and personal autonomy spring from the recognition that, as distinct individuals with distinct interests and points of view, in order to view life as valuable, each of us must live according to what we believe has value. If our lives are directed from outside us, according to beliefs we cannot endorse or conditions we cannot accept, our lives are thereby diminished.

The rub is that personal and political autonomy often pull in opposing directions. In Western culture, demands for greater personal autonomy have always accompanied the exercise of political autonomy in the form of democratic participation. But across the world today political autonomy is often advocated at the expense of personal autonomy—for instance, many Muslims demand political autonomy, insisting on the right to worship in an Islamic state free of the distractions from other political and religious actors, while brutally suppressing personal autonomy. How best to live in accordance with this ideal of self-direction is a question very much up for grabs in many parts of the world.

By contrast, in the United States, that issue has largely been decided in favor of personal autonomy—its steady growth is perhaps the dominant trend in our recent history. As the sociologist Alan Wolfe reports in his study of American's moral attitudes: "On the surface, America seems as conformist as ever. . . . But deep inside, Americans are exploring a new frontier. Though they still believe in God, uphold the family and love their country, they increasingly decide which God best suits their temperament; which family structure works for them; and whether their country's government is worthy of their trust."[6] On a variety of moral questions, such as what counts as happiness, and how and when to be honest, loyal, forgiving, and caring,

Americans tend to resist moral authorities and think of these issues as matters of personal decision. "The defining characteristic of the moral philosophy of the Americans can therefore be described as the principle of moral freedom. Moral freedom means that individuals should determine for themselves what it means to lead a good and virtuous life."[7]

Yet, many people argue that moral freedom is precisely the source of moral decline. Moral freedom is troubling to social critics who argue that if moral commitments and values are a matter of individual choice, then there are no standards for what we should choose except what each of us desires. If our individual desires are all that guide us, then morality no longer enables us to resist temptation, get rid of inappropriate desires, and cannot nudge us toward cooperating with others and serving the common good. In other words, if moral freedom has become our moral philosophy, the development of moral character is impossible. This is the source of our moral crisis. For these critics, morality requires some measure of authority—God's laws or the coercive power of the state, community, or tradition in order to reinforce moral norms.

Increasingly, most of our debates in society break down into two opposing camps, one side insisting on greater personal autonomy and moral freedom, the other insisting that some form of governmental, religious, or conventional authority is required to avoid social chaos and moral decline

Our interest in moral freedom arises from the more general interest in personal autonomy that is so deeply embedded in Western culture. The desire for personal control over the circumstances of life is the source of most of the impulses that drive contemporary society. The pursuit of wealth is not merely a product of wanton greed but an extension of our desire for independence and self-direction. Similarly, the impulse to create more and better technology is not merely indulgence for the lazy or a fascination with expensive toys, but an attempt to break down the limits to our control that nature, time, and space impose on us. The American experience has been an experiment because never before have ordinary men and women had so much freedom and so much power to control their own destiny and the destiny of Civilization.

Yet, the critics of autonomy and moral freedom have a point. Recently, we have been discovering that personal autonomy has a darker side. When we try to live in accordance with this ideal of autonomy, it often vanishes like a fickle friend in hard times. As we strive to control time by using it more efficiently, we become slaves to the clock and to the devices that help us save time. When we no longer require our neighbors to help sustain and protect us, we gain self-sufficiency and dispose of the burdens neighbors impose on us. As a result, we may be less likely to care deeply about them or trust them, and thus are less likely to be able to influence them, again suffering a loss of autonomy. We gain control by establishing networks of distant and dispersed acquaintances through improvements in transportation and communication, but at significant cost to relationships closer to home. We are free to reject traditional values and vastly increase the range of choices available to us, but this often leaves us with little guidance regarding how to live and diminished resources for self-directedness.

Wealth and technology extend autonomy by easing hardships and removing obstacles, but in the process may eliminate the adversity essential to developing moral character. The crucible of hard knocks forces us to acquire courage, honesty, compassion, and justice, traits that enhance our autonomy since we can govern our lives more effectively when equipped with the tools to overcome adversity. Ironically, as we gain control over the circumstances of our lives, we make self-control more difficult to achieve by eliminating the adversity that character development requires.

Autonomy is a dissolute seductress, lovely and exhilarating but in danger of consuming herself in her own excesses. The drive to control our circumstances when coupled with too many choices and the devaluing of traditional wisdom is an unstable mixture. It is not surprising that the social pathologies of fragmented families, malaise, and excessive criminal behavior arise in a wealthy, technologically advanced society.

Many Americans think there are limits to the value of autonomy and, as a solution to a perceived moral crisis, seek grounding in a moral authority more stable and enduring such as religion, communal traditions, or transcendent moral truths. Only the recognition of a greater power outside the control of contemporary human beings can keep our appetites in check, so they argue. But the world in which such grounding seemed secure is but a memory. We no longer live in organic communities held together by the sheer impossibility of living elsewhere; neither can we believe in something with unfettered conviction since challenge and disputation are constant companions. For better or ill, the array of choices available allows us to opt in or opt out of any association or system of belief and provides inducements for doing so as well. Consequently, the pursuit of autonomy may be the only attraction in town.

WHAT IS AUTONOMY?

If we are to understand the complex dilemmas that autonomy poses, and resolve these vexing moral issues that confront modern societies, we need to gain a clearer understanding of what precisely it means to have autonomy. If one is autonomous, does that really mean he must be able to do whatever he wants to do? "Autonomy" refers to the capacity of an individual to govern herself, to direct the course of her life, according to her own sense of what has value and significance. Two intuitions guide philosophical thinking on this issue. One intuition is that to be self-governing is to have control over one's urges, impulses, desires, etc. It is important to us that we are not guided by unwanted impulses or desires that are not compatible with who we really are or want to be, and so our actions must be deliberate and intended, at least most of the time. The second intuition is that to be self-governing is to be relatively free of external influences, so that one's actions reflect his own will and not the will of someone else.

But what does it mean to be free of external influence and to have desires that are truly one's own? We do not choose most of our desires—we just find ourselves with them. Furthermore, parents, friends, teachers, and a variety of experts have substantial influence over us, and often we simply accept their authority. Society establishes norms and legal constraints that we are obliged to follow, and the social environments in which we live shape us in a variety of subtle ways of which we may not be fully aware. As we learn more about the science of genetics, we discover that much of the explanation of human action must include a biological component as well. In what sense do we ever govern ourselves, given the external factors that influence us? The challenge for a theory of autonomy is to provide a precise answer to this question.

In general, there are two competing philosophical views on how we should understand this concept of autonomy. The first view, which I will call self-sufficiency, requires that an autonomous person establish her independence from the external factors that typically influence human beings. It is a bad thing to be subject to someone else's will. Thus, the judgment of others should never be decisive in determining what one does, and there should be as few humanly created impediments to our actions as possible. External authorities can influence us, but in the end, we must decide whether those influences are worthy or not.

Self-sufficiency is an exceedingly strong characterization of moral freedom. Self-sufficiency values a pattern of life that seeks to maximize personal control over events and circumstances. Because socialization processes are so powerful and pervasive, autonomous individuals must actively cultivate the competence to critically assess their commitments and revise their values when they judge them unworthy of allegiance. It follows from this that legal constraints on the actions of individuals should be as minimal as possible, and government power should require only those activities essential for maintaining a functioning society.

Critics of self-sufficiency argue that this ideal is neither achievable nor desirable. They argue that our identities are the product of influences that we do not choose and these identities involve value commitments and qualities of character that are often so deeply embedded in our psychologies and ways of life that they are not subject to our will. Moreover, genuine caring relationships can succeed only when we are sometimes willing to let the judgment of others determine our actions. Finally, some critics argue that we cannot avoid appeals to authority. Just as we depend on experts when we lack technical expertise, in the domain of morality we must accept the authority of legal regulations, community norms, or religious beliefs.

In light of these criticisms, theorists have developed an alternative account of autonomy, which I will call self-direction. A self-directed person leads life from the inside according to her own beliefs and desires. But on this view an autonomous person can be guided by moral authorities, anchor her identity in inherited social environments not of her own choosing, and sustain commitments that limit one's liberty as long as these external influences are constrained by the appropriate autonomy-conserving procedures.[8]

There is substantial disagreement among philosophers about what procedures are sufficient to preserve autonomy. In any case, self-direction is typically understood to require a psychology organized as follows. Our will is partly reflected in our immediate desires to do something—to have an ice cream, call a friend on the phone, apply to law school. However, these first-order desires to act are only part of the picture, because we often ask ourselves whether it would be good to act on these first order desires. Perhaps that ice cream would disrupt my diet, perhaps the friend I want to call has been spreading scurrilous rumors about me, perhaps law school is my parent's idea of a future, not mine. Thus, we have second order desires and values—a desire for a healthy life-style, a meaningful career, committed relationships—in light of which we evaluate our first order desires. A person is self-directed when she identifies with her desires—when her lower order desires are consistent with her higher order values and she reflects critically on her desires and values and approves of having them. Thus, it does not matter what our desires are, we are autonomous if we have thought about them and approve of them. An action is autonomous as long as it is the product of the agent's assessment of her situation rather than an unthinking, passive, or coerced response. It is this active assessment that enables the agent to "own" the action.

Self-direction embodies a practical standard that many people can achieve, because it does not require heroic acts of separation or critical assessment in order to become autonomous. A person who is deeply influenced by external factors—religion, parents, cultural norms, etc.—whose will is guided by the will of others, can be autonomous on this view if, upon critical reflection, she endorses those influences and the resulting system of values.

However, although many philosophers would grant that self-direction is a necessary condition for autonomy, some doubt that it is sufficient. The difficulty is that various forms of social conditioning often coerce or manipulate people into conforming to oppressive values and principles, and such manipulation may be severe enough to interfere with their capacity to critically evaluate their situation. For instance, a woman may continue in an abusive marriage because her upbringing has convinced her that it is appropriate for a woman to submit to her husband's absolute authority. She may lack understanding of the possibilities for woman so that even upon reflection she endorses her situation. Yet, implausibly, on the self-direction model such a person would be considered autonomous.

The problem is that factors that interfere with our autonomy can affect our deepest values and rational capacities as well as our impulses and urges. Thus, any account of autonomy that requires merely that our desires be compatible with our deeper values will not identify such a person as lacking autonomy, though intuitively she clearly is not autonomous.

Thus, there are problems with both conceptions of autonomy. Self-sufficiency sets the conditions for autonomy too high, requiring that one live a particular kind of uncommitted life to be autonomous. Self-direction sets the conditions for autonomy too low, requiring no specific content to autonomy but only a process of evaluation that is too friendly to external influence to establish the independence autonomy requires.

Finally, many thinkers argue that neither self-sufficiency nor self-direction can be fundamental values. The problem with both is that the standards of assessment we use to judge whether our actions and values are appropriate are purely subjective. They involve no appeal to something outside the self that can provide adequate guidance to individuals. Without a moral authority external to the individual to support and enforce a strong sense of duty, there is nothing to prevent our strongest impulses from overwhelming our values and principles. Although the weaker notion of autonomy, self-direction, permits the influence of external authority, it does not require it. Thus, autonomy, if it is our most basic value, is incompatible with morality according to autonomy's severest critics.

AUTONOMY AND THE CRISIS OF VALUES

This is the point at which these philosophical concerns join with the cultural debate concerning a crisis of values. Social critics who claim that our morality is eroding typically claim that we have allowed the pursuit of moral freedom (autonomy in the moral sphere) to go too far. These critics will deny that autonomy can be a basic value, or they will adopt a weak version of autonomy such as the self-direction model, which is compatible with the acceptance of moral authorities.

However, this position will be subject to the philosophical objections discussed above that the self-direction model is too weak to capture our intuitions about autonomy. Furthermore, if moral freedom is the moral philosophy of contemporary Americans, it is likely that contemporary Americans have in mind a more robust account of autonomy, one that denies the significance of moral authorities as Wolfe's research suggests. However, as I argued above, the difficulty with endorsing a stronger conception of autonomy, such as the self-sufficiency model, is that self-sufficiency may not be a coherent and livable conception of autonomy. If the self-sufficiency model is the one to which Americans aspire, critics of autonomy may have a point. Thus, the resolution of cultural debates on a variety of topics appears to depend on the development of a more coherent account of autonomy, a task to which I hope this book can contribute.

The American experiment pits the desire to make our own choices and control the circumstances of our lives against the potentially destructive forces unleashed by that very same desire. The pursuit of autonomy is invigorating and fecund. However, in addition to autonomy, we value deep and abiding relationships, moral commitments, and traditional forms of life that often conflict with autonomy. How we balance the gains against the losses will determine whether we flourish or not.

This balancing act will have not the clarity of dogma but the opacity of a work in progress. We lack clear answers to moral questions because we confront novelty and uniqueness at every turn, because reality stubbornly resists our attempts to control it, and because the passion to control one's own life can readily become an obsession to control others. Although, in response to this lack of clarity, many issue a call to arms and engage in political posturing exhorting us to lurch in one direction or another, the most important thing each of us can do is thoughtfully engage the circumstances of our own life. Genuine autonomy that enhances rather than diminishes the quality of experience is possible only when we understand the consequences of our actions and the forces that influence us.

The following essays take competing positions on a variety of central issues in contemporary debates about values. Few of the essays discuss autonomy directly, but each essay presupposes a conception of how we should resolve the tension between the passion for autonomy and the variety of other things we value. These assumptions about autonomy in part explain the disagreements between the various contributors to this volume. Thus, each chapter includes a section entitled "Interventions" that highlight and assess the conception of autonomy at work in the essays. In these sections, I develop arguments designed to advance our understanding of autonomy in hopes of indicating how our society might resolve some of these debates.

NOTES

1. Statistics are from David G. Myers, *The American Paradox: Spiritual Hunger in the Age of Plenty* (New Haven: Yale University Press, 2000), 68.

2. See 1998 Report Card on the Ethics of American Youth, Josephson Institute survey, www.josephsoninstitute.org?98Survey/98Survey.htm.

3. See A Surgeon General's Call to Action to Promote Sexual Health and Responsible Sexual Behavior, June 2001. The report can be accessed at www.surgeongeneral.gov/library/sexualhealth/.

4. Statistics on depression are from Martin Seligman, "Explanatory Style: Predicting Depression, Achievement, and Health," in *Brief Therapy Approaches to Treating Anxiety and Depression,* ed. Michael D. Yapko (New York: Brunner/Mazel, 1989). Data on happiness are from Richard Gene Niemi, John Mueller, and Tom W. Smith, *Trends in Public Opinion: A Compendium of Survey Data* (New York: Greenwood, 1989). Statistics on child suicide are from *Healthy People 2000 Review, 1998–1999,* report from the Center for Disease Control.

5. The decline in social connections is measured in Robert Putnam, *Bowling Alone: The Collapse and Revival of American Community* (New York: Simon and Schuster, 2000). For data on trust, see Myers, 180.

6. Alan Wolfe, "The Pursuit of Autonomy," *The New York Times*, May 7, 2000.

7. Alan Wolfe, *Moral Freedom: The Search for Virtue in a World of Choice* (New York: W. W. Norton and Company, 2001), 195.

8. These two philosophical views of autonomy represent simplified amalgamations of a variety of more complex theories of autonomy. Self-sufficiency is inspired by such theorists as Robert Paul Wolff, Jean Paul Sartre, and Will Kymlicka. Self-direction is inspired by the work of Harry Frankfurt, Gerald Dworkin, and John Christman. Neither self-sufficiency nor self-direction does justice to the nuances of the work of these theorists. See "Suggestions for Further Reading" for bibliographic information.

I

MORALS AND MONEY

Defenders of capitalism assert that, from a moral point of view, capitalism provides the best system of economic production and consumption. This defense centers on three claims: (1) the operations of a free market give people the quantity and quality of goods and services they want; (2) the institutions of private property protect our basic liberties and preserve the dignity of individual human beings by enabling citizens to make free and rational choices; and (3) the competition enabled by free markets encourages the development of good qualities of character required to function effectively in the market, such as the capacity for hard work, delayed gratification, the ability to anticipate the needs of others, honesty, etc. Free markets enable individuals to develop their own life plans, to choose what sort of work to do, how to spend their time and money, how to use their property, etc. Thus, at bottom, capitalism is valuable because it encourages autonomy, enabling individuals to be the authors of their own lives.

The worry that contemporary society faces a moral crisis is in part a concern that capitalism, as it functions today, does not measure up to these claims made in its defense. Critics of capitalism have long argued that the wealth and liberty that capitalism produces are unevenly distributed. Part 2's discussion of equality will take up this criticism. The present chapter focuses on the complaint that the choices that contemporary capitalism provides are not free and rational and the qualities of character it encourages are not virtuous.

Capitalism has proven to be remarkably efficient at producing goods the value of which is determined by how much people are willing to pay for them—automobiles, stylish clothing, entertainment, and other goods that stimulate our imaginations and make our lives easier. However, critics claim that less tangible goods, which cannot easily be assigned a price, are pushed to the side when market forces invade all aspects of our lives. Thus, in contemporary life, spiritual and moral values, self-sacrifice in the service of others, environmental protection, and other public goods have receded in importance. We may pay lip service to them but can rarely act on these values in a society where the incentives are overwhelmingly skewed toward market goods. Consequently, the qualities of character we develop to serve others— courage, honesty, kindness, etc.—atrophy as we increasingly become self-interested consumers.

This critique of capitalism invites a variety of questions. Are moral values becoming less important to us as a culture? If so, is capitalism the culprit or is some other explanation more plausible? Or do changes in our moral point of view signal not a decline, but a shift in the focus of our moral concern toward a materialist ethic more appropriate for contemporary life than traditional morality?

1

The Spirit of Capitalism 2000

David Bosworth

David Bosworth is a fiction writer, essayist, and Professor of English at University of Washington in Seattle. Bosworth condemns contemporary capitalism because it encourages immaturity—an unwillingness to allow basic facts about the human condition to circumscribe our actions. He argues that we must accept the reality of death, human weakness, and the fact we are dependent beings, and thus recognize the necessity of commitments to moral principles, civic responsibility, family, and religious traditions.

Each of us brings his favorite examples to the table when the subject of contemporary adult immaturity is raised. From the multitude of news items that by turns offend and amaze, I offer the following two as especially illustrative of our postmodern, postindustrial, indisputably American age.

The first, which captured the attention of nightly newscasts all across the nation, related the story of a white, middle-class, Midwest couple, an engineer and a homemaker, who decided they needed a winter vacation and so flew south to warmer climes, leaving their two pre-teenage children behind for nine full days, including Christmas, unattended.

When their daughters, ages four and nine, accidentally set off a smoke alarm in their suburban home, a neighbor notified the police who then arrested the parents when they finally deplaned from their Acapulco getaway. This so-called Home Alone case was especially troubling to the national conscience, I think, because it seemed to exhibit a purely hedonistic motivation

From David Bosworth, "The Spirit of Capitalism 2000" in *The Public Interest*, Winter 2000. Reprinted by permission from the Institute for American Values and the author.

for offensive behavior, absent any apparent pathological or political sub-strate, such as drug addiction or an attempt to manipulate welfare rules. It was even more troubling, perhaps, in that all the various ways of categoriz-ing the offending couple refuted our easiest, self-exculpatory presumptions about antisocial behavior: that the desertion of America's children is primar-ily a problem of single-parent families, or of men, or of a mostly black and urban underclass, or of a corrupt liberal cultural elite that has taken up resi-dence on the two coasts.

The second example is even stranger but no less troubling to our easy pre-sumptions about the origins of irresponsible behavior. Back in 1990, a termi-nally ill Californian was involved in an unusual legal suit. Credentialed in pre-cisely those ways we now soberly respect, this Silicon Valley computer consultant, with a doctorate in mathematics from the University of Chicago, wanted the court to permit doctors to fulfill his final wish, which was, grotesque as it seems, to have his head cut off before his disease actually killed him. His intention was not some bizarre form of euthanasia (Dr. Kevorkian meets "Chain Saw Massacre") but its opposite: He didn't want to die in peace so much as to live forever. The plan was to have himself instantly frozen "alive," in hopes of being revived when the advances of science might cure his disease. And because he believed his true self to reside in his brain (recall his profession), and because the private companies that offer cryonic deep-freeze charge far less for preserving a head than a whole human body ($35,000 ver-sus $100,000 at that time), he was requesting decapitation so that he could af-ford a procedure which he had come to believe might eventually save him.

The great naturalist Louis Agassiz is said to have commanded a graduate student to study a single dead fish for weeks to make him intimate with the form (and deformation) of animal anatomy. What I would suggest is that the computer consultant's judicial request might serve as an equally instructive specimen. I would suggest that if we think, and think hard, about a justice system that would entertain such a suit, about an economy that would spawn such a company, about the philosophy that predicated the man's rea-soning, and about the ethical implications of investing one's resources in such a way, we might achieve an intimate comprehension of our culture's anatomy, its current form and deformation.

Let it be noted first that this man's decision making was rooted in the ba-sic premises of the prevailing practical philosophy of our day—which is, I would assert, a form of rational materialism largely stripped of Judeo-Christian values. Although his request seems extreme to the point of absurdity, he was not being rash; his reasoning, to the contrary, was highly methodical, rational, and (some might even say) brave. After studying the medical evidence, he had accepted the terrible truth of a terminal diagnosis, researched his options, and made a kind of cost-benefit analysis. Unlike so many today, he wasn't asking for a government handout, only for the right to exercise a unique opportunity offered to him by the combined creativity of science and the marketplace. One could argue, in short, that the man was a good capitalist consumer, acting out of precisely the kind of enlightened self-interest thought to produce both economic prosperity and social progress, and that he was a model democratic citizen, using the peaceful means of the law to pursue his constitutional right to direct his own destiny.

Is it fair to call such a request immature? If maturity can be defined as those character traits necessary for the sustenance of a harmonious society, and if the sustaining of such a society depends on adults who have adapted to the realities of the human condition, including the reality of death, and who are willing, therefore, to bequeath both their wisdom and their wealth to the next generation—then, yes, I believe it is fair. Although opposite in apparent temper, this "rational" request for decapitation is no less self-centered in its own way than the rash desertion of the vacationing couple, and, as a model for adult decision making, no less destructive to society.

THE NEW MAJORITY

But is it fair to use two such extreme examples as somehow representative of the nation's immaturity? Society, after all, officially condemned the couple (they were pilloried in the press, convicted of neglect, and lost custody of their children), and the court finally refused the dying consultant's request. Yet, although these individuals did transgress the borders of permissible behavior, their ways of thinking are, alas, not that far removed from the newly emerging cultural norms. Middle-class children are left on their own every day in postindustrial America, often by parents who are off satisfying their "own needs" as defined ever more expansively (and expensively) by our consumer economy; and the denial of death is an urgent and still burgeoning industry here. Millions of medical dollars are spent mechanically prolonging the lives of the mortally comatose and thousands of puffy words expended avoiding the pronouncement of the one-word sentence we all must share: i.e., death. Although our movies are notorious for their abundant body counts, our own real-life relation to the inescapable fact of our mortality is best captured by the perhaps apocryphal octogenarian lady who, when informed that she was dying, responded plaintively: "Why me?"

It is crucial to note, too, that such delusions are by no means limited to the uneducated or to a willfully superstitious laity. Supposedly serious scientists, associated with prestigious institutions like M.I.T.'s Media Lab, continue to make claims that we shall eventually invent our way into an actual immortality. (True to the ruling philosophy of the day, these claims are of two schools: the rationalists, like Hans Moravec from Carnegie Mellon, who believe that we will eventually "download" our individual minds into computers and, enacting a Cartesian escape from our merely mortal flesh, live

forever as continuously evolving "software"; and the more traditional materialists who still focus on perfecting the flesh itself through drug protocols
and genetic engineering.) Nor do political affiliation or philosophy seem to
exempt one from these now pandemic temptations to immature behavior.
Republican, Democrat, and Independent alike invest in cosmetic surgery,
throw adolescent road-rage fits, flatter their "inner child," variously defined,
to the detriment of their actual children.

I open with this complementary pair of incidents, then, because I believe
they illustrate my larger point: The behavior that disturbs us now is very
broadbased and is performed by men and women of the middle class, by
"us," exercising our freedom of choice as directed implicitly and explicitly by
the values of our postindustrial economy—an economy that increasingly en-
closes and invades the everyday lives of both liberals and conservatives. Although most of us still cling to the traditional rhetoric of religious and civic
responsibility, which has long counterbalanced America's radical experiment in individual liberty, these incidents illustrate the ways in which we
have been drawn, often unconsciously, toward entirely different schedules
of ideal behavior, schedules hostile to both the temper and the habits of a
democratic community. That is to say, what we actually believe and what we
think we believe no longer mesh. While some of that discrepancy may be at-
tributable to an intentional deception—i.e., to the self-conscious hypocrisy
that the opposing critics in our culture wars love to dissect—much of it occurs below the level of articulate self-awareness. Such a claim, that these destructive changes are both ubiquitous and largely unconscious, strongly suggests that, even as we admit the urgency of the problem, we ought to tone
down the partisan scorn that has come to characterize these analyses. It also
poses the grand question that haunts all our current cultural conflicts: Exactly
how has our behavior shifted so dramatically without our self-conscious
knowledge or consent?

CAPITALISM'S TWO SELVES

Thirty-five years ago, Marshall McLuhan supplied a partial answer when he
observed that "everyone experiences far more than he understands. Yet it is
experience, and not understanding, that influences behavior." McLuhan was
primarily concerned, of course, with the shift in communications from print
to the electronic media, and the statement can be seen as a brief elaboration
of his catchy aphorism, "the medium is the message." But the principle applies more broadly as well. To the extent that our daily experience is at all
humanly mediated—"brought to us by" human ideas, technologies, archi-
tectures—it is necessarily suffused with implicit moral values. Churches and
synagogues can tell us what we should believe, continuing to teach tradi-

tional virtues, but if the grounds and rounds of daily life are calibrated differently, our behavior will begin to shift accordingly. We can continue to "talk the talk" but won't "walk the walk" as, in Hamlet's words, "that monster, custom, who doth all sense eat," silently reconfigures our daily actions.

That since World War II our capitalist economy—its ventures, ambitions, procedures, and "messages"—has become the new primary calibrator of our daily experience is not a controversial claim. My subsequent assertion that its new predominance has led to the very patterns of rash and rational immaturity cited above, however, requires a more elaborate analysis. To begin, we can cite and extend the central thesis of Daniel Bell's recently reissued *The Cultural Contradictions of Capitalism*—which is, in essence, a postindustrial updating of Max Weber's 1904 classic, *The Protestant Ethic and the Spirit of Capitalism*. Among the contradictions astutely analyzed by Bell is that between the ethos of capitalist production—which still requires obedience, hard work, and self-sacrifice through delayed gratification—and the ethos of capitalist consumption, with its idealizing of hedonism, rebellion against authority, and impulsive behavior (such as deserting your children for a sudden vacation).

Simply stated, the two main divisions of capitalist commerce, production and sales, have come to require two opposing regimens of ideal behavior—one rational, the other rash—and these regimens suggest two discordant identities, a coolly mechanical and narrowly accountable Producing Self (Dr. Jekyll) and a hotly appetitive Consuming Self (Mr. Hyde). In the gotcha game of the culture wars, each side cleverly identifies and "outs" the antisocial excesses of its opponent's Consuming Self even as it ignores its own. The conservative spotlights, in alternating tones of contempt and alarm, the dangers of the liberal's sexual and aesthetic excesses while the liberal satirizes and sermonizes against the excessive greed and conspicuous consumption of the corporate elite. Not only does each side see the moral ugliness of the other's Hyde while missing its own, both tend to miss the ongoing conflict all of us face in attempting to follow two essentially incompatible models of behavior. Neither side acknowledges the emotional stress and cognitive dissonance of being asked to play, often in the very same day, both an abstemious Jekyll and an avid Hyde.

It is not simply commerce, then, but commerce's two separate moral regimens for production and consumption that are the new primary calibrators of our daily experience; they are "the monster[s] . . . who doth all sense eat"—who, that is, have become so customary that, like the air we breathe, we cease to actively sense their influence. What I wish to emphasize here, however, is that both prospective identities are potentially destructive, the Producing Self no less than the Consuming Self, whose depravations are more commonly noted. Not only can a good employee be an awful parent, neighbor, or citizen; that employee is, I would contend, more likely to be an ineffective parent or neighbor if he or she continues to follow the customary values of the postmodern workplace beyond the bounds of the office, factory, or store. If, for example, delayed gratification were sufficient in itself to good citizenship, then who could be a more exemplary citizen than our computer consultant, a man willing to "sacrifice" his body now and put his head on ice for untold years before experiencing the "gratification" of his revival?

THE END OF ADULTHOOD

If I am right, then a recovery of moral maturity would require a new sort of abstinence, more expansively defined. In our struggle to relearn what it means to be good parents and neighbors, we would need to withdraw from those spheres where the narrow schedules of both the Avid Consumer and the Efficient Producer overly determine our daily experience.

Yet everywhere we turn these tacitly moral customizers now intrude. They have converted the public square, which has been subsumed by the commercial mall. They have infiltrated the private home, which has been saturated with commercial solicitation through radio, television, and now the Web. They have co-opted the processes of democratic government, which has become increasingly beholden to commercial interests, whether "left-wing" Hollywood or "right-wing" Wall Street, through the necessities of campaign financing, and increasingly rationalized into an "information product" by for-hire election technicians like Dick Morris. They have invaded our public schools, where advertising has been allowed to intrude into the hallways and even into the curriculum in return for badly needed funding. They have been taking command of our universities, whose laboratories and classrooms are rapidly being transformed into duchies of the postindustrial economy—the new sites for product invention and employee training—and whose humanities curricula increasingly ape the fashion-line model of planned obsolescence. They taint the studio, movie house, and literary bookstore, which continue to contain paintings, movies, and novels espousing a robotic "anti-bourgeois" sentiment that is, in fact, obedient to the hedonistic ethos of consumerism. And, finally, they have even co-opted our religious organizations, which have become increasingly obsessed with publicity and the marketing of product lines. (This is truest of the most energetic and fastest-growing movements in postmodern America, including "right-wing" fundamentalism and "left-wing" New Age sects.)

If we survey the list above, the corruption of academia, art, and religion are especially telling—insofar as these were the most likely critics of the commercial order. They demonstrate vividly how one can still talk the talk of critical independence while walking the walk of tacit compliance. The infiltration of the private home by commerce also holds a special significance in that it helps measure the stunning rapidity of the changes that have taken place. As recently as the mid-sixties, most of America's women and young children still spent a high percentage of their waking hours outside the official producer economy. (The consumer economy, of course, had already entered with a vengeance via the Trojan horse of commercial TV.) Today's mass entry of women into the work force (and, consequently, of children into professional child care) has meant that the entire middle-class family is now being modeled not only by the seductions of the Avid Consumer but also by the over-specializations of the Efficient Producer—by Weber's "iron cage" of highly rationalized, narrowly motivated social structures. As a result of these omnipresent, if contradictory, forms of modeling, our clothing is now stamped with the logos of commerce, our minds are now stocked with the jingles of commerce, our hours are now structured by either the rational regimens of commerce or those of bureaucratic government, and our humane responsibilities—whether as momentary as expressing a "sentiment" to our newly married friend or as monumental as caring for our aging parents—are increasingly purchased rather than performed.

What happened to adulthood with its full panoply of emotions, duties, competencies—its capacity for grace under multiple pressures? Adulthood has been disappearing because we now live in a place (both physical and social) radically different from the one we occupied even 40 years ago. This new habitat is a place fundamentally hostile to the virtues traditionally associated with maturity. This "new and improved" American place "grows" profit but eviscerates character; it renders our experience rationally efficient yet spiritually impoverished. Where has adulthood gone? It has been ramified, outsourced, divided into specialties for expert study and for product creation in the service economy. It has been rationalized and merchandised into non-existence.

What are the deeper sources of such a dramatic conversion? This is obviously a very complex historical question, one I can only address here in summary form as a means of framing the examples to come. To begin with, it is the logical result of the increasing triumph in American life of rational materialism, which is adept at manipulating the physical world but is also, and by design, humanly indifferent, metaphysically dumb, and morally blind. The cultural dangers of such a cluster of traits were largely avoided in America because our own version of rational materialism, "scientific capitalism," was preceded by, and (at first) politically allied with, strong traditions of both local governance and religious freedom—i.e., the original, still spiritually grounded Protestant ethic. Given those origins, our society managed to maintain a humane balance of power.

But this balance was severely challenged in the mid nineteenth century by the Industrial Revolution, with its widespread mechanization of work, specialization of thought, and urbanization of living space—here begins in earnest the still ongoing institution of Weber's iron cage. This balance was further challenged in the early twentieth century by the rise of consumerism, with its widespread boosting of new "needs" through instant credit and the constant proselytizing of advertising—here begins the seductive phase of scientific capitalism (and its cultural contradictions), its paradoxical use of the techniques of the iron cage to create the mirage of what we might call "the gilded carrot," the ever-changing and marketable object of constant desire. The full effects of this second challenge (when added to the first) were delayed by an extended depression and an all-consuming war and thus couldn't be seen until an entire generation, the Boomers, had been raised in relative peace and unprecedented prosperity under its influence.

The failure of that generation (my own) to mature into responsible adulthood, especially into responsible parenthood, is dramatic proof of both the ideological power and social destructiveness of the current economic order. Such a failure is also a sign that the precarious, but necessary, balance between scientific capitalism and Judeo-Christianity has been lost, that the former has subsumed, co-opted, and superseded the latter to our current detriment and future moral peril.

GREAT EXPECTATIONS (1960)

The discrepancy between the hope invested in the post-War generation and our actual performance has been so severe that the anticipation itself invites further examination. By the mid-fifties, giddy on the optimism of consumerism and global political domination, America really seemed to believe that its children, like its products, would necessarily be "new and improved"—that every day, in every way, we were indeed getting better and better. Year after year, in classrooms, assemblies, and convocation halls, we were told in confident tones how special we were: the richest, best educated, most technologically advanced, and implicitly—because it was naively supposed, our character must "rise" with the surging tide of our GNP—the most righteous generation in the history of the planet. Both the oratory of officialdom and the messages of advertising were glad to agree that we were the ones destined to redeem the golden promise of the American dream: heirs not simply to the pursuit of happiness but to its purchase and possession.

The extremity of that hope (and its secret folly) is one of the stronger memories of my own, mostly benign suburban upbringing. I recall especially a posh reception following a classmate's bar mitzvah during which we, his seventh-grade friends, were made to enter an enormous dining hall as though a wedding party or a royal procession. Two by two, a boy beside a girl, to the beat of a band's ceremonial music, we were marched up an aisle, parting a sea of damp-eyed adults, and then onto a raised platform where we ate, conversed, and later even danced, elevated above, yet surrounded by, the parents of suburbia, hundreds in number.

Occasionally, one of the men would slip up the steps, but then only briefly, to pass to my friend an envelope thick with congratulatory cash, as if only this, his propitiatory offering, gave him license to approach. Otherwise we remained there in exalted isolation, on perpetual display. And what I remember most now, beyond my own discomfort, was how the stares of the adults kept drifting up, from their plates of prime rib, to locate us; how they would touch and then hold the hem of the moment—this carefully composed, happy tableau of "youth on the cusp." My unrelenting desire to disappear was, of course, mostly the result of a social awkwardness befitting my age. But even then I sensed that there was something wrong in this reversal of status; something fundamentally (and frighteningly) false about the veneration we received in expressions that seesawed between proprietary joy and solemn awe.

Now, a parent myself, I better understand the temptations of such love, the ways in which our vanities survive, subversive to the end, through projecting parent fantasies onto the lives of our reluctant kids. Now, glancing backward, I see that scene as especially representative of the post-War era: how religious rites of passage were being co-opted then into celebrations of materialist status; how Catholics, Protestants, and Jews alike—all of whom sat at the elevated table—were being converted to Mammon's melting-pot version of the mortgaged Good Life. What I see, when I glance back now, is the idolatry of childhood: the little god and goddess of Self-Esteem being raised on the altar of the secular dream.

About five years later, in the year of my own graduation, *Time* actually put the yearbook photos of a high-school senior class (from California, of course) on its glossy cover, confirming, as only a *Time* cover could then, the ascension of America's "youth culture." Not long thereafter, *Time* also ran a cover daring to wonder if God were dead, thus completing the dual prophecy already implicit in that bar mitzvah scene. For the boosting of youth and the debunking of God were (and are) associate phenomena, each arising from the true cover story of the post-War age: the triumph of the consumer economy over traditional spirituality as the arbiter of social values.

The way that we, as a generation, were so oversold only shows how much the temper of commercial salesmanship had already tainted the raising of families by the 1950s. And our failures as a group in middle age speak painfully now to this economy's own failure as the dominant model for daily behavior. Its vaunting of self-interest, its reduction of people to contacts or products, its disingenuous blurring of moral improvement with material progress: these were the values that, in the midst of our "rebellions," we were stooping to obey, blind to the results until it was too late. That our becoming "better off" might actually make a worse human place was the sort of savvy calculation that an economy programmed to Great Expectations could not, and still cannot, make.

GREAT EXPECTATIONS (1860)

To understand the nature of the economic assault on the contemporary family, we might profitably turn back to the era and nation where industrial capitalism first took hold (nineteenth-century England), and to the artistic form that evolved, in part, to study the manners and morals of middle-class life: the social novel. Charles Dickens was one of the first and most astute critics of the ways in which the then new regimens of scientific capitalism could imperil the rhythms of domestic life; and nowhere are both the dangers and adaptive responses more entertainingly drawn than in *Great Expectations* when the orphan Pip, suddenly and mysteriously made rich, is brought to London.

For there, Pip is placed under the care of the new priesthood of the Industrial Age—"the Law"—in the form of the austere and intimidating criminal lawyer Jaggers and his clerk, Mr. Wemmick. At first, Wemmick appears to be punctilious and dry, a man so bereft of civil human gestures that he has actually forgotten that people shake hands. When Wemmick brings Pip to his home, however, we learn that he hasn't lost his capacities for amiability and affection so much as been forced to specialize the locale of their expression. His particular job (and, by implication, the larger economy that defines that job) has required a rigid partition of his behavior—between workplace and homestead, between a strict obedience to the protocols of the law and a strong conformity to the rituals of the heart.

Dickens makes clear which of these two locales (and the separate schedules of behavior they allow) is "under siege" by providing a delightfully comic depiction of a "man's house is his castle." For Wemmick's house, although the smallest Pip has ever seen, is a miniature redoubt. With painted Gothic windows, a ditch as a moat, a plank for a bridge, a lattice fence for stone walls, and a small gun as armament, Wemmick has self-consciously constructed his own symbolic castle to keep the modern world out.

While the castle's physical protection is merely symbolic, the psychological border it demarks is very real. Inside his castle walls, Wemmick practices the old economies of farming and craftsmanship—he is a self-reliant, independent "jack of all trades"; outside, he works a middle stratum within one of the new economy's white-collar professions—he is a highly specialized, wage employee. Inside, Wemmick maintains the old allegiances to country and clan—he raises a flag every Sunday and, much more important, he lovingly cares for his deaf father, whom he affectionately dubs "the aged parent"; outside, his sole allegiance is to his employer, Jaggers, and Jaggers's often disreputable clients—his loyalty is literally for hire. The man-at-home in his castle is affectionate, generous, gregarious; the man-at-work in his office is pinched, acquisitive, dutifully discreet.

Dickens's comic depiction of Wemmick's divided life captures, a full century earlier, a key ambition behind the suburban adventure of the 1950s and 1960s: the attempt to build a green-belt moat around the American family to protect it not only from physical danger but from the psychological depredations of the postwar economy. And when Pip narrates how the once gracious Wemmick becomes "dryer and harder" as he heads back to work, he might be describing the psychological transformation required of any of ten million American fathers commuting daily then to their white-collar jobs.

THE INFORMATION AGE

Wemmick's challenge is the perennial one of the democratic citizen living under scientific capitalism: how to partake of its unprecedented material bounty without succumbing to its spiritual depravations; how to use its machines without, in effect, becoming one. Although always problematic, his ironic solution—to use the economy's means to build, in a sense, a fortress against that economy's beliefs—was far more feasible in 1860 than in 1960, when the penetrations of the Information Age made any large-scale segregation of private from public impossible, and when the economy's own shift to boosting consumption made the family itself a necessary target for ideological instruction. The commuting fathers of postwar America might keep their family circumstances a secret from their bosses, as Wemmick did from Jaggers, but the economy's propaganda was still invading their homes daily through radio and TV, and no moat, wall, or remote locale could block its reach.

Although Dickens died long before the Information Age, one of the subplots in David Copperfield does metaphorically suggest the insidious nature of its coming threat to the family's domain. Here, too, law is the profession, but Mr. Wickfield's focus is financial, not criminal; his small office is in his home; and he practices in suburban Canterbury rather than fast-paced London. In character, too, Wickfield is nearly the opposite of Wemmick's master, soft to Jaggers' hard, more devoted to his wife and daughter than to his job. He is an honest man, but after his wife dies, he increasingly retreats from the details of his practice into solitude and drink—a retreat that is encouraged and, in fact, secretly stage-managed by his single employee, the clerk, Uriah Heep.

Perpetually present, always volunteering to take over for his distracted boss, Heep flatters and fawns, and behind his unctuous protestations of his own "'umbleness," the resentful underling relentlessly plots: first taking control of Wickfield's practice, then tricking him into complicity in illegal dealings, then bribing his way into a formal partnership. Eventually, he not only runs Wickfield's business as if it were his own; he completes his domination by actually moving both his mother and himself into Wickfield's home. While Wemmick's virtual castle managed to maintain a safe space for the practice of "family values," Wickfield's family castle has now been invaded—its spaces occupied, its practices subverted.

As the central vehicle for consumerist ideology, postwar TV was very much the Uriah Heep of technologies: always hanging about the house and bowing obsequiously, always claiming to be our servant, our ever so 'umble and unworthy servant. Like Heep, commercial TV perpetually flattered its viewers, playing on our weaknesses while subtly subverting our traditional beliefs. Like Heep, it quietly became a household fixture, so mundane and demeaned that we ceased to see this high-tech, servile "employee" for what it actually was. We failed to note, as Wickfield failed to note, how dependent we had become on its "companionship" and "services." And we failed to suspect, as the domain of its influence rapidly spread, that its offerings weren't free after all, that the interests it served were not ours but its own, and that, like Heep's, its aims were insidious—de facto control of our business, our bodies, our children in our homes.

In Dickens's story, the climax of Heep's attempted usurpation of the head, house, and heart of the Wickfield family is his plot to marry Agnes, Wickfield's only daughter. It is a plot rich with symbolic overtones, for as the novel's highly idealized heroine, Agnes practices those very same traits of modesty, solicitude, and self-abnegation (true "humbleness") that Heep can duly fake. Through his blackmail, then, Heep is aiming to take possession not only of the home's sole, beloved child but of the incarnation of goodness itself. Simulated virtue is on the verge of conquering actual virtue—a triumph of fakery only foiled in the end by a comic-heroic intervention.

In our story, though, the tale of the postwar generation as stalked by the avid industries of consumerism through the "'umble" appliance of commercial TV, there is no intervention. We, the culture's "new and improved" kids, overfed and overfeted, are gradually co-opted, subtly possessed. Actual virtue is gradually subverted by simulated virtue as, in true Heepian fashion, private resentments and personal ambition assume the guise of public compassion. In our story, unlike Dickens's story, "the helping hand" is subsumed by "self-help" while charity becomes an industry itself, complete with commission sales forces and perk-laden chief executives. In our story, self-interest on both the Left and the Right borrows the language of the idealistic ("liberation from oppression or creative destruction") as we manage to progress from civil rights to self-esteem; from "keeping the world safe for democracy" to the sanctification of selfishness and the commodification of everything.

In Dickens's world, imagined at the height of the Industrial Age, the family in distress is usually saved; the regimens of industry and the rituals of domesticity manage finally to coexist in their separate domains. In our world, as reinvented by the Information Age, their domains are no longer separate. Whether in child-, health-, or "aged parent" care, the industrial increasingly runs the rituals of the domestic, and the family in distress increasingly fails.

FAUX REBELLION: THE SALESMANSHIP OF "LIBERATION"

Because the business of America has been business for so long, because commerce is our establishment, we lose sight of the ways in which modern capitalism is necessarily anti-establishment: how it promotes disruption, dissatisfaction, mini-revolutions in tastes, habits, and so, inevitably, moral behavior.

In the American economy proper, the specific recognition that certain qualities of personal rebelliousness, rather than overthrowing capitalism, might actually be exploited to expand its base, dates back to the origins of consumerism. Not only did selling the "new" mean, implicitly at least, discounting the "old"; the very nature of some of the earliest consumer products, such as the radio and the car, radically undermined both parental and communal authority, changing the moral landscape in the 1920s and fueling a new hedonism in American life. The initial establishment response to these commercially driven shifts in behavior was a kind of crude denial and displacement of causes—to immigrants, to radicals, to urban and "un-American" sinners, to demon rum. (The grossest example of such scapegoating was Henry Ford's highly public and poisonously proselytizing anti-Semitism.) Yet by the sixties, driven by the desire to cultivate the enormous potential of the youth market, rebellion was being embraced as an explicit theme in advertising itself. Initially, Madison Avenue idealized the pose of liberation through traditional images of American individualism like the Marlboro Man, but soon it would learn to exploit even specifically political expressions of revolt.

This opportunistic strategy of converting social protest into marketable product was best exemplified in the seventies by the Virginia Slims ad campaign. Launching the first cigarette targeted exclusively for women, these familiar and highly successful ads typically featured two photos, in an ironically staged before-and-after scenario, dramatizing the change from pre- to postliberation American womanhood. In the first, a young woman who is fettered in a frumpy Victorian dress has been caught attempting to sneak a cigarette by an oppressive husband or father figure—a veritable starched phallus of paternalism complete with wagging finger, stern stare, and Germanic walrus mustache. In the second, her contemporary and now "liberated" sister poses, sassy, slender, joyous, and free, her cigarette transformed into a kind of elegant fashion accessory, her progress proclaimed in the now famous phrase: "You've come a long way, baby!"

With its arch tone, its hip address, its mockery of the past and of prudishness, its trivializing of political change into selfhood's triumph, its blurring of active accomplishment with passive sexiness, and, of course, with its overall masking of solicitation with flattery—this one campaign exemplified three decades of advertising themes. Like most seductions, it played on the twin emotions of resentment and self-love, but its particular genius lay in locating the language of vanity best fitted to the age: independence, self-liberation.

That by "celebrating" freedom, these ads actually intended to enslave—a deadly addiction the hook concealed by flattery's bait—is a dark but instructive irony. It describes, in extreme, a key strategy of consumerism in the postmodern age: how each apparent inducement to rebellion can be fashioned to conceal a tacit order to obey.

"BORN (AGAIN) GANGSTAZ"

By the nineties, faux rebellion had become a marketing shtick so banal that some marketers were driven to casting their products in ever more outrageous terms of darkness, violence, and sexual excess. (One of the most notorious mainstream examples of this was a Calvin Klein ad campaign that seemed little more than a collection of pinups for pedophiles.) Ever in search of new and profitable borders to cross, pop music provided its own extreme examples, as Brett Pulley of the Wall Street Journal discovered.

Pulley was investigating the career of Boss Laws, a new female rapper whose first album, "Born Gangstaz," featured cover photos of Laws striking "various poses clutching automatic weapons," and whose songs included the now almost standard cop-killer lyrics: "'I loaded the clip and took the nine to the copper's brain.'" Fond of slugging down malt liquor from 40-ounce bottles, cursing out her audience, and boldly pronouncing in public her desire to kill, Laws spoke often of life on the streets. Her menacing persona, and the gritty "art" it had produced, had arisen apparently from her experiences as gang member, drug pusher, and prison inmate.

As it happens, Laws had never been in jail, nor could her other mean-street stories be verified. She wasn't in fact born a gangster but delivered to two protective parents who raised her in a comfortable, middle-class Detroit neighborhood. There, she had been educated in Catholic schools and had been the beneficiary of lessons in ballet, modern dance, and piano. Laws also had attended church and gone to college, where she had majored in business and had become a fraternity sweetheart.

Majoring in business is probably the most significant biographical detail in that privileged list. As Laws herself said to Pulley in defense of her new persona: "I'm both a gangster and a smart business person. I know what I'm doing." Indeed, she did. That she chose to entitle her first album "Born Gangstaz," rather than something more biographically accurate, such as "Born Bourgeois," tells us much about the selling of popular art through faux rebellion, the reinvention of self as commercial product, and the inherent amorality of marketing on the postmodern stage.

In the Christian faith within which Laws was raised, being "born again" meant having one's soul realigned with the experience of the divine and a subsequent obedience to the laws of God. In the consumerist faith that has taken its place as the primary shaper of public behavior, being "born again" means reshaping one's image according to the fashions of the Market, obedient to its laws of publicity and promotion.

RELATIVISM AND CAPITALISM

"Born Gangstaz" provides a useful and sobering transition out of stereotype. The careerist maneuvers of Boss Laws remind us that although we have come to expect the proselytizing of immaturity, vulgarity, and violence from the entertainment industry, it is still, in fact, an industry. Like any industry in postmodern America, the primary beneficiaries of pop music's offensive values are both the investing rich and a highly diversified professional class: lawyers, publicists, accountants, graphic artists, marketing and computer consultants, all rationally and efficiently assisting in the creation of a product, the core values of which are (in the case of Boss Laws) irrational and anarchic.

This professional assistance, it is important to remember, is usually provided without any self-conscious political or social intent. We cannot presume, for example, that the large cast of co-conspirators listed above consists primarily of misguided liberals, much less self-proclaimed anarchists—a group that seems to reside almost exclusively now in academic tenure dens and the tony galleries of art investors. Many a conservative's stock portfolio has been fattened, and soccer mom's all-terrain vehicle financed, through supporting clients like Calvin Klein. And would anyone really be surprised if the tobacco company that was flattering feminism through its Virginia Slims campaign was simultaneously contributing to the reelection coffers of Jesse Helms? The ethos of commerce—with its scientific methods pressed to monetary ends, with its strict rationalism placed in the service of a narrow materialism—has neither the language nor the appetite for such scrupulous discriminations. Rather, its democracy of profit wants to decree that all money is good money while its standard of service wants to insist that the customer is always right.

When practiced in moderation, these commercial ideals of toleration and solicitude are indeed necessary for a civil, democratic marketplace. But when the market expands to enclose the whole of society so that even the most intimate of activities becomes economically defined, when the primary shapers of allowable behavior are the imperatives of the bottom line, then toleration gives way to decadent license, civil solicitude to venal solicitation, as everything becomes "good" and anything "right." So enclosed, we can rationalize the most offensive of behaviors. Access to the morgue photos of a murdered child, JonBenet, becomes yet one more entrepreneurial opportunity, their purchase and publication justified under the banners of "freedom of expression" and the public's "right to know."

How has such moral relativism come to define our social sphere? The answer is both so pervasive and so near that it is hard for us to see: Relativism is the standard operating procedure of scientific capitalism, the working premise of commercial life. To say so is merely to restate the premises of capitalism's cultural contradictions, and show again how the Producing Self has become complicit with, and dependent on, the depredations of the Consuming Self.

POSTMODERN PARENTING

As a last example of the insidious effects of these economically shaped identities, I want to return to parenting and balance the "rash" with a "rational" model. Let's imagine a slightly upscale, much more admirably motivated version of the family mentioned on the first page: a white, married, Midwest couple, college educated, with two pre-teenage children, Adam and Amy. Although both parents now work full-time, the mother gladly stayed home a full year after each child's birth and then relentlessly sought out the very best child care, regardless of price. In fact, committed to both gender equality and responsible parenthood, this couple had planned to alternate working half-time until Amy reached junior high. But when the father's company was downsized, he had to take on more work rather than less, and although the mother was still willing to sacrifice the career advantage of full-time employment, they found that, without the extra income, they couldn't afford a home in the community with the best public schools. So she extended her hours—as did the father, for his commute was lengthened an hour each day after the move.

Such sacrifices are, in fact, characteristic of this couple. They have no desire to take impulsive vacations free of their children's company. To the contrary, their fondest fantasy, discussed over takeout dinners or whispered above the soundtrack of the children's Friday night video, is to have a more relaxed and natural family life. But everything they read, including the President's speeches, and their own employment experiences together warn them that their children must be highly trained to survive the changes that the new economy is likely to require. So they take out a loan to buy the very best home computers, which they upgrade, then upgrade again. When Adam has trouble learning to read, they send him to a nationally franchised Sylvan Learning Center for after-school training and then to a private tutor who specializes in dyslexia. When Amy shows ability in math, it only seems fair that they offer her tutoring as well, so they send her to the local Kumon Math Center (also nationally franchised) and pay for skating lessons as well.

All of this, of course, means more expense and less time spent together, but they try to adjust by using cell phones and e-mail to stay in touch. Furthermore, Adam and Amy are guaranteed "quality time" on the weekend (there's a sign-up sheet over the microwave): four full hours when each gets to choose favorite activities and special foods, when each has the right to be "spoiled" by the intensity of their parents' total attention. The couple also attends every conference, game, and performance they can. There, too, the intensity of their attention doesn't flag; there, as their children's passionate advocates, they work "the system"—lobby teachers, network neighbors, argue with refs—whatever it takes to wrest the best for Amy and Adam.

I could go on, but the portrait is complete enough and, perhaps, painfully familiar. What I find so insidious here is the extent to which the totality of domestic life is being shaped by economic models, motives, fears, and values: how much the grimly anxious pace of the postmodern workplace has come to command the postmodern household. And, of course, for clarity's sake, I have removed all the potentially corrupting effects of contemporary consumerism, the hedonistic half of the mixed message the economy presents. Statistically speaking, this is a uniquely ascetic postmodern couple. Here, we have no divorce, infidelity, rampant careerism; no alcoholism, drug addiction, compulsive shopping or gambling—none of the many forms of self-centered dysfunction that darken our day and rend family life. Here, we have nothing so rash, just a perversely rational schedule of pervasive separation, a desertion of one's own children "on their behalf."

This household has been purged of sexist inequalities, but it has also been stripped of wonder, curiosity, improvisational fun. Mother and father have merged into one cooperative, unisexual provider. The good parent has been reduced to the Good Producer whose job as parent is to supply society with a new generation of good producers—i.e., employees who are already accustomed to highly rationalized social environments and whose skills are upgraded to the ever-evolving specs of the time. The new parent doesn't teach by example; he hires tutors, coaches, experts "in the field." His role is less to cherish and chasten than to outfit and facilitate; less to shape meaning than to make money, furnishing each child with all the materialist gear and rationalist techniques the economy requires.

Even this household's happier moments have been reinvented in the economy's terms. The notion of prescheduled "quality time," for example, converts parenting to corporate standards of executive efficiency. As in the rest of the technological economy, enhanced technique is supposed to reduce the need for management "face time," leading to an implicitly absurd rationalization by which, nevertheless, many of us now run our lives. We believe that the better parents we are, the less time we actually will spend with our children. The parent as passionate advocate—the one lobbying hard on her child's behalf without broader concerns for truth, justice, or even common courtesy—is likewise a rote reenactment of workplace roles, especially as defined by the ever-expanding service domain. Such behavior accurately reflects the highly specialized code of conduct—the so-called professional ethics—of the lawyer, the therapist, the consultant, or the licensed accountant whose firm does the books for both a local church and an S&M supply house. Our job at home, like our job in the field, is not to reprimand but to represent. All clients are good clients. Our children have become our customers, and the customer is always right.

LOST HAVENS AND LOST VIRTUES

When our children become our clients, then even the family has ceased to be a possible sphere for moral instruction. When our domestic rituals are set to the beat and drawn toward the goals of our workaday schedules, then home itself ceases to be a sanctuary. Even at night, we have no respite from the anxieties of the marketplace where the buyer must beware and only the fittest are supposed to survive. Even in our living rooms, we find no alternative to the economy's reductive, yet contradictory, commands to produce and consume, produce and consume. The strict division that Wemmick drew—the symbolic border that allowed him to be productive at work and humane at home—has been dissolved. Today's Wemmick has no place where he can be generous and genial, no time to be metaphysically curious, humanly kind. The old compromise with the wealth-producing engine of scientific capitalism has collapsed. Although small, lightly armored, and comically appointed, Wemmick's house was still an effective castle, but that castle has now been sacked.

Our current distress arises, in part, from an inarticulate sense that we have lost that last bastion of our humanity, what Christopher Lasch called our "haven in a heartless world." And the best measure of the dread that such a loss can excite is our urgent attempt now to rebuild the moat of separateness: more private schools to teach, more guards to police, a new maze of walled-in communities. Once again we circle our wagons in suburban cul-de-sacs, where, ever anxious, we stare out at the world through tinted glass. But physical removal is an insufficient defense when the hearts and minds of the family we would protect, adult and child alike, have been aligned to the values of the very world we are trying to escape.

Those values are intrinsically hostile to the disciplined tenderness that makes a meaningful haven out of a merely physical house. In truth, the economy that now pervades American life does not "want" people who are capable of creating and sustaining the rituals of domesticity. It wants instead, and paradoxically, pure rationalists and pure materialists; it wants efficient producers and avid consumers. And even if we could harmonize its increasingly contradictory demands for perfect efficiency and unending appetite, the merged model could only supply an impoverished definition of human life. Acting out of such a model, which reduces us to the "mechanical" and the "animal," we still could not mature into a fully competent, deeply caring, communally committed adulthood. If we wish to become such adults—and most of us still profess that we do—we need to admit, then, not only scientific capitalism's internal contradictions but its ultimate insufficiency as the primary shaper of our daily behavior. We need to confront the very specific ways in which its regimens for profitability are hostile to the cultivation of maturity's most necessary traits.

Maturity requires both the acquisition of a broad, commonsense intelligence and a commitment to truth-telling. The economy rewards instead both the narrow expertise of producership and the utopian fantasies of salesmanship with its commodified dreams of omniscience, omnipotence, immortality. Maturity requires emotional endurance. The new economy promotes the habit of complaint; it hypes the latest "injustice" or psychic pain, which then can be medicated, adjudicated, serviced for a fee.

Maturity requires the selflessness of social commitment; the economy promotes the selfishness of "self-liberation." Maturity depends on a transfer of tradition between the generations through daily example. The economy eradicates tradition through insisting that the new is always improved, and it segregates the generations—into day-care, workplace, retirement communities—for more efficient service and marketing.

Maturity directs the submission of both physical desires and intellectual schemes to the discipline of higher meaning. The postmodern economy co-opts and consumes all traditional forms of meaningfulness. It relentlessly converts quality into quantity, spirit into commodity, the organism of symbolism into the mechanism of market value, the self-sacrificial hero into the sponsoring star.

Maturity requires, above all, a meaningful acceptance of the human condition. It depends on our acknowledging those Facts which remain the same for every culture and generation, uniting the first with the last: that death is real; that our knowledge is limited; that even in an age of technological advance our rational control (both as individuals and as a community) remains provisional—that, in the words of Ecclesiastes, "time and chance happen to us all." Not only do common sense, compassion, and self-discipline emerge out of an acceptance of those first and final facts, so does humility. And humility is the necessary temperamental grounding for any system of ethics aspiring to be practical—aspiring, that is, to shape our beliefs in actual practice. As the temperament that (to use a carpenter's term) constantly trues us to the shape of the real, humility is the source of the most profound sort of pragmatism—a fact that our earliest American ancestors well knew.

"Every man has just as much and no more truth in him, as he hath humility," wrote a New England Puritan. Where, we might ask, in this economy of rank self-promotion and rational utopias, can such a truthful man or woman be found? The relative rarity of such a person illuminates why, for all the multiplication of our material wealth and the explosion of our rational knowledge, this postindustrial society of ours seems so shallow, so phony—not only immature but fundamentally false.

SPECIALISTS WITHOUT SPIRIT, SENSUALISTS WITHOUT HEART

At the very end of the *Protestant Ethic*, Max Weber briefly emerged from his sober and objective analysis to speculate on the coming character of the West's iron cage of capitalist endeavor. "No one knows," he wrote:

> who will live in this cage in the future, or whether at the end of this tremendous development entirely new prophets will arise, or whether there will be a great rebirth of old ideas and ideals, or, if neither, mechanized petrification, embellished with a sort of convulsive self-importance. For of the last stage of this cultural development, it might truly be said: Specialists without spirit, sensualists without heart; this nullity imagines that it has attained a level of civilization never before achieved.

As with "convulsive self-importance," we now proclaim America's global dominance, we might wonder at the extent to which we have achieved just such a nullity: a society of both rational and rash immaturity; a civilization of "specialists without spirit, sensualists without heart." For their eloquence as well as their prophetic accuracy, these words of Weber, written at the very start of the twentieth century, are frequently cited. Few note, however, the unintended irony of the very next sentence: "But this brings us to the world of judgments of value and of faith, with which this purely historical study need not be burdened."

We now have had a full century of such intellectual purity—a hundred years of purely historical, purely financial, purely aesthetic, purely scientific study and practice. Yet that very "world of judgments" which such practices would shun, is not apart from, but encoded within, all human activity. The purging of value—this vaunted purity of rationalized study—is a fiction. Historically, it has been a very useful fiction. It has allowed us to imagine ourselves apart from the world so that we might see it more sharply and to achieve, as a consequence, a series of truly astonishing technological triumphs. But, as the narrow compass of that fiction has become all-pervasive, its temporary respite from value has stretched instead into a kind of permanent estrangement. As domain after domain has been converted to its strategic pretense of objectivity, we have become enclosed within an interlocking maze of morally opaque systems, places, methodologies. Trapped inside this ethical blind, customized to its selective unawareness, our actions and beliefs begin to divide, and we lose "all sense" of both how we are behaving and why.

To open that blind and reinfuse our overly rationalized sites and minds with the "world of judgments" can indeed, as Weber observed, become a burden; for it threatens us with a renewed awareness that most of our actions are, in fact, judgments of value, and so reminds us that neither the regimens of expertise nor the fantasies of self-esteem can exempt us from the constant accountability of the moral life. To readmit that world is also dangerous, for if done in the wrong spirit—which is to say, if our judging is not trued by humility—we will only poison the air with more of the self-righteous scorn that has characterized the "gotcha game" of the culture wars. But surveying our scene of rash and rational immaturity, I am convinced that now is the time to embrace that burden and to brave the danger. Now is the time to recover those practices and refashion those places where, as in Wemmick's castle, "the judgments of value and of faith" have a home.

STUDY QUESTIONS

1. What does Bosworth mean when he claims that the decisions of some contemporary Americans are immature?
2. According to Bosworth, what is the cause of this increasing immaturity?
3. How do the contradictions of capitalism contribute to moral decline, according to Bosworth?
4. Explain how capitalism contributes to instability and the disruption of traditional forms of life.
5. Does Bosworth make a convincing case for the claim that capitalism pushes a variety of values aside? Explain.
6. How does our desire to be in control of our lives contribute to what Bosworth views as a decline in morality?

INTERVENTIONS: AUTONOMY,
HUMILITY, AND SELF-DIRECTION

Bosworth's critique of capitalism suggests that autonomy is only one value among others. In striving for economic and technological control, we fail to acknowledge the important role that moral and spiritual values should play in our lives, which often require that we accept the influence and authority of a higher purpose or commitments to others that bind our will to their needs, thus inhibiting our autonomy. Moreover, according to Bosworth, the sort of autonomy capitalism promotes is an ersatz autonomy. It provides us with an infinite number of choices regarding consumer goods and entertainment but demands that we regulate our lives according to the rhythms of the workplace and marketplace, leaving little time for family, genuine relaxation, or contemplation. For Bosworth, autonomy is not merely the capacity to get what one wants, but requires the ability to assess our wants in light of more deeply held values. But, since those deeper values are allegedly less available in a capitalist society, we lose the capacity for critical thinking that enables us to make wise choices regarding how to live. The net effect is a loss of autonomy since we no longer possess the self-awareness that is an essential component of autonomy.

Bosworth clearly rejects self-sufficiency as the proper account of autonomy in favor of self-direction. [See the Introduction, pp. xix–xxii, for descriptions of these accounts of autonomy.] Upon reflection, he argues, we should realize the spiritual poverty of modern life and turn toward the traditional virtues born in humility that have nurtured human beings throughout history in our confrontation with the fixed features of reality.

But is Bosworth's view sufficiently cognizant of the genuine new possibilities that exist in modern life? After all, not every feature of reality is unalterable or outside our control, and advances in science seem to promise even greater control over life's circumstances. Moreover, many traditions have proven to be so oppressive that they prevent people from living life from the inside—traditions supporting racism, sexism, religious intolerance, or class distinctions interfere with autonomy. How do we distinguish those elements of our condition that cannot or should not be changed from those that must change if we are to lead self-directed lives?

2

Markets and the Social Structure of Morality

David Marsland

David Marsland is Director of Research in the Department of Health and Social Care at Brunel University in the United Kingdom. He is the author of several books, including *Seeds of Bankruptcy*, *Understanding Youth*, and *Welfare or Welfare State?* Marsland's libertarian defense of the moral basis of capitalism rests on the premise that only decisions made freely can be genuine moral choices. Thus, free markets are required as a condition of morality. Symptoms of social decay are a product of the purposelessness people experience when they become dependent and choices are made for them, as is the case in societies that have too many government regulations and government sponsored welfare. By contrast, when people must compete in a free market, the discipline imposed by the possibility of failure encourages the development of rational capacities and strength of character.

Even supporters of free-market principles tend to believe that markets are "morally neutral," denying or ignoring their positive human value. I argue here that this is a mistaken judgment and a dangerous concession to enemies of freedom. It constitutes a foolish encouragement to their inclination to remainder markets to a subordinate and merely instrumental role in the structure of society.

Markets are not morally neutral. They both presuppose and generate virtue. Like any human institution they can in the short term be misused and abused, but in and of themselves they must be judged by any dispassionate observer to be morally beneficial. Like other naturally evolved spontaneous

From David Marsland, "Markets and the Social Structure of Society" in *Society*, March 2001. Reprinted by permission.

human institutions—such as the family, the local community, and the nation state—they are constitutively moral.[1] The argument presented here is
that freedom and personal autonomy are pre-conditions of genuine morality, that freedom and personal autonomy are optimized in market societies,
and that market participation facilitates and stimulates virtuous action. I
then turn to examine the various enemies of the market and the damage
which their arguments and action do to freedom and morality alike.

Markets are not mere instruments of economic efficiency, though certainly
they are at least that, as even socialists now reluctantly admit.[2] Markets are
also key arenas for the expression and development of fundamental human
virtues, and indispensable nurseries of moral action. We need a coherent
philosophical and sociological analysis of the grounding of morality in freedom, and ipso facto in market institutions, if the plaintive socialist critique of
capitalism is to be answered once and for all.

PRECONDITIONS OF MORALITY

Moral action presupposes choice. Virtue entails an opportunity for vice fore-
gone. The gravest charge against totalitarianism is that its ruthless suppres-
sion of liberty dissolves the distinction between virtue and vice, and empties
the concept of morality of any meaning. Hence the banality discovered in the
perpetrators of the Holocaust and the barren amoralism of the Gulag regime.
Thus, morality is feasible only in conditions of liberty. Without personal autonomy, I can do neither good nor evil. Freedom is the logical, psychological, and sociological pre-condition of virtue.[3] Apparent virtue displayed in
conditions of unfreedom is mere habit, a product of unconsidered custom,
or a lingering trace effect of some long-lost freedom. Morally correct behavior arising as a response to external sanctions rather than as a result of autonomous, rational choice is properly to be classified as conformity—and its
contrary as deviance, rather than as moral action—with its contrary in immorality. Admittedly this analysis involves a substantial simplification of the
complexities of the real world. Most social circumstances are characterized
by a mixture of freedom and unfreedom. Even in free societies, conformity
induced by external sanctions and the inculcation of good habits is an essential stage in the development of morality in children. Even indeed among
the adult members of free societies, some few may be so degraded by habitual vice that the imposition of punitive sanctions may be necessary in order to restore their capacity for genuinely autonomous moral action.

In principle and in general, however, morality is linked to freedom and
virtue to choice as breathing is associated with oxygen. Deprivation of liberty is a poisonous gas which fatally destroys the essential hallmark of
humanity—our capacity to make rational moral decisions. Morality is consti-

tutively rooted in freedom. Self-reliant autonomy is the indispensable source of creativity, excellence, concern for others, and virtue in general.[4]

FREEDOM, MARKETS, AND MORALITY

If liberty is the essential pre-condition of virtue, and if we are concerned to preserve or restore the rule of morality, we must study closely the social pre-requisites of freedom. For unfree societies permit at best domesticated beasts behaving well out of mere habit and custom, and at worst a jungle of amoral-ism fit only to be ruled by the Lenins, Hitlers, Stalins, and Mao Tse-tungs of modern socialism.

Analysis of the social structure of freedom is a more challenging and a more complex task than I can address comprehensively here.[5] The history of the development of freedom covers many thousands of years of subtle evo-lution, involving many distinct peoples and civilizations, from biblical Israel, through ancient Greece and Rome, Renaissance Italy, the Low Countries, Britain in many eras, and the United States. The social functioning of free-dom is conditioned by many, various, and mysterious structural factors whose operations have not so far been better than fitfully illuminated even by the powerful intellects of such as Aristotle, Hobbes, Locke, Kant, Mon-tesquieu, Burke, Smith, Spencer, Acton, and Hayek.

The development of individualism as a concept and as a practice, repre-sented archetypically in Antigone's resistance to Creon, is essential. A frame-work of law such as Israel, Greece, and Rome in combination have be-queathed to us is necessary. Arnold Toynbee is surely correct in his claim that a sufficiency of external challenge is necessary if a people is to fracture the cake of custom and develop the scope for innovation which freedom re-quires. But so too is an adequate level of economic prosperity and institu-tional strength sufficient to resist external pressures and defend incipient lib-erty against its internal and external enemies. Not least essential is a constitutional state which facilitates the gradual evolution of democracy while confidently inhibiting pseudo-democratic tendencies such as those represented by Jacobins and Leninists.

The list of structural pre-conditions of liberty should no doubt be ex-tended beyond this short-list of mine substantially. But however long we make it, it has to include, and in a position of high priority, the market. Cer-tainly in the optimal case of the genuinely and securely free society, the mar-ket is absolutely essential. And even at the earliest stages of the development of freedom, and in societies where liberty is much more partial and fragile than we trust we can take for granted in Britain and the USA, the role of markets—as instruments of innovative challenge to outmoded authority and as mechanisms of protection for threatened liberties—is crucial.

The free market is an essential component of the social structure of liberty, and ipso facto, given my argument above about the relations between morality and freedom, an indispensable component of the social structure of virtue. Thus, other than in free market societies, genuine freedom is infeasible better than occasionally, partially, and accidentally. By the same token, bona fide moral action and authentic virtue are impossible in societies lacking free markets except at best as pale, anticipatory shadows of themselves.

Markets are thus neither morally negative, as their most incoherently severe critics (from Marx, through Lenin, to Hitler and Stalin) have alleged, nor even, as more moderate enemies of the market (from J. S. Mill, through Lloyd George Liberals, to the British Labour Party and modern Social Democrats worldwide) persistently claim, morally neutral. They are, on the contrary, in several distinct senses, resoundingly and constitutively positive in their moral implications and effects.

First, markets are one of the several indispensable social preconditions of liberty, and as such prerequisite to any genuinely moral action. In the medium term, if not in the short term, no market, no freedom, no virtue.

Second, in the nature of their modus operandi, markets require quite stringent moral underpinnings—the concept and practice of honesty, for example, to ensure fair dealing, and the virtues of thrift, diligence, and curiosity as guarantors of the self-reliant enterprise without which, as Russia's current parlous condition sadly demonstrates, markets are infeasible.

Third, over and above and separate from their pre-requisite requirement of moral behavior, markets are also among the most important arenas for the display, practice, and learning of moral behavior. It is in the marketplace rather than in the private confines of the family or the parochial domesticity of the local community (let alone the superficial milieu of high society and the media) that real reputations are made on the basis of genuine images of authentically virtuous action. It is in the continually challenging, competitive environment of a market society, unprotected by family, ascribed status, or political privileges, that we can best rehearse the psychological and social skills which underlie the virtues—of diligence, discretion, honesty, fortitude, and all the rest of the repertoire of Judaeo-Christian morality. It is in worlds of work shaped by tough market criteria that young men and women learn what it really means to behave well. Hollywood's Gordon Gecko is as much a fictional projection of anti-capitalist prejudice as Dickens's Mr. Gradgrind.

Fourth and not least, it is the market which, much more reliably than any charter of human rights or the latest politically correct commitment to "multiculturalism" and "gender-equality," underwrites the genuine equality of all human beings. Capitalism cannot perpetrate holocausts or subject minorities to underclass serfdom or bind women to exclusive concern with *kinder und kuche*. These are political, and usually socialist or primitivist, actions, to which the markets of capitalist society are in principle antagonistic—since in the market it is only money, and effort which is worth money, which counts. Every other human characteristic is strictly and completely irrelevant.

Thus it is the concept of the market and the practice of capitalist institutions which in the last resort provide the ultimate guarantee of democracy, of that equality to which democracy gives realistic, practical expression, and of the whole moral system of our civilization out of which equality and democracy have sprung.

ULTRA-SOCIALIST ENEMIES OF VIRTUE

Since the market is a pre-condition of freedom, and since freedom is prerequisite to virtue, opponents of the market are enemies of virtue. If we wish to restore, preserve, and enhance the sway of morality in our decadent societies, we must vigorously resist the arguments, the media campaigning, and the politics of those who denigrate the market. In defending the market, we are standing up for morality itself.

The enemies of the market are for the most part, unsurprisingly, socialists. In this section and the next I address two brands of socialist opposition to free markets. I consider first the damage done to morality by the hard-line socialism of communists and fascists. National and Bolshevik socialism are at one in their complete opposition to free markets and their undiluted commitment to subjecting markets to centralized political control by the state apparatus. Alleged differences between fascism and communism in this respect are as inconsequential as Orwell recognized correctly in *1984*.[6]

However, since fascism has been crushed by force of arms and communism by economic implosion, why worry, the reader might ask, about either of these primitive ideologies at this late stage of history? The answer is simple. Fascism, like the Hydra, is forever revivified however many of its ugly heads we cut off. We should expect it in Africa, in Asia, in South America, and even perhaps restored in Europe. Communism is an even worse case, since, although the media and social scientists may forget it, it is still alive and well in China, where the duplicitous "market socialism" initiated by Deng is the equivalent of the Leninist New Economic Policy which facilitated Stalin's puritanical restoration of thoroughgoing communist terror. In Russia the forces of communism remain, despite welcome movement towards democracy and a market economy, strong and threatening. They loom like a shambling ideological zombie, dead yet hauntingly powerful in the hearts and minds of millions of ex-Soviets.

We must, then, still grapple with the ultra-socialist opposition of fascists and communists to free markets. In this endeavor, it is not enough to condemn fascism narrowly for its anti-Semitism or to dismiss communism simply because its utopian economic policies have failed completely. Beyond and underlying these grave deficiencies, the fundamental error of National and Bolshevik socialism alike is their antagonism to the liberty inherent in the market.

Everything else follows from that: their incapacity to distinguish right from wrong; their willingness to resort routinely to genocide as an instrument of normal policy; their easy inclination to aggressive war; and their incompetence in scientific and technological development. Germany lost the Second World War and Russia the Cold War primarily because the anti-capitalist ideology of their leaderships and their elites destroyed the morality of their people. Robbed of virtue, these two great peoples were left incapable of the persistent, effortful, energetic action which the Free World under Roosevelt, Truman, Churchill, Reagan, and Thatcher were able to call on from the citizens of liberal market societies.

The lesson is straightforward. Destroy the market and you condemn the people to purposeless amoralism. Yield to ultra-socialism in any of its tempting varieties, and within decades your country will lie in ruins.

PSEUDO-DEMOCRATIC SOCIALISTS

A more immediate and more realistic threat to liberty, and hence to virtue, is presented by the soft or pseudo-democratic Third Way socialism into which fundamentalist socialism has conveniently transformed itself in much of the world. Its primary expression, which the market apparently or allegedly accepted, after decades of vitriolic condemnation, in the industrial sphere is support for the welfare state.

The ideology and apparatus of state welfare, with whatever benevolent intentions it may be established, inevitably stifles the responsible, adaptive behavior which freedom requires of those who would claim its precious benefits. Its bureaucratic structures strangle the natural, spontaneously developing cooperative institutions on which freedom depends—the family, the market, the legal system, and the local community foremost amongst them. Its tangled web of rules and obligations destroys the capacity of free men and women to choose freely for themselves and to pursue their individual interests rationally. Its illegitimate seizure of moral control abandons the people to purposeless drifting, subservient dependency, and aimless incapacity to choose and act responsibly and freely for themselves.

Fundamentalist socialism has failed, and is apparently being replaced. The soft socialists' welfare state has failed at least as badly. We need to replace it with institutions more appropriate to a free people. If we are to maintain our liberties and defend virtue, we should liberate welfare from the shackles of the state, and provide for ourselves a system of welfare which in turn liberates from the cramping oppression of the State that capacity for responsible autonomy which is of the essence of moral action.

We should, therefore, turn the welfare state over expeditiously and lock, stock, and barrel to the free market and voluntary agencies. Given the very substantial reductions in taxation and the considerable improvements in efficiency which privatization would permit, most of the population—all except perhaps 10 or at most 15 percent—would be much better served than they are under the established state monopoly system. They would, moreover, and even more importantly, have restored to them with the marketization of welfare, the liberties and the scope for moral action and the exercise of virtue of which the nationalization of welfare has for decades—with disastrous consequences for the moral condition of the population—deprived them.[7]

Nor should these moral advantages be forfeited by mistaken arrangements in the Special Assistance Programme which would certainly be needed for the unfortunate and feckless minority for whom moral and economic self-reliance is in the short term too challenging. Its fundamental mission would be to shift people out of state dependency and back into the normal self-provisioning system as rapidly as possible. This is essential if we are to reverse and prevent the major destructive effect of the welfare state as currently organized—its moral and psychological impact on the character of free people. For the most damaging effect of the welfare state is its impact on the character, motivations, and behavior of the individual men and women subjected to its comprehensive expropriation of their capacity for free and independent action, for self-reliance, for enterprising initiative, and for moral autonomy. By nationalizing care and by expropriating personal responsibility, the welfare state creates and reproduces dependency.

This process affects every level of society and every sphere of social life. Welfare by right and on demand inevitably destroys what free and civilized societies have always defined as the fundamental characteristic of human beings—the capacity to make rational moral choices as a basis for independent action.

Collectivist welfare damages the economy, cripples the dynamism of enterprise culture, fails to help those who most need help, and worst of all positively harms those it is most meant to help—by creating out of temporary unfortunates among our fellow citizens an underclass of welfare dependents. Still worse, their dependency is transmitted from one generation to the next by the fractured families which inappropriate welfare encourages and multiplies, generating a permanent and expanding underclass of moral incompetents.

If we are to halt and reverse this tide of decay, radical reform of welfare is essential. Unless we cut the welfare state back to size by contracting out the prosperous majority and by handling minority special needs more rationally, its destructively damaging effects will worsen still further as its expansionary growth continues at an accelerating rate.

Thus even the soft socialism of supporters of state welfare consists essentially, like the fundamentalist socialism of fascists and communists, of a program for restricting the operations of the free market. And the consequences are identical in both cases: economic efficiency is reduced substantially and the scope for virtue is rendered nugatory. Socialist antagonism to the market produces at one and the same time economic and moral bankruptcy.

CAMPAIGNING AGAINST THE MARKET

Even if we can manage to keep the hands of ultra-socialists off business, and persuade the soft-left to acknowledge the necessity of reforming welfare, we shall still face resistance to the market and thus a restriction on the scope for virtuous action which genuine liberty, uninhibited by state interventions, would permit. This continuing opposition to the free market will come from campaigning liberal, conservative, Christian, and other non-socialist paternalists and collectivists, actively led no doubt by socialists otherwise beneficially unemployed as a result of the demise of socialism. Indeed, resistance to the pseudo-moralistic campaigning against the market organized by such people is already as important as the fight against socialism. In the media, in higher education, and in the schools, in relation to the environment, the privatized industries, multi-culturalism, gender, gay liberation, Third World poverty, the arms trade, and so on, active campaigns are afoot to impose still further bureaucratic state controls on the operations of the free market. Manned by a combination of ex-socialists and willfully utopian idealists, these campaigns ground their arguments not in socialist ideology as such, but directly in moral rhetoric targeted at the market.

They should be answered unapologetically without the slightest concession to their merely fashionable concerns. For on all these fronts the case for the market is overwhelmingly powerful, and the campaigners' moral arguments are incoherent and empty. They rest on adolescent appeals to emotionalism (the meat trade, modern farming, road building), on fraudulent or grossly oversimplified science (Brent Spar, global warming, nuclear energy, smoking), on muddled and heretical theology ("ethical" investment, public service so-called, profits and incentives), and on bizarrely amateur philosophical analysis (feminism, gay liberation, equality).

Across the whole range of these campaigning fronts, the cant is mistaken and the market is more efficient and more effective by a large margin than the bureaucratic systems which these pseudo-moralists prefer.[8] Moreover, unlike the state-regulatory alternatives, which would close up moral debate, market solutions to all these problems would leave the public, the media, and politicians free, as they should be in a free and open society, to carefully debate the complex moral issues involved and to make considered, pragmatic policy decisions appropriate to such challenging issues.

SOCIALISM OR VIRTUE?

Even quite sensible people construe the pair "morals and markets" as a contrast instead of a coupling. I recall my late father—a working-class, proto-Thatcherite Yorkshireman of considerable native intelligence—insisting that while socialism obviously couldn't work, it was a valuable ideal. I never managed to dislodge this pseudo-Christian hangup of his, or to persuade him that an ideology as unrealistic, morally incoherent, and infantile as socialism was quite as unattractive as an ideal as in practice.

Of course the market needs moral and legal regulation, but so too does every institutional sphere in a democratic society, especially the state itself. The lesson of history and of commonsense is that keeping the state under effective control is exceedingly difficult: "unfettered capitalism" is a socialist myth, while unfettered socialism is a reality whose murderous effects have been endured across the face of the earth.[9]

The key to keeping the state under control is to keep its scope minimal, and in particular to prevent it intruding on the proper, expansive sphere of free market institutions. For the market is not only incomparably more efficient than the state in the production and distribution of goods and services of every sort. It is also—and this is why it is efficient—better attuned to the moral concerns of the mass of ordinary people, and allows them the scope, which the state can never provide, for deploying and displaying the whole range of human virtues.

Virtue is a function of freedom, of which the market is a key component. Socialists are in the business of restricting markets and thus of curtailing freedom. We must choose, therefore, between socialism and virtue, between the liberty and morality of capitalism and the slavely amoralism of state domination, between the programmed condition of mere ants and a life of freedom and personal responsibility as human beings.[10]

STUDY QUESTIONS

1. Why are free markets a necessary condition for morality, on Marsland's view?
2. According to Marsland, morality is more effectively learned in the market than in the family or community. Is he correct? Explain.

3. How does Marsland explain contemporary immorality? Is this a plausible explanation of wrongdoing? Explain.
4. Are there forms of wrongdoing that Marsland's view cannot explain?
5. In a society organized according to Marsland's conception of freedom, would the bonds between people be stronger or weaker than in contemporary society. Why?

NOTES

1. See F. A. Hayek, *The Constitution of Liberty* (London: Routledge, 1960).

2. See Tony Blair, *New Britain: My Vision of A Young Country* (London: Fourth Estate, 1996).

3. See H. Arkes, *First Things: An Enquiry into the First Principles of Morality and Justice* (Princeton: Princeton University Press, 1986).

4. See D. C. Anderson, ed. *The Loss of Virtue: Moral Confusion and Social Disorder in Britain and America* (London: Social Affairs Unit, 1992).

5. Gertrude Himmelfarb, *The De-Moralization of Society: From Victorian Virtues to Modern Values* (New York: Knopf, 1995), and Wilhelm Roepke, *The Moral Foundations of Civil Society* (Baton Rouge: Louisiana State University Press, 1995).

6. See I. Shafarevich, *The Socialist Phenomenon* (New York: Harper and Row, 1990).

7. See David Marsland, ed. *Self Reliance: Reforming Welfare in Advanced Societies* (New Brunswick, NJ: Transaction Publishers, 1995).

8. See D. O'Keeffe, *Political Correctness and Public Finance* (London: Institute of Economic Affairs, 1999), and Thomas Sowell, *Markets and Minorities* (London: Blackwell, 1981).

9. See F. A. Hayek, *The Fatal Conceit: The Errors of Socialism* (London: Routledge, 1988).

10. See Edward Shils, *The Virtue of Civility: Selected Essays on Liberalism, Tradition and Civil Society,* ed. by S. Grosby (Indianapolis: Liberty Fund, 1997).

INTERVENTIONS: AUTONOMY AS SELF-SUFFICIENCY

For Marsland, the capacity to make independent decisions and act on them without undue external influence is essential to building moral character. Each person is the best judge or his/her interests, and when individuals are left alone to act on the powerful motive of self-interest, and compete against others who are advancing their self-interest, they will acquire the qualities of character enabling them to compete. We have much more incentive to be honest, fair, curious, and hard-working when these characteristics contribute to our self-interest. When we act on a motive other than self-interest, we extinguish our most powerful motive to be good. Marsland's view suggests that government regulations as well as some traditions, customs, and other moral authorities inhibit self-interested actions by placing artificial barriers to social and economic mobility and thus inhibit the acquisition of moral character. Thus, capitalism's disruptive effect on tradition enhances both liberty and morality.

Marsland's account supports self-sufficiency as the appropriate understanding of autonomy. (See the Introduction, p.xx, for a discussion of self-sufficiency.) In competitive environments there are winners and losers. People who are adversely affected by competition must be prepared to move to areas of the market in which they can compete. This entails that they be prepared to sacrifice commitments to persons, places, and values if these impede participation in the market. Unlike traditional forms of social life, no part of our identity can be immune to revision if it is incapable of participation in the market.

But how revisable are our beliefs, values, and commitments? Are there components of our personal and social identities that cannot be changed without significant loss? Moreover, Marsland thinks our sense of directing our lives from within is best nurtured by being free from external control. But are we free from control when we are forced to submit to market forces?

3

Two Cheers for Capitalism

James B. Twitchell

James B. Twitchell is a professor of English at the University of Florida, Gainesville. He is the author of several books, including *Living It Up: America's Love Affair With Luxury* (2002). This article is adapted from *Lead Us Into Temptation: The Triumph of American Materialism* (1999). Twitchell argues that capitalism exemplifies the fact that human beings love things and this fascination with objects is a source of happiness and emancipation. Although perhaps superficial and uninspiring when compared to other sources of value, consumer goods satisfy needs, reduce suffering, and are a central component in the formation of modern identities.

Of all the strange beasts that have come slouching into the 20th century, none has been more misunderstood, more criticized, and more important than materialism. Who but fools, toadies, hacks, and occasional loopy libertarians have ever risen to its defense? Yet the fact remains that while materialism may be the most shallow of the 20th century's various "-isms", it has been the one that has ultimately triumphed. The world of commodities appears so antithetical to the world of ideas that it seems almost heresy to point out the obvious: most of the world most of the time spends most of its energy producing and consuming more and more stuff. The really interesting question may be not why we are so materialistic, but why we are so unwilling to acknowledge and explore what seems the central characteristic of modern life.

When the French wished to disparage the English in the 19th century, they called them a nation of shopkeepers. When the rest of the world now wishes to disparage Americans, they call us a nation of consumers. And they

From James B. Twitchell, "Two Cheers for Capitalism" in *The Wilson Quarterly*, Spring 1999. Reprinted by permission.

are right. We are developing and rapidly exporting a new material culture, a mallcondo culture. To the rest of the world we do indeed seem not just born to shop, but alive to shop. Americans spend more time tooling around the mallcondo—three to four times as many hours as our European counterparts—and we have more stuff to show for it. According to some estimates, we have about four times as many things as Middle Europeans, and who knows how much more than people in the less developed parts of the world. The quantity and disparity are increasing daily, even though, as we see in Russia and China, the "emerging nations" are playing a frantic game of catch-up.

This burst of mallcondo commercialism has happened recently—in my lifetime—and it is spreading around the world at the speed of television. The average American consumes twice as many goods and services as in 1950; in fact, the poorest fifth of the current population buys more than the average fifth did in 1955. Little wonder that the average new home of today is twice as large as the average house built in the early years after World War II. We have to put that stuff somewhere—quick!—before it turns to junk.

Sooner or later we are going to have to acknowledge the uncomfortable fact that this amoral consumerama has proved potent because human beings love things. In fact, to a considerable degree we live for things. In all cultures we buy things, steal things, exchange things, and hoard things. From time to time, some of us collect vast amounts of things, from tulip bulbs to paint drippings on canvases to matchbook covers. Often these objects have no observable use.

We live through things. We create ourselves through things. And we change ourselves by changing our things. In the West, we have even developed the elaborate algebra of commercial law to decide how things are exchanged, divested, and recaptured. Remember, we call these things "goods," as in "goods and services." We don't—unless we are academic critics—call them "bads." This sounds simplistic, but it is crucial to understanding the powerful allure of materialism.

Our commercial culture has been blamed for the rise of eating disorders, the spread of "affluenza," the epidemic of depression, the despoliation of cultural icons, the corruption of politics, the carnivalization of holy times like Christmas, and the gnat-life attention span of our youth. All of this is true. Commercialism contributes. But it is by no means the whole truth. Commercialism is more a mirror than a lamp. In demonizing it, in seeing ourselves as helpless and innocent victims of its overpowering force, in making it the scapegoat du jour, we reveal far more about our own eagerness to be passive in the face of complexity than about the thing itself.

Anthropologists tell us that consumption habits are gender-specific. Men seem to want stuff in the latent and post-midlife years. That's when the male collecting impulse seems to be felt. Boys amass playing marbles first, Elgin marbles later. Women seem to gain potency as consumers after childbirth, almost as if getting and spending is part of a nesting impulse.

Historians, however, tell us to be careful about such stereotyping. Although women are the primary consumers of commercial objects today, they have enjoyed this status only since the Industrial Revolution. Certainly in the pre-industrial world men were the chief hunter-gatherers. If we can trust works of art to accurately portray how booty was split (and cultural historians such as John Berger and Simon Schama think we can), then males were the prime consumers of fine clothes, heavily decorated furniture, gold and silver articles, and of course, paintings in which they could be shown displaying their stuff.

Once a surplus was created, in the 19th century, women joined the fray in earnest. They were not duped. The hegemonic phallocentric patriarchy did not brainwash them into thinking goods mattered. The Industrial Revolution produced more and more things not simply because it had the machines to do so, and not because nasty producers twisted their handlebar mustaches and whispered, "We can talk women into buying anything," but because both sexes are powerfully attracted to the world of things.

Karl Marx understood the magnetism of things better than anyone else. In *The Communist Manifesto* (1848), he wrote:

> The bourgeoisie, by the rapid improvement of all instruments of production, by the immensely facilitated means of communication, draws all, even the most barbarian nations into civilization. The cheap prices of its commodities are the heavy artillery with which it batters down all Chinese walls. . . . It compels all nations on pain of extinction, to adopt the bourgeois mode of production; it compels them to introduce what it calls civilization into their midst, i.e. to become bourgeois themselves. In one word, it creates a world after its own image.

Marx used this insight to motivate the heroic struggle against capitalism. But the struggle should not be to deter capitalism and its mad consumptive ways, but to appreciate how it works so its furious energy may be understood and exploited.

Don't turn to today's middle-aged academic critic for any help on that score. Driving about in his totemic Volvo (unattractive and built to stay that way), he can certainly criticize the bourgeois afflictions of others, but he is unable to provide much actual insight into their consumption practices, much less his own. Ask him to explain the difference between "Hilfiger" inscribed on an oversize shirt hanging nearly to the knees and his rear-window university decal (My child goes to Yale, sorry about yours), and you will be met with a blank stare. If you were then to suggest that what that decal and automotive nameplate represent is as overpriced as Calvin Klein's initials on a plain white T-shirt, he would pout that you can't compare apples and whatever. If you were to say next that aspiration and affiliation are at the heart of both displays, he would say that you just don't get it, just don't get it at all.

If you want to understand the potency of American consumer culture, ask any group of teenagers what democracy means to them. You will hear an extraordinary response. Democracy is the right to buy anything you want. Freedom's just another word for lots of things to buy. Appalling perhaps, but there is something to their answer. Being able to buy what you want when and where you want it was, after all, the right that made 1989 a watershed year in Eastern Europe.

Recall as well that freedom to shop was another way to describe the right to be served in a restaurant that provided one focus for the early civil rights movement. Go back further. It was the right to consume freely which sparked the fires of separation of this country from England. The freedom to buy what you want (even if you can't pay for it) is what most foreigners immediately spot as what they like about our culture, even though in the next breath they will understandably criticize it.

The pressure to commercialize—to turn things into commodities and then market them as charms—has always been particularly Western. As Max Weber first argued in *The Protestant Ethic and the Spirit of Capitalism* (1905), much of the Protestant Reformation was geared toward denying the holiness of many things that the Catholic church had endowed with meanings. From the inviolable priesthood to the sacrificial holy water, this deconstructive movement systematically unloaded meaning. Soon the marketplace would capture this off-loaded meaning and apply it to secular things. Buy this, you'll be saved. You deserve a break today. You, you're the one. We are the company that cares about you. You're worth it. You are in good hands. We care. Trust in us. We are here for you.

Materialism, it's important to note, does not crowd out spiritualism; spiritualism is more likely a substitute when objects are scarce. When we have few things we make the next world holy. When we have plenty we enchant the objects around us. The hereafter becomes the here and now.

We have not grown weaker but stronger by accepting the self-evidently ridiculous myths that sacramentalize mass-produced objects; we have not wasted away but have proved inordinately powerful; have not devolved and been rebarbarized, but seem to have marginally improved. Dreaded affluenza notwithstanding, commercialism has lessened pain. Most of us have more pleasure and less discomfort in our lives than most of the people most of the time in all of history.

As Stanley Lebergott, an economist at Wesleyan University, argues in *Pursuing Happiness* (1993), most Americans have "spent their way to happiness." Lest this sound overly Panglossian, what Lebergott means is that while consumption by the rich has remained relatively steady, the rest of us—the intractable poor (about 4 percent of the population) are the exception—have now had a go of it. If the rich really are different, as F. Scott Fitzgerald said, and the difference is that they have longer shopping lists and are happier for it, then we have, in the last two generations, substantially caught up.

The most interesting part of the book is the second half. Here Lebergott unloads reams of government statistics and calculations to chart the path that American consumption has taken in a wide range of products and services: food, tobacco, clothing, fuel, domestic service, and medicine—to name only a few. Two themes emerge strongly from these data. The first, not surprisingly, is that Americans were far better off by 1990 than they were in 1900. And the second is that academic critics—from Robert Heilbroner, Tibor Scitovsky, Robert and Helen Lynd, and Christopher Lasch to Juliet Schor, Robert Frank, and legions of others—who've censured the waste and tastelessness of much of American consumerism have simply missed the point. Okay, okay, money can't buy happiness, but you stand a better chance than with penury.

The cultural pessimists counter that it may be true that materialism offers a temporary palliative against the anxiety of emptiness, but we still must burst joy's grape. Consumption will turn sour because so much of it is based on the chimera of debt. Easy credit = overbuying = disappointment = increased anxiety.

This is not just patronizing, it is wrongheaded. As another economist, Lendol Calder, has argued in *Financing the American Dream* (1999), debt has been an important part of families' financial planning since the time of Washington and Jefferson. And although consumer debt has consistently risen in recent times, the default rate has remained remarkably stable. More than 95.5 percent of consumer debt gets paid, usually on time. In fact, the increased availability of credit to a growing share of the population, particularly to lower-income individuals and families, has allowed many more "have nots" to enter the economic mainstream.

There is, in fact, a special crippling quality to poverty in the modern Western world. For the penalty of intractable, transgenerational destitution is not just the absence of things; it is also the absence of meaning, the exclusion from participating in the essential socializing events of modern life. When you hear that some ghetto kid has killed one of his peers for a pair of branded sneakers or a monogrammed athletic jacket you realize that chronically unemployed poor youths are indeed living the absurdist life proclaimed by existentialists. The poor are the truly self-less ones in commercial culture.

Clearly what the poor are after is what we all want: association, affiliation, inclusion, magical purpose. While they are bombarded, as we all are, by the commercial imprecations of being cool, of experimenting with various presentations of disposable self, they lack the wherewithal to even enter the loop.

The grandfather of today's academic scolds is Thorstein Veblen (1857–1929), the eccentric Minnesotan who coined the phrase "conspicuous consumption" and has become almost a cult figure among critics of consumption. All of his books (save for his translation of the *Lexdaela Saga*) are still in print. His most famous, *The Theory of the Leisure Class*, has never been out of print since it was first published in 1899.

Veblen claimed that the leisure class set the standards for conspicuous consumption. Without sumptuary laws to protect their markers of distinction, the rest of us could soon make their styles into our own—the Industrial Revolution saw to that. But since objects lose their status distinctions when consumed by the hoi polloi, the leisure class must eternally be finding newer and more wasteful markers. Waste is not just inevitable, it is always increasing as the foolish hounds chase the wily fox.

Veblen lumped conspicuous consumption with sports and games, "devout observances," and aesthetic display. They were all reducible, he insisted, to "pecuniary emulation," his characteristically inflated term for getting in with the in-crowd. Veblen fancied himself a socialist looking forward to the day when "the discipline of the machine" would be turned around to promote stringent rationality among the entire population instead of wasted dispersion. If only we had fewer choices we would be happier, there would be less waste, and we would accept each other as equals.

The key to Veblen's argumentative power is that like Hercules cleaning the Augean stables, he felt no responsibility to explain what happens next. True, if we all purchased the same toothpaste things would be more efficient and less wasteful. Logically we should all read Consumer Reports, find out the best brand, and then all be happy using the same product. But we aren't. Procter & Gamble markets 36 sizes and shapes of Crest. There are 41 versions of Tylenol. Is this because we are dolts afflicted with "pecuniary emulation," obsessed with making invidious distinctions, or is the answer more complex? Veblen never considered that consumers might have other reasons for exercising choice in the marketplace. He never considered, for example, that along with "keeping up with the Joneses" runs "keeping away from the Joneses."

Remember in *King Lear* when the two nasty daughters want to strip Lear of his last remaining trappings of majesty? He has moved in with them, and they don't think he needs so many expensive guards. They whittle away at his retinue until only one is left. "What needs one?" they say. Rather like governments attempting to redistribute wealth or like academics criticizing consumption, they conclude that Lear's needs are excessive. They are false needs. Lear, however, knows otherwise. Terrified and suddenly bereft of purpose, he bellows from his innermost soul, "Reason not the need."

Lear knows that possessions are definitions—superficial meanings, perhaps, but meanings nonetheless. And unlike Veblen, he knows those meanings are worth having. Without soldiers he is no king. Without a BMW there can be no yuppie, without tattoos no adolescent rebel, without big hair no Southwestern glamor-puss, without Volvos no academic intellectual, and, well, you know the rest. Meaning is what we are after, what we need, especially when we are young.

What kind of meaning? In the standard academic view, growing out of the work of the Frankfurt school theorists of the 1950s and '60s (such as Antonio Gramsci, Theodor Adorno, and Max Horkheimer) and later that of the Center for Contemporary Cultural Studies at the University of Birmingham, it is meaning supplied by capitalist manipulators. What we see in popular culture, in this view, is the result of the manipulation of the many for the profit of the few.

For an analogy, take watching television. In academic circles, we assume that youngsters are being reified (to borrow a bit of the vast lexicon of jargon that accompanies this view) by passively consuming pixels in the dark. Meaning supposedly resides in the shows and is transferred to the sponge-like viewers. So boys, for example, see flickering scenes of violence, internalize these scenes, and willy-nilly are soon out jimmying open your car. This is the famous Twinkie interpretation of human behavior—consuming too much sugar leads to violent actions. Would listening to Barry Manilow five hours a day make adolescents into loving, caring people?

Watch kids watching television and you see something quite different from what is seen by the critics. Most consumption, whether it be of entertainment or in the grocery store, is active. We are engaged. Here is how I watch television. I almost never turn the set on to see a particular show. I am near the machine and think I'll see what's happening. I know all the channels; any eight-year-old does. I am not a passive viewer. I use the remote control to pass through various programs, not searching for a final destination but making up a shopping basket, as it were, of entertainment.

But the academic critic doesn't see this. He sees a passive observer who sits quietly in front of the set letting the phosphorescent glow of mindless infotainment pour over his consciousness. In the hypodermic analogy beloved by critics, the potent dope of desire is pumped into the bleary dupe. This paradigm of passive observer and active supplier, a receptive moron and a smart manipulator, is easily transported to the marketplace. One can see why such a system would appeal to the critic. After all, since the critic is not being duped, he should be empowered to protect the young, the female, the foreign, the uneducated, and the helpless from the onslaught of dreck.

In the last decade or so, however, a number of scholars in the humanities and social sciences have been challenging many of the academy's assumptions.[1] What distinguishes the newer thinking is that scholars have left the office to actually observe and question their subjects. Just one example: Mihaly Csikszentmihalyi, a psychology professor at the University of Chicago, interviewed 315 Chicagoans from 82 families, asking them what objects in the home they cherished most. The adult members of the five happiest families picked things that reminded them of other people and good times they'd had together. They mentioned a memento (such as an old toy) from their childhood 30 percent of the time. Adults in the 5 most dissatisfied families cited such objects only 6 percent of the time.

In explaining why they liked something, happy family members often described, for example, the times their family had spent on a favorite couch, rather than its style or color. Their gloomier counterparts tended to focus on the merely physical qualities of things. What was clear was that both happy and unhappy families derived great meaning from the consumption and interchange of manufactured things. The thesis, reflected in the title of his co-authored 1981 book, *The Meaning of Things: Domestic Symbols and the Self*, is that most of the "work" of consumption occurs after the act of purchase. Things do not come complete; they are forever being assembled.

Twentieth-century French sociologists have taken the argument even further. Two of the most important are Pierre Bourdieu, author of *Distinction: A Social Critique of the Judgement of Taste* (1984), and Jean Baudrillard, whose books include *The Mirror of Production* (1983) and *Simulacra and Simulation* (1994). In the spirit of reader-response theory in literary criticism, they see meaning not as a single thing that producers affix to consumer goods, but as something created by the user, who jumbles various interpretations simultaneously. Essentially, beneath the jargon, this means that the Budweiser you drink is not the same as the one I drink. The meaning tastes different. The fashion you consider stylish, I think is ugly. If we buy the package not the contents, it is because the package means more.

The process of consumption is creative and even emancipating. In an open market, we consume the real and the imaginary meanings, fusing objects, symbols, and images together to end up with "a little world made cunningly." Rather than lives, individuals since midcentury have had lifestyles. For better or worse, lifestyles are secular religions, coherent patterns of valued things. Your lifestyle is not related to what you do for a living but to what you buy. One of the chief aims of the way we live now is the enjoyment of affiliating with those who share the same clusters of objects as ours. Mall-condo culture is so powerful in part because it frees us from the strictures of social class. The outcome of material life is no longer preordained by coat of arms, pew seat, or trust fund. Instead, it evolves from a never-ending shifting of individual choice. No one wants to be middle class, for instance. You want to be cool, hip, with it, with the "in" crowd, instead.

One of the reasons terms like Yuppie, Baby Boomer, and GenX have elbowed aside such older designations as "upper middle class" is that we no longer understand social class as well as we do lifestyle, or what marketing firms call "consumption communities." Observing stuff is the way we understand each other. Even if no one knows exactly how much money it takes to be a yuppie, or how young you have to be, or how upwardly aspiring, everybody knows where yuppies gather, how they dress, what they play, what they drive, what they eat, and why they hate to be called yuppies.

For better or worse, American culture is well on its way to becoming world culture. The Soviets have fallen. Only quixotic French intellectuals and anxious Islamic fundamentalists are trying to stand up to it. By no means am I sanguine about such a material culture. It has many problems that I have glossed over. Consumerism is wasteful, it is devoid of otherworldly concerns, it lives for today and celebrates the body, and it overindulges and spoils the young with impossible promises.

"Getting and spending" has eclipsed family, ethnicity, even religion as a defining matrix. That doesn't mean that those other defining systems have disappeared, but that an increasing number of young people around the world will give more of their loyalty to Nike than to creeds of blood, race, or belief. This is not entirely a bad thing, since a lust for upscale branding isn't likely to drive many people to war, but it is, to say the least, far from inspiring.

It would be nice to think that materialism could be heroic, self-abnegating, and redemptive. It would be nice to think that greater material comforts will release us from racism, sexism, and ethnocentrism, and that the apocalypse will come as it did at the end of romanticism in Shelley's "Prometheus Unbound," leaving us "Scepterless, free, uncircumscribed . . . Equal, unclassed, tribeless, and nationless."

But it is more likely that the globalization of capitalism will result in the banalities of an ever-increasing worldwide consumerist culture. The French don't stand a chance. The untranscendent, repetitive, sensational, democratic, immediate, tribalizing, and unifying force of what Irving Kristol calls the American Imperium need not necessarily result in a Bronze Age of culture. But it certainly will not produce what Shelley had in mind.

We have not been led into this world of material closeness against our better judgment. For many of us, especially when young, consumerism is our better judgment. We have not just asked to go this way, we have demanded. Now most of the world is lining up, pushing and shoving, eager to elbow into the mall. Getting and spending has become the most passionate, and often the most imaginative, endeavor of modern life. While this is dreary and depressing to some, as doubtless it should be, it is liberating and democratic to many more.

STUDY QUESTIONS

1. What does consumerism tell us about human beings, according to Twitchell?

2. On Twitchell's view, what are the underlying motives of consumerism?
3. Twitchell argues that, for most of us, social meanings and personal identity are wrapped up in the pursuit and enjoyment of material goods. Is he correct? Explain.
4. What does Twitchell mean when he writes that "things do not come complete; they are forever being assembled"? Is this one of the primary ways we exercise autonomy in contemporary culture?
5. Overall, is a worldwide consumerist culture a good thing or a bad thing?
6. Is a life devoted to consumption a kind of life we have chosen? Explain.

NOTE

1. This reconsideration of consumption is an especially strong current in anthropology, where the central text is *The World of Goods: Towards an Anthropology of Consumption* (1996), by Mary Douglas and Baron Isherwood. It can also be seen in the work of scholars such as William Leiss in communication studies; Dick Hebdige in sociology; Jackson Lears in history; David Morley in cultural studies; Michael Schudson in the study of advertising; Sidney Levy in consumer research; Tyler Cowan in economics, Grant McCracken in fashion; and Simon Schama in art history. There are many other signs of change. One of the more interesting recent shows at the Museum of Modern Art, "Objects of Desire: The Modern Still Life," actually focused on the salutary influence of consumer culture on high culture.

INTERVENTIONS: DOES CAPITALISM
SUBVERT OR SUPPORT AUTONOMY?

Capitalism is often accused of subverting autonomy. According to some critics, advertising and envy create wants that subvert our reasoning and spin out of control without the restraint of strong moral character grounded in spiritual values and a critical response to materialism. This criticism of capitalism raises the specter of oppressive socialization. If we grow up under social conditions in which we are rendered passive victims of powerful social forces like advertising, autonomy will be difficult to achieve. Under such conditions, our desires are not our own since we had no role in shaping them. Twitchell takes issue with this equation, arguing that our desire to possess material goods is not the irrational product of corrupted deliberative processes but constitutes genuine, reflectively endorsed preferences. Consumption is an active process of conferring meaning on objects and can supply us with a meaningful sense of community.

Though we might grant Twitchell's point that human beings find meaning in material objects, autonomy theorists worry that much of modern consumer society is devoted to the satisfaction of first-order desires—immediate wants and pleasures that may have little lasting significance. However, autonomy construed as self-direction requires that these immediate desires be reflectively endorsed by assessing their consistency with deeper values. To what degree does society promote and encourage reflection about these desires? Is it relatively easy to adopt a critical, informed perspective on the worth of consumer goods and our consumer habits? Do the institutions of capitalism impede or enhance our ability to recognize distorted desires and false norms?

On the other hand, the concept of self-direction assumes that the real self is the self we exhibit when we step back and take a reflective look at our immediate desires from the perspective of long-term commitments, deeply held values, etc. Yet, in countless moments of daily life, the body fuses intelligently with the world through interaction with objects, and the fabric of intuitions, perceptions, and feelings that make up our interactions with objects powerfully shapes our habits and actions. It is doubtful that these habits can be dissolved through deliberation.

Twitchell argues that our identities are in part a product of this active, imaginative engagement with material objects that reflect back to us and to others who we are. The diversity of accessible lifestyles made available by consumerism enables agents to "try on" self-definitions in order to determine which ones confer social recognition and a sense of self-worth. If objects are not merely things to be accumulated and assigned value but represent a fundamental way of knowing the world and ourselves, then perhaps the sort of experiential exploring that consumerism enables is important for autonomy.

II

THE PROMISE OF EQUALITY

Egalitarian liberalism asserts that the best explanation of social conflict, crime, family breakdown, and other indicators of social decay is that they are the result of social injustices such as racial prejudice, sexism, and economic inequality. Although these injustices have been with us for a long time, many argue that our persistent inability to reduce social and economic inequality suggests that modern liberal societies have failed to live up to their moral ideals and are losing their legitimacy. In this view, the notion that all human beings deserve equal respect is a fundamental moral principle and the inability of social institutions to sustain policies of equal treatment in accordance with equal rights is a moral failing.

By contrast, libertarians argue that a crisis of values arises from attempts to rectify most inequalities. Resistance to affirmative action and government spending on welfare, education, and health care rests on the belief that our basic liberty rights are compromised when we tax the property of some citizens in order to improve the welfare of others. On this view, inequalities in wealth result from natural differences in abilities and are thus deserved by the people who benefit from them. Attempts by government to redistribute wealth violate the autonomy of individuals by using their property and labor to help others without their consent.

Theoretically, this debate is not about the value of equality as a moral ideal—both sides agree that equality is a fundamental principle. The disagreement is over the meaning of equality, a disagreement driven by contrasting assumptions regarding the nature and scope of autonomy.

What does it mean to say that all human beings deserve equal respect? It obviously does not mean that all human beings are equal in ability, intelligence, or moral character. For both libertarians and egalitarian liberals it means that each individual has an interest in choosing how to live—our autonomy matters to us equally. This leads libertarians to argue that political institutions must not impose values on citizens by favoring the interests of some citizens over others but must treat each citizen equally. Thus, our interest in autonomy gives rise to rights not to be coerced by government power as long as we do not interfere with the autonomy of others. This is a political conception of autonomy that treats government power as the main threat to a person's capacity for autonomy.

However, egalitarian liberals view autonomy not merely as a political right but as a psychological capacity to govern oneself. Autonomy in this sense has to do with my capacity to be aware of a variety of choices and critically assess desires and preferences in a way that enables me to act on them. To the extent that an individual lacks self-respect, access to education, health care, or adequate housing she will lack crucial elements of her capacity for autonomy. Equal respect for the capacity to lead an autonomous life thus involves guaranteeing that each individual has the goods required to exercise this capacity. For egalitarian liberals freedom from excessive government interference is only one of a variety of conditions that give rise to autonomy. This justifies at least some degree of wealth redistribution.

Thus, the disagreement between competing positions in this debate concerns the nature of the threat to autonomy. Does the government's power to tax and regulate individuals threaten autonomy, or is autonomy threatened when individuals lack resources and access to positions in society?

4

Nihilism in Black America

Cornel West

Cornel West is Alphonse Fletcher Jr. University Professor of Divinity at Harvard University. He is the author of numerous books including *Beyond Ethnocentrism and Multiculturalism, Jews and Blacks: Let the Healing Begin, The Cornel West Reader, The African-American Century*, and *Race Matters*, from which the following essay is taken. Cornel West argues that the history of inequalities suffered by African Americans have led not only to lost opportunities in the competition for a piece of the American dream, but to a pervasive sense of meaninglessness and lack of self-respect within the poorest African-American communities. This sense of meaninglessness, though a product of racial prejudice and discrimination, is deepened and fortified by hedonistic market values that crowd out an ethic of care and service to others. Thus, solutions to problems of racial inequality in America involve not just economic and political change but a transformation in values that will revitalize a sense of agency within communities.

Recent discussions about the plight of African Americans—especially those at the bottom of the social ladder—tend to divide into two camps. On the one hand, there are those who highlight the *structural* constraints on the life chances of black people. Their viewpoint involves a subtle historical and sociological analysis of slavery, Jim Crowism, job and residential discrimination, skewed unemployment rates, inadequate health care, and poor education. On the other hand, there are those who stress the *behavioral* impediments on black upward mobility. They focus on the waning of the Protestant ethic—hard work, deferred gratification, frugality, and responsibility—in much of black America.

Those in the first camp—the liberal structuralists—call for full employment, health, education, and child-care programs, and broad affirmative action practices. In short, a new, more sober version of the best of the New Deal and the Great Society: more government money, better bureaucrats, and an active citizenry. Those in the second camp—the conservative behaviorists—promote self-help programs, black business expansion, and non-preferential job practices. They support vigorous "free market" strategies that depend on fundamental changes in how black people act and live. To put it bluntly, their projects rest largely upon a cultural revival of the Protestant ethic in black America.

Unfortunately, these two camps have nearly suffocated the crucial debate that should be taking place about the prospects for black America. This debate must go far beyond the liberal and conservative positions in three fundamental ways. First, we must acknowledge that structures and behavior are inseparable, that institutions and values go hand in hand. How people act and live are shaped—though in no way dictated or determined—by the larger circumstances in which they find themselves. These circumstances can be changed, their limits attenuated, by positive actions to elevate living conditions.

Second, we should reject the idea that structures are primarily economic and political creatures—an idea that sees culture as an ephemeral set of behavioral attitudes and values. Culture is as much a structure as the economy or politics; it is rooted in institutions such as families, schools, churches, synagogues, mosques, and communication industries (television, radio, video, music). Similarly, the economy and politics are not only influenced by values but also promote particular cultural ideals of the good life and good society.

Third, and most important, we must delve into the depths where neither liberals nor conservatives dare to tread, namely, into the murky waters of despair and dread that now flood the streets of black America. To talk about the depressing statistics of unemployment, infant mortality, incarceration, teenage pregnancy, and violent crime is one thing. But to face up to the monumental eclipse of hope, the unprecedented collapse of meaning, the incredible disregard for human (especially black) life and property in much of black America is something else.

The liberal/conservative discussion conceals the most basic issue now facing black America: *the nihilistic threat to its very existence*. This threat is not simply a matter of relative economic deprivation and political powerlessness—though economic well being and political clout are requisites for meaningful black progress. It is primarily a question of speaking to the profound sense of psychological depression, personal worthlessness, and social despair so widespread in black America.

The liberal structuralists fail to grapple with this threat for two reasons. First, their focus on structural constraints relates almost exclusively to the economy and politics. They show no understanding of the structural character of culture. Why? Because they tend to view people in egoistic and rationalist terms according to which they are motivated primarily by self-interest and self-preservation. Needless to say, this is partly true about most of us. Yet, people, especially degraded and oppressed people, are also hungry for identity, meaning, and self-worth.

The second reason liberal structuralists overlook the nihilistic threat is a sheer failure of nerve. They hesitate to talk honestly about culture, the realm of meanings and values, because doing so seems to lend itself too readily to conservative conclusions in the narrow way Americans discuss race. If there is a hidden taboo among liberals, it is to resist talking *too much* about values because such discussions remove the focus from structures and especially because they obscure the positive role of government. But this failure by liberals leaves the existential and psychological realities of black people in the lurch. In this way, liberal structuralists neglect the battered identities rampant in black America.

As for the conservative behaviorists, they not only misconstrue the nihilistic threat but inadvertently contribute to it. This is a serious charge, and it rests upon several claims. Conservative behaviorists talk about values and attitudes as if political and economic structures hardly exist. They rarely, if ever, examine the innumerable cases in which black people do act on the Protestant ethic and still remain at the bottom of the social ladder. Instead, they highlight the few instances in which blacks ascend to the top, as if such success is available to all blacks, regardless of circumstances. Such a vulgar rendition of Horatio Alger in blackface may serve as a source of inspiration to some—a kind of model for those already on the right track. But it cannot serve as a substitute for serious historical and social analysis of the predicaments of and prospects for all black people, especially the grossly disadvantaged ones.

Conservative behaviorists also discuss black culture as if acknowledging one's obvious victimization by white supremacist practices (compounded by sexism and class condition) is taboo. They tell black people to see themselves as agents, not victims. And on the surface, this is comforting advice, a nice cliche for downtrodden people. But inspirational slogans cannot substitute for substantive historical and social analysis. While black people have never been simply victims, wallowing in self-pity and begging for white giveaways, they have been—and are—*victimized*. Therefore, to call on black people to be agents makes sense only if we also examine the dynamics of this victimization against which their agency will, in part, be exercised.

What is particularly naive and peculiarly vicious about the conservative behavioral outlook is that it tends to deny the lingering effect of black history—a history inseparable from though not reducible to victimization. In this way, crucial and indispensable themes of self-help and personal responsibility are wrenched out of historical context and contemporary circumstance—as if it is all a matter of personal will.

This ahistorical perspective contributes to the nihilistic threat within black America in that it can be used to justify right-wing cutbacks for poor people struggling for decent housing, child care, health care, and education. As I pointed out above, the liberal perspective is deficient in important ways, but even so liberals are right on target in their critique of conservative government cutbacks for services to the poor. These ghastly cutbacks are one cause of the nihilist threat to black America.

The proper starting point for the crucial debate about the prospects for black America is an examination of the nihilism that increasingly pervades black communities. *Nihilism is to be understood here not as a philosophic doctrine that there are no rational grounds for legitimate standards or authority; it is, far more, the lived experience of coping with a life of horrifying meaninglessness, hopelessness, and (most important) lovelessness.* The frightening result is a numbing detachment from others and a self-destructive disposition toward the world. Life without meaning, hope, and love breeds a coldhearted, meanspirited outlook that destroys both the individual and others.

Nihilism is not new in black America. The first African encounter with the New World was an encounter with a distinctive form of the Absurd. The initial black struggle against degradation and devaluation in the enslaved circumstances of the New World was, in part, a struggle against nihilism. In fact, the major enemy of black survival in America has been and is neither oppression nor exploitation but rather the nihilistic threat—that is, loss of hope and absence of meaning. For as long as hope remains and meaning is preserved, the possibility of overcoming oppression stays alive. The self-fulfilling prophecy of the nihilistic threat is that without hope there can be no future, that without meaning there can be no struggle.

The genius of our black foremothers and forefathers was to create powerful buffers to ward off the nihilistic threat, to equip black folk with cultural armor to beat back the demons of hopelessness, meaninglessness, and lovelessness. These buffers consisted of cultural structures of meaning and feeling that created and sustained communities; this armor constituted ways of life and struggle that embodied values of service and sacrifice, love and care, discipline and excellence. In other words, traditions for black surviving and thriving under usually adverse New World conditions were major barriers against the nihilistic threat. These traditions consist primarily of black religious and civic institutions that sustained familial and communal networks of support. If cultures are, in part, what human beings create (out of antecedent fragments of other cultures) in order to convince themselves not to commit suicide, then black foremothers and forefathers are to be applauded. In fact, until the early seventies black Americans had the lowest suicide rate in the United States. But now young black people lead the nation in suicides.

What has changed? What went wrong? The bitter irony of integration? The cumulative effects of a genocidal conspiracy? The virtual collapse of rising expectations after the optimistic sixties? None of us fully understands why the cultural structures that once sustained black life in America are no longer able to fend off the nihilistic threat.

I believe that two significant reasons why the threat is more powerful now than ever before are the saturation of market forces and market moralities in black life and the present crisis in black leadership. The recent market-driven shattering of black civil society—black families, neighborhoods, schools, churches, mosques—leaves more and more black people vulnerable to daily lives endured with little sense of self and fragile existential moorings.

Black people have always been in America's wilderness in search of a promised land. Yet many black folk now reside in a jungle ruled by a cut-throat market morality devoid of any faith in deliverance or hope for freedom. Contrary to the superficial claims of conservative behaviorists, these jungles are not primarily the result of pathological behavior. Rather, this behavior is the tragic response of a people bereft of resources in confronting the workings of U.S. capitalist society. Saying this is not the same as asserting that individual black people are not responsible for their actions—black murderers and rapists should go to jail. But it must be recognized that the nihilistic threat contributes to criminal behavior. It is a threat that feeds on poverty and shattered cultural institutions and grows more powerful as the armors to ward against it are weakened.

But why is this shattering of black civil society occurring? What has led to the weakening of black cultural institutions in asphalt jungles? Corporate market institutions have contributed greatly to their collapse. By corporate market institutions I mean that complex set of interlocking enterprises that have a disproportionate amount of capital, power, and exercise a disproportionate influence on how our society is run and how our culture is shaped. Needless to say, the primary motivation of these institutions is to make profits, and their basic strategy is to convince the public to consume. These institutions have helped create a seductive way of life, a culture of consumption that capitalizes on every opportunity to make money. Market calculations and cost-benefit analyses hold sway in almost every sphere of U.S. society.

The common denominator of these calculations and analyses is usually the provision, expansion, and intensification of *pleasure*. Pleasure is a multivalent term; it means different things to many people. In the American way of life pleasure involves comfort, convenience, and sexual stimulation. Pleasure, so defined, has little to do with the past and views the future as no more than a repetition of a hedonistically driven present. This market morality stigmatizes others as objects for personal pleasure or bodily stimulation. Conservative behaviorists have alleged that traditional morality has been undermined by radical feminists and the cultural radicals of the sixties. But it is clear that corporate market institutions have greatly contributed to undermining traditional morality in order to stay in business and make a profit. The reduction of individuals to objects of pleasure is especially evident in the culture industries—television, radio, video, music—in which gestures of sexual foreplay and orgiastic pleasure flood the marketplace.

Like all Americans, African Americans are influenced greatly by the images of comfort, convenience, machismo, femininity, violence, and sexual stimulation that bombard consumers. These seductive images contribute to the predominance of the market-inspired way of life over all others and thereby edge out non-market values—love, care, service to others—handed down by preceding generations. The predominance of this way of life among those living in poverty-ridden conditions, with a limited capacity to ward off self-contempt and self-hatred, results in the possible triumph of the nihilistic threat in black America.

A major contemporary strategy for holding the nihilistic threat at bay is a direct attack on the sense of worthlessness and self-loathing in black America. This *angst* resembles a kind of collective clinical depression in significant pockets of black America. The eclipse of hope and collapse of meaning in much of black America is linked to the structural dynamics of corporate market institutions that affect all Americans. Under these circumstances black existential *angst* derives from the lived experience of ontological wounds and emotional scars inflicted by white supremacist beliefs and images permeating U.S. society and culture. These beliefs and images attack black intelligence, black ability, black beauty, and black character daily in subtle and not-so-subtle ways.

Toni Morrison's novel, *The Bluest Eye*, for example, reveals the devastating effect of pervasive European ideals of beauty on the self-image of young black women. Morrison's exposure of the harmful extent to which these white ideals affect the black self-image is a first step toward rejecting these ideals and overcoming the nihilistic self-loathing they engender in blacks.

The accumulated effect of the black wounds and scars suffered in a white-dominated society is a deep-seated anger, a boiling sense of rage, and a passionate pessimism regarding America's will to justice. Under conditions of slavery and Jim Crow segregation, this anger, rage, and pessimism remained relatively muted because of a well-justified fear of brutal white retaliation. The major breakthroughs of the sixties—more psychic than political—swept this fear away. Sadly, the combination of the market way of life, poverty-ridden conditions, black existential *angst*, and the lessening of fear of white authorities has directed most of the anger, rage, and despair toward fellow black citizens, especially toward black women who are the most vulnerable in our society and in black communities. Only recently has this nihilistic threat—and its ugly inhumane outlook and actions—surfaced in the larger

American society. And its appearance surely reveals one of the many instances of cultural decay in a declining empire.

What is to be done about this nihilistic threat? Is there really any hope, given our shattered civil society, market-driven corporate enterprises, and white supremacism? If one begins with the threat of concrete nihilism, then one must talk about some kind of *politics of conversion*. New models of collective black leadership must promote a version of this politics. Like alcoholism and drug addiction, nihilism is a disease of the soul. It can never be completely cured, and there is always the possibility of relapse. But there is always a chance for conversion—a chance for people to believe that there is hope for the future and a meaning to struggle. This chance rests neither on an agreement about what justice consists of nor on an analysis of how racism, sexism, or class subordination operate. Such arguments and analyses are indispensable. But a politics of conversion requires more. Nihilism is not overcome by arguments or analyses; it is tamed by love and care. Any disease of the soul must be conquered by a turning of one's soul. This turning is done through one's own affirmation of one's worth—an affirmation fueled by the concern of others.

A love ethic must be at the center of a politics of conversion. A love ethic has nothing to do with sentimental feelings or tribal connections. Rather it is a last attempt at generating a sense of agency among a downtrodden people. The best exemplar of this love ethic is depicted on a number of levels in Toni Morrison's great novel, *Beloved*. Self-love and love of others are both modes toward increasing self-valuation and encouraging political resistance in one's community. These modes of valuation and resistance are rooted in a subversive memory—the best of one's past without romantic nostalgia—and guided by a universal love ethic. For my purposes here, *Beloved* can be construed as bringing together the loving yet critical affirmation of black humanity found in the best of black nationalist movements, the perennial hope against hope for trans-racial coalition in progressive movements, and the painful struggle for self-affirming sanity in a history in which the nihilistic threat *seems* insurmountable.

The politics of conversion proceeds principally on the local level—in those institutions in civil society still vital enough to promote self-worth and self-affirmation. It surfaces on the state and national levels only when grassroots democratic organizations put forward a collective leadership that has earned the love and respect of and, most important, has proved itself *accountable* to these organizations. This collective leadership must exemplify moral integrity, character, and democratic statesmanship within itself and within its organizations.

Like liberal structuralists, the advocates of a politics of conversion never lose sight of the structural conditions that shape the sufferings and lives of people. Yet, unlike liberal structuralism, the politics of conversion meets the nihilistic threat head-on. Like conservative behaviorism, the politics of conversion openly confronts the self-destructive and inhumane actions of black people. Unlike conservative behaviorists, the politics of conversion situates these actions within inhumane circumstances (but does not thereby exonerate them). The politics of conversion shuns the limelight—a limelight that solicits status seekers and ingratiates egomaniacs. Instead, it stays on the ground among the toiling everyday people, ushering forth humble freedom fighters—both followers and leaders—who have the audacity to take the nihilistic threat by the neck and turn back its deadly assaults.

STUDY QUESTIONS

1. What is the difference between liberal structuralists and conservative behaviorists? Why, according to West, are these categories inadequate for understanding the situation in the African-American community?
2. Why do liberals tend to ignore the nihilistic threat, on West's view? Why do conservatives ignore it?
3. What does West mean by nihilism? Why does nihilism threaten to undermine black struggles?
4. How did traditions help to counter the threat of nihilism in earlier generations of African Americans?
5. Why are the traditions and institutions that nurtured black society in earlier generations no longer effective?
6. What does West mean by a "market morality"?
7. What is the antidote for nihilism and how will this encourage a sense of agency among African Americans, according to West? Do you agree?

5

Life, Liberty, Property

Richard Pipes

Richard Pipes, Baird research professor of history at Harvard, is the author of numerous works, including *Russia Under the Old Regime*, *The Unknown Lenin*, *The Russian Revolution*, and *Property and Freedom*. Pipes argues for the libertarian view that the essence of autonomy is the protection of private property from the coercive power of government. He argues that government programs that mandate equal treatment of minority groups and use tax dollars to provide economic security to citizens inevitably rob people of the ability to use their property as they wish. The tendency of modern governments to infringe on property rights threatens our deepest value—liberty. The only coherent notion of equality is that each individual be equally free of government coercion.

As the 20th century draws to a close, the traditional threats to liberty no longer loom large. The downfall of Communism has eliminated the most direct and dangerous challenge, while the economic failures of socialism have discredited the notion that the abolition of private ownership in the means of production solves all social ills. Even though tyrannies still manage to hang on to power here and there, they are either isolated or else slowly yielding to the spirit of the times: the slogans of the day are democracy and privatization.[1]

Yet these welcome changes by no means signify that liberty's future is secure: it is still at peril, although from a different and novel source. The main threat to freedom today comes not from tyranny but from equality—equality defined as identity of reward. Related to it is the quest for security.

Liberty is by its nature inegalitarian, because living creatures differ in strength, intelligence, ambition, courage, perseverance, and all else that makes for success. Equality of opportunity and equality before the law—in the sense laid down to the Israelites through Moses in Leviticus 24:22: "Ye shall have one manner of law, as well for the stranger as for the home-born; for I am the Lord your God"—are not only compatible with liberty but essential to it. Equality of reward is not. Indeed, it is attainable only by coercion, which is why all utopian schemes presuppose despotic authority and all despots insist on the equality of their subjects. As Walter Bagehot observed over a century ago, "there is no method by which men can be both free and equal."

Ironically, the enforcement of equality destroys not only liberty but equality as well, for as the experience of Communism has demonstrated, those charged with implementing social equality claim for themselves privileges that elevate them high above the common herd. It also results in pervasive corruption, inasmuch as the elite that monopolizes goods and services—as must be done if those goods and services are to be equitably distributed—expects, in return for distributing them, rewards for itself. And yet the ideal of a Golden Age when all were equal because there was no "mine and thine" has never ceased to appeal to humanity: it is one of our persistent and seemingly indestructible myths. In the contest between equality and liberty, the former holds the stronger hand, because the loss of liberty is felt only when it occurs, whereas the pain of inequality rankles every moment of the day.

The trend of modern times appears to indicate that citizens of democracies are willing heedlessly to surrender their freedoms to purchase social equality (along with economic security), apparently oblivious of the consequences. And the consequences are that their ability to hold on to and use what they earn and own, to hire and fire at will, to enter freely into contracts, and even to speak their mind is steadily eroded by governments bent on redistributing private assets and subordinating individual rights to group rights. Despite the commendable reforms of recent years in the United States, the entire concept of the welfare state as it has evolved in the second half of the 20th century stands in tension with individual liberty, for it allows various groups with common needs to combine and claim the right to satisfy those needs at the expense of society at large, in the process steadily enhancing the power of the state that acts on their behalf.

This reality is currently masked by the immense wealth generated by the industrial economies operating on a global scale in time of peace. It could become painfully apparent, however, should the economic situation drastically deteriorate and the controls established by the state in time of prosperity enable it to restore social stability at the cost of freedom.

Returning the responsibilities for social assistance to the family or private charities, which shouldered them prior to the 20th century, would undoubtedly go a long way toward resolving this predicament. But such a radical solution is neither feasible nor desirable. The libertarian ideal of a society in which the government runs nothing is as unrealistic as the utopian ideal of one in which it runs everything. Even at the height of laissez-faire, government everywhere intervened in some measure in economic and social affairs: the notion of a passive state is as much a myth as that of primitive Communism.

This does not mean, however, that it is impossible to find a sensible alternative to the two extreme positions. In dealing with the scope of state power, the question is not either/or—either none or all-embracing—but more or less. When, in the 19th century, the Supreme Court found it necessary to intervene in private contractual engagements—and it did so with great reluctance—the interference was often accompanied by the cautionary adjective "reasonable." Today, although the state must regulate more than ever, such caution is correspondingly more necessary than ever. It must be remembered that the economic rights of citizens (rights to property) are as essential as their civil rights (rights to equal treatment), and that, indeed, the two are inseparable.

Although the concept of human nature has fallen into disfavor, it is difficult to escape the conclusion that there do indeed exist certain constants in human behavior. One of these constants, impervious to legislative and pedagogic manipulation, is acquisitiveness.

In and of itself, the desire to possess manifests greed no more than the appetite for food manifests gluttony, or love lechery. Acquisitiveness is common to all living things, being universal among animals and children as well as adults at every level of civilization. On the most elementary level, it is an expression of the instinct of survival. But beyond this, it constitutes a basic trait of the human personality, for which achievements and acquisitions are means of self-fulfillment. And since fulfillment of the self is the essence of liberty, liberty cannot flourish when property and the inequality to which it gives rise are forcibly eliminated.

In addition to being the most important of liberties, acquiring property is the universal engine of prosperity. The close relationship between property and prosperity is demonstrated by the course of history. Although property in personal belongings is well-nigh universal and known since the dawn of humanity, the ownership of agricultural land—the principal source of livelihood until very modern times—originated in ancient Greece and Rome, and since the Middle Ages spread to the rest of Europe and regions populated by Europeans. One of the main reasons for the rise of the West to its position of global economic preeminence lies in this institution of property, which in much of the rest of the world has led and still leads a rather precarious existence.

The indispensability of property for prosperity can be demonstrated empirically for the contemporary world. The results are impressive in their consistency. Countries that provide the firmest guarantees of economic independence, including private property rights, are virtually without exception the richest. They also enjoy the best civil services and judicial institutions. Today this holds true not only for countries populated by Europeans but also for Japan, South Korea, Hong Kong, Chile, and Taiwan. Conversely, countries that rate lowest in terms of property rights and market freedom—Cuba, Somalia, and North Korea, for instance—languish at the bottom of the scale.

The relationship of property to freedom is more complex, because unlike prosperity, "freedom" has more than one meaning. Thus it is possible to enjoy firm property (economic) rights without political rights, that is, the right to vote. In Western Europe, property rights were respected long before citizens were granted the franchise. Today, some of the most prosperous countries (Singapore, Hong Kong, Taiwan) with the firmest guarantees of property are run in an authoritarian fashion.

It is a serious mistake, unfortunately often committed by the U.S. government in its foreign dealings, to define freedom to mean exclusively democracy, for ordinary citizens may enjoy a wide range of economic and legal freedoms along with personal rights without being able to choose their government. The mistake is probably due to the fact that Americans, as heirs and beneficiaries of English constitutional development, take such freedoms and rights so much for granted that they identify freedom with representative government. The historical evidence indicates that property can coexist with arbitrary and even oppressive political power. Democracy, however, cannot do without it.

The symbiotic relationship between property and freedom does not preclude the state from imposing reasonable restraints on the uses made of objects owned, or ensuring the basic living standards of the neediest strata of the population. Clearly, one cannot allow property rights to serve as a license for ravaging the environment or ignoring the fundamental needs of the unemployed, sick, and aged. Hardly anyone contests this proposition today: even Friedrich Hayek, an implacable foe of state intervention in the economy, agreed that the state has the duty to ensure for all citizens "a minimum of food, shelter, and clothing, sufficient to preserve health and the capacity to work."

But to say this is not to grant the state the authority to use the powers at its disposal to interfere with the freedom of contract, to redistribute wealth on a large scale, or to compel one part of the population to bear the costs of the government-defined "rights" of special constituencies. This is precisely the situation we now face, in particular in the form of limitations on the use of property imposed by various environmental or zoning laws and regulations.

Such limitations should surely be interpreted as "takings" under the Fifth Amendment and adequately compensated. Unfortunately, as the political scientist William Riker has written, this runs counter to the entrenched attitude of the highest organs of the judiciary, which since the late 1930's have assumed "that civil rights and property rights can be sharply distinguished, and that civil rights . . . merit greater judicial protection than property rights."[2] Yet only by a redress of the balance—through court decisions and deregulatory rulings of the government—can the rights of ownership be restored to their proper place in the scale of values instead of being sacrificed to the unattainable ideal of social equality and all-embracing economic security.

Not only do "civil" and "property" rights need to be balanced if we care about freedom, but the whole concept of civil rights requires reexamination. The Civil Rights Act of 1964 gave the government no license to set quotas for hiring personnel in private enterprise or for admitting students to institutions of higher learning; and yet for decades the federal bureaucracy has acted as if it had. Even less did the Act authorize interference with freedom of speech in the workplace in matters of so-called "sexual harassment." But even as property rights have been steadily narrowed in application, the category of "civil rights" has been broadened to include the claims of any group—women, minorities, the disabled, and so forth—to goods and services that fellow citizens must pay for either by sacrificing some of their own rights or else by footing the bill.

The plain truth is that the so-called "social rights" of today, having been bestowed by legislative fiat, are not "rights" in any meaningful sense and certainly not "entitlements," since no one is entitled to anything at someone else's expense; they are, rather, claims on society that it may or may not grant. Nevertheless, in the name of such spurious rights, a large number of citizens in modern industrial democracies are now required to work for the support of others.

In Sweden, the most retrograde state in this respect, for each citizen who earns his own living, 1.8 other citizens are fully or partially maintained by taxes that he is required to pay; in Germany and Great Britain, the ratio is 1:1, and in the U.S., 1:0.76. Because the population dependent on the state includes a heavy proportion of the elderly while the taxpayers are younger wage and salary earners, an unhealthy generational conflict may well develop in welfare societies as the population ages. We see glimmerings of such a conflict in the current dispute in this country over Social Security.

Unless the greatest care is exercised in protecting the rights to property, we may well end up with a regime that, without being tyrannical in the customary sense of the word, is nevertheless unfree. The framers of the American Constitution did not anticipate this possibility: in the words of the 20th-century jurist Roscoe Pound, "They intended to protect the people against their rulers, not themselves." But, as it has turned out, under conditions of modern, welfare-oriented democracy, the threat to liberty can also emanate from one's fellow citizens, who, increasingly dependent on government largesse, often care more about their personal security than about general freedom.

"Experience," wrote Justice Brandeis,

> should teach us to be most on our guard to protect liberty when the government's purposes are beneficent. Men born to freedom are naturally alert to repel invasion of their liberty by evil-minded rulers. The greatest dangers to liberty lurk in insidious encroachments by men of zeal, well-meaning but without understanding.

The reason for this is that despotism appears in two distinct guises. There is the arbitrary rule of absolutist monarchs or dictators, elected by no one and subject neither to constitutional nor parliamentary restraints. And there is the tyranny in democratic societies of one part of the population over another: that of the majority over the minority but also—where elections are won with pluralities—of minorities over the majority.

Czarist Russia in its classical guise provided an extreme example of traditional despotism. There, the authorities could detain, imprison, or exile any subject without due process; they could confiscate his properties; they legislated as they saw fit. And yet, in practice, the average Russian under the old regime had scarcely any contact with the government and felt little interference from it, because the scope of government activity was very narrow, being largely confined to the collection of taxes, the drafting of recruits, and the preservation of the established order.

Today, the scope of government activity is immeasurably broader, and not only in authoritarian regimes but in a democracy like our own. Our government is elected, to be sure, but its interference in the life of citizens is greater than it has ever been. This is true at every level, from the federal down to that of the states and localities; in the latter, indeed, the recent expansion of government, partly under the aegis of "devolution," has reached striking proportions.

As Hayek pointed out, the broadening of the scope of government, in and of itself, carries seeds of a despotism at least as invidious as the traditional kind. Hayek's main concern was with protecting liberty from the seemingly unstoppable trend in Western democracies to subject the national economy to planning, which, he felt, would inevitably lead to tyranny. His fears in this respect proved unfounded. But his observations on the dangers implicit in the extension of the government's reach retain their validity:

> [T]he probability of agreement of a substantial portion of the population upon a particular course of action decreases as the scope of state activity expands. . . . Democratic government worked successfully so long as, by a widely accepted creed, the functions of the state were limited to fields where real agreement

among a majority could be achieved. The price we have to pay for a democratic system is the restriction of state action to those fields where agreement can be obtained; and it is the great merit of a liberal society that it reduces the necessity of agreement to a minimum compatible with the diversity of opinions which in a free society will exist.

This reasoning explains why government interference in the life of the citizenry even for benevolent purposes endangers liberty: it posits a consensus that does not exist and hence requires coercion.

But well-meaning patriarchalism also enervates people by robbing them of the entrepreneurial spirit implicit in freedom. What harm long-term dependence on the welfare state can inflict became apparent after the collapse of the Soviet Union, when a substantial part of the population, suddenly deprived of comprehensive state support and unaccustomed to fending for itself, came to yearn for the restoration of the despotic yoke.

To be sure, Soviet Communism represented the most determined effort ever undertaken to condition people's thoughts and behavior, and nothing remotely like it is on the horizon in today's United States. Moreover, one can even point to a number of hopeful countervailing trends here, including recent decisions of the Supreme Court favoring property owners in their disputes with local authorities, the reform of welfare, and limitations on racial preferences in employment and higher education.

Nevertheless, for a variety of reasons, including the fact that our schools fail to teach history, the vast majority of today's citizens have no inkling as to what they owe their liberty and prosperity—namely, a long and successful struggle for rights of which the right to property is the most fundamental. They are therefore unaware of what debilitating effect the restrictions on property rights will, over the long run, have on their lives.

The aristocrat Tocqueville, observing the democratic United States and his native bourgeois France a century and a half ago, had a premonition that the modern world faced dangers to liberty previously unknown. "I have no fear that they will meet with tyrants in their rulers," he wrote of future generations, "but rather with guardians." Such "guardians" would deprive people of liberty by gratifying their desires and would then exploit their dependence on such generosity. He foresaw a kind of democratic despotism in which "an innumerable multitude of men, all equal and alike," would incessantly strive to pursue "the petty and paltry pleasures with which they glut their lives." Hovering over them would be the benign paternalistic government—the modern welfare state:

> For their happiness such a government willingly labors, but it chooses to be the sole and only arbiter of that happiness; it provides for their security, foresees and supplies their necessities, facilitates their pleasures, manages their principal concerns, directs their industry, regulates the descent of property, and subdivides

their inheritances: what remains, but to spare them all the care of thinking and all the trouble of living?

Is this what we want?

STUDY QUESTIONS

1. What does Pipes mean by "equality"? Why does equality threaten liberty on his view?
2. Why, according to Pipes, are property rights more fundamental than civil rights? Is his defense of this view convincing? Explain.
3. What policies and court decisions does Pipes claim threaten individual liberties?
4. According to Pipes, why does government intervention threaten democracy?
5. Pipes endorses the view that all citizens have a right to "a minimum of food, shelter, and clothing, sufficient to preserve health and the capacity to work." Why do citizens have such a right, on his view, and does he provide reasons for restricting basic goods to a minimum of food, shelter, and clothing?

NOTES

1. This holds true despite the fact that the ex-Communist countries which have recently adopted democracy and privatization, most notably Russia, are experiencing immense difficulties in adopting the Western model. It must be borne in mind that even the Communist parties of these countries no longer talk of a return to the Soviet model. They want to blend democracy and the market with social-welfare policies and a certain degree of government intervention in the economy—not an infeasible combination.

2. The fictitious contrast between the "rights of property" and the "rights of men" was drawn as early as 1910 by Theodore Roosevelt and restated by Franklin Delano Roosevelt in 1936. See Tom Bethell, *The Noblest Triumph*, which I reviewed in the November 1998 *Commentary*.

6

Still the Land of Opportunity?

Isabel V. Sawhill

Isabel V. Sawhill is a senior fellow at the Brookings Institution and author of *One Percent for the Kids: New Policies, Brighter Futures for America's Children* (2003). Sawhill advocates a meritocracy in which inequalities are justified if based on the choices people make. Those who choose to work hard and acquire skills necessary to succeed deserve greater compensation than those who choose otherwise. However, such a meritocracy can exist only if each individual has an equal opportunity to acquire skills and make choices that contribute to success. In the absence of equal opportunity, people succeed not based on their choices but because of accidents of birth and good fortune. Thus, for Sawhill, "equality" means equal opportunity.

America is known as "the land of opportunity." But whether it deserves this reputation has received too little attention. Instead, we seem mesmerized by data on the distribution of incomes, which show that incomes are less evenly distributed than they were twenty or thirty years ago. In 1973, the richest 5 percent of all families had eleven times as much income as the poorest one-fifth. By 1996, they had almost twenty times as much. But it is not only the distribution of income that should concern us. It is also the system that produces that distribution.

Indeed, I would argue that one cannot judge the fairness of any particular distribution without knowing something about the rules of the game that gave rise to it. Imagine a society in which incomes were as unequal as they are in the United States but where everyone had an equal chance of receiving any

Reprinted with permission of the author. C National Affairs, Inc., *The Public Interest,* No. 135, Spring 1999, Washington, D.C.

particular income—that is, in which the game was a completely unbiased lottery. Although some, especially those who are risk-adverse, might blanch at the prospect of losing, and might wish for a more equal set of outcomes a priori (as most fatuously argued by John Rawls), others might welcome the chance to do exceedingly well. But—and this is the important point—no one could complain that they hadn't had an equal shot at achieving a good outcome. So the perceived fairness of the process is critical, and the rules governing who wins and who loses matter as much as the outcomes they produce.

In talking about this issue, we often invoke the phrase "equal opportunity," but we seldom reflect on what we really mean by "opportunity," how much of it we really have, and what we should do if it's in short supply. Instead, we have an increasingly sterile debate over income equality. One side argues for a redistribution of existing incomes, through higher taxes on the wealthy and more income support for the poor. The other side argues that inequality reflects differences in individual talent and effort, and as such is a spur to higher economic growth, as well as just compensation for unequal effort and skill. If there is any common ground between these two views, it probably revolves around the idea of opportunity and the measures needed to insure that it exists.

OPPORTUNITY FIRST

The American public has always cared more about equal opportunity than about equal results. The commitment to provide everyone with a fair chance to develop their own talents to the fullest is a central tenet of the American creed. This belief has deep roots in American culture and American history and is part of what distinguishes our public philosophy from that of Europe. Socialism has never taken root in American soil.

Public opinion is only one reason to refocus the debate. Another is that the current emphasis on income inequality begs the question of how much inequality is too much. Virtually no one favors a completely equal distribution of income. Inequality in rewards encourages individual effort and contributes to economic growth. Many would argue that current inequalities far exceed those needed to encourage work, saving, and risk taking, and further that we need not worry about the optimal degree of inequality in a society that has clearly gone beyond that point. But the argument is hard to prove and will not satisfy those who believe that inequality is the price we pay for a dynamic economy and the right of each individual to retain the benefits from his or her own labor. In light of these debates, if any public consensus is to be found, it is more likely to revolve around the issue of opportunity than around the issue of equality.

A final reason why opportunity merits our attention is that it gets at the underlying processes that produce inequality. It addresses not just the symptoms but the causes of inequality. And a deeper understanding of these causes can inform not only one's sense of what needs to be done but also one's sense of whether the existing distribution of income is or is not a fair one.

THREE SOCIETIES

Consider three hypothetical societies, all of which have identical distributions of income as conventionally measured. The first society is a meritocracy. It provides the most income to those who work the hardest and have the greatest talent, regardless of class, gender, race, or other characteristics. The second one I will call a "fortune-cookie society." In this society, where one ends up is less a matter of talent or energy than of pure luck. The third society is class-stratified. Family background in this society is all important, and thus you need to pick your parents well. The children in this society largely end up where they started, so social mobility is small to nonexistent.

The United States and most other advanced countries are a mixture of these three ideal types. Given a choice among the three, most people would probably choose to live in a meritocracy. Not only do the rules determining success in a meritocracy produce greater social efficiency but, in addition, most people consider them inherently more just. Success is dependent on individual action. In principle, by making the right choices, anyone can succeed, whereas in a class-stratified or fortune-cookie society, people are buffeted by forces outside their control. So, even if the distribution of income in each case were identical, most of us would judge them quite differently. We might even prefer to live in a meritocracy with a less equal distribution of income than in a class-stratified or fortune-cookie society with a more equal distribution. Indeed, social historians have found this to be the case. The American public accepts rather large disparities in income and wealth because they believe that such disparities are produced by a meritocratic process. Even those at the bottom of the distribution believe that their children will do better than they have. It is this prospect, and the sense of fairness that accompanies it, that has convinced the American body politic to reject a social-welfare state.

For the last twenty-five years, the top one-fifth of the population has been improving their prospects while the other 80 percent has lagged behind. Yet no one has rebelled. The many have not imposed higher taxes on the few. (Small steps in this direction were taken in 1993, but the Democratic president who proposed them later apologized to a group of wealthy donors for doing so.) Even welfare recipients tell survey researchers that they consider the new rules fair that require them to work at whatever job they can get. They plan on "bettering themselves." Such optimism flies in the face of studies suggesting that women on welfare (and those similar to them) will earn poverty-level wages for most of their lives. But it is an optimism that is characteristically, if in this case poignantly, American.

Several points need to be made about our purported meritocracy. The first is that even a pure meritocracy leaves less room for individual agency than is commonly believed. Some of us are blessed with good genes and good parents while others are not. The second is that the United States, while sharing these inherent flaws with other meritocracies, remains a remarkably dynamic and fluid society. Although it is not a pure meritocracy, it has moved closer to that ideal than at any time in its past. The third point is that, in the past, a rapid rate of economic growth provided each new generation with enhanced opportunities. It was this fact, in large part, that contributed to our image as the land of opportunity. But a mature economy cannot count on this source of upward mobility to leaven existing disparities; it needs instead to repair its other two opportunity-enhancing institutions: families and schools. The remainder of this essay elaborates on each of these points.

THE INHERENT LIMITS OF A MERITOCRACY

In a meritocracy, one would expect to find considerable social and economic fluidity. In such a system, the abler and more ambitious members of society would continually compete to occupy the top rungs. Family or class background, per se, should matter little in the competition while education should matter a lot.

The social-science literature contains a surprising amount of information on this topic. Based on my own reading of this literature, I would argue that social origins or family background matter a good deal. Not everyone begins the race at the same starting line. The kind of family into which a child is born has as much or more influence on that child's adult success than anything else we can measure. Yes, education is important too, but when we ask who gets a good education, it turns out to be disproportionately those from more advantaged backgrounds. Well-placed parents are much more likely to send their children to good schools and to encourage them to succeed academically. In short, although not as evident as in a class-stratified society, even in a meritocracy one had better pick one's parents well.

Why do families matter so much? There are at least three possibilities. The first is that well-placed parents can pass on advantages to their children without even trying: They have good genes. The second is that they have higher incomes, enabling them to provide better environments for their children. The third is that they are simply better parents, providing their children an appropriate mix of warmth and discipline, emotional security and intellectual stimulation, and preparation for the wider world.

It has proved difficult to discover which of these factors is most important. However, as Susan Mayer demonstrates in her recent book, *What Money Can't Buy*, the role of material resources has probably been exaggerated. Most studies have failed to adjust for the fact that parents who are successful in the labor market have competencies that make them good parents as well. It is these competencies, rather than the parents' income, that help their children succeed. I don't want to leave the impression that income doesn't matter at all. It enables families to move to better neighborhoods; it relieves the stresses of daily living that often produce inadequate parenting; and, most obviously, it enables parents to purchase necessities. Still, additional income assistance, although possibly desirable on other grounds, is not likely to produce major changes in children's life prospects.

Genes clearly matter. We know this from studies of twins or siblings who have been raised apart. However, IQ or other measures of ability are at least somewhat malleable, and differences in intelligence only partially explain who ends up where on the ladder of success. Good parenting and an appropriate home environment are much harder to measure, but studies suggest that they may explain a substantial portion of the relationship between family background and later success in school or in the labor market. In addition, children with two parents fare much better than those with only one, in part because they have higher incomes but also because the presence of a second parent appears, according to all of the evidence, to be beneficial in and of itself.

So, for whatever reason, families matter. Unless we are willing to take children away from their families, the deck is stacked from the beginning. And even if one could remove children from their homes, there would still be the pesky little matter of differences in genetic endowments. Since a meritocracy has no good way of dealing with these two fundamental sources of inequality, it is a pipe dream to think that it can provide everyone with an equal chance. If we want a society in which there is less poverty and more equality, we will have to work harder and more creatively to compensate for at least some of these initial advantages and disadvantages.

HOW MUCH SOCIAL MOBILITY?

Whatever its flaws, a meritocracy is clearly better than some of the alternatives. Although economic and social mobility may be inherently limited, it exists. But just how much of it do we actually have in the United States? Do families matter so much that children can rarely escape their origins? Do people move up and down the economic ladder a little or a lot? Before attempting to answer these questions, let us consider a simple example of a society consisting of only three individuals: Minnie, Mickey, and Mighty.

Assume that Minnie, Mickey, and Mighty start with incomes (or other valued goods) of $20,000, $30,000, and $40,000, respectively. Now imagine that Minnie's children do extremely well, moving from an income of $20,000 to one of $40,000. Mighty's children, by contrast, fall in status or well-being from $40,000 to $20,000. Mickey's situation doesn't change. This is the sort of social mobility we would expect to find in a meritocracy. It is a story of rags to riches (or the reverse) in a generation. Note that the distribution of income, as conventionally measured, has not changed at all. As Joseph Schumpeter once put it, the distribution of income is like the rooms in a hotel—always full but not necessarily with the same people.

This same rags-to-riches story can occur over a lifetime as well as between generations. Those at the bottom of the income scale often move up as they accumulate skills and experience, add more earners to the family, or find better jobs. Those at the top may move down as the result of a layoff, a divorce, or a business failure. Thus any snapshot of the distribution of incomes in a single year is unlikely to capture the distribution of incomes over a lifetime. For example, in a society in which everyone was poor at age 25 but rich at age 55, the distribution of annual incomes for the population as a whole would be quite unequal, but everyone would have the same lifetime incomes!

Now note that it is theoretically possible for the distribution of income to become more unequal at the same time that the Minnies of the world are improving their status. Is this what happened over the last few decades in the United States? The answer is yes and no. On the one hand, we know that there is a lot of income mobility within the population. Every year, about 25 percent or 30 percent of all adults move between income quintiles (say, from being in the bottom one-fifth of the income distribution to being in the second lowest fifth). This rate increases with time, approaching 60 percent over a ten-year period. So there is considerable upward and downward movement. A lot of the Minnies in our society move up, and a lot of the Mightys move down. A few of the Minnies may even trade places with the Mightys of the world, as in our example. On the other hand, most people don't move very far; many remain stuck at the bottom for long periods; and some apparent moves are income reporting errors. (These are particularly large among the very poor and the very wealthy whose incomes tend to come from unearned sources that are difficult to track and that they may be reluctant to reveal.) Most importantly, from the data we have, there is no suggestion of more mobility now than there was twenty or thirty years ago. So one can't dismiss complaints about growing income inequality with the argument that it has been accompanied by more opportunity than in the past for everyone to share in the new wealth.

But what about Minnie's and Mighty's children? Suppose we look at mobility across generations instead of looking at it across their own life cycles? Here, the news is much more positive. Social mobility in America appears to have increased, at least since 1960, and probably going back to the middle of the last century (though the data for measuring such things is much better for the more recent period). This conclusion is based on studies done by Michael Hout, David Grusky, Robert Hauser, David Featherman, and others—studies that show less association between some measure of family background and eventual adult career success now than in the past. This association has declined by as much as 50 percent since the early 1960s, according to Hout.

What has produced this increase in social mobility? The major suspects are a massive broadening of educational opportunities, the increased importance of formal education to economic success, and more meritocratic procedures for assigning workers to jobs (based on "what you know rather than who you know"). In addition, the extension of opportunities to some previously excluded groups—most notably women and blacks—has produced greater diversity in the higher, as well as the lower, ranks.

HOW MUCH ECONOMIC MOBILITY?

Now return to our three-person society and consider a second scenario. In this one, the economy booms, and Minnie, Mickey, and Mighty all double their initial incomes from $20,000, $30,000, and $40,000 to $40,000, $60,000, and $80,000. Clearly, everyone is better off, although the relative position of each (as well as the distribution of income) is exactly the same as before. It is this sort of economic mobility, rather than social mobility per se, that has primarily been responsible for America's reputation as the land of opportunity. In other words, the growth of the economy has been the most important source of upward mobility in the United States; it is the reason that children tend to be better off than their parents. In a dynamic economy, a farmer's son can become a skilled machinist, and the machinist's son a computer programmer. Each generation is better off than the last one even if there is no social mobility. (Class-based differentials in fertility aside, social mobility—as distinct from economic mobility—is, by definition, a zero-sum game.)

But, as important as it was historically, economic mobility has been declining over the past few decades for the simple reason that the rate of economic growth has slowed. Young men born after about 1960, for example, are earning less (in inflation-adjusted terms) than their fathers' generation did at the same age. It would be nice to assume that a higher rate of growth is in the offing as we enter a new century. Certainly, new technologies and new markets abroad make many observers optimistic. But whatever the force of these developments, they haven't yet improved the fortunes of the youngest generation.

In sum, both these factors—the increase in social mobility and the decline in economic mobility—have affected prospects for the youngest generation. The good news is that individuals are increasingly free to move beyond their origins. The bad news is that fewer destinations represent an improvement over where they began. For those concerned about the material well-being of the youngest generation, this is not a welcome message. But for those concerned about the fairness of the process, the news is unambiguously good.

CLASS STRATIFICATION

Not only has economic growth slowed but its benefits now accrue almost entirely to those with the most education. Simply being a loyal, hard-working employee no longer guarantees that one will achieve the American dream. Whatever progress has been made in extending educational opportunities, it has not kept pace with the demand. Men with a high-school education or less have been particularly hard hit. The combination of slower growth and a distribution of wage gains that have favored women over men and the college educated over the high-school educated since the early 1970s has hurt poorly educated men. Their real incomes are less than one-half what they otherwise would have been in 1995. Education is, to put it simply, the new stratifying variable in American life. This, of course, is what one would hope for in a meritocracy, but only if everyone has a shot at a good education.

It is said that Americans would rather talk about sex than money. But they would rather talk about money than class, and some would rather not talk about the underclass at all. Many people consider the label pejorative, but research completed in the past decade suggests that such a group may indeed exist. Its hallmark is its lack of mobility. This group is not just poor but persistently poor, often over several generations. It is concentrated in urban neighborhoods characterized by high rates of welfare dependency, joblessness, single parenthood, and dropping out of school. It is disproportionately made up of racial and ethnic minorities. Although still relatively small (a little under three million people in 1990, according to an Urban Institute analysis of census data), it appears to be growing. Anyone who doubts the existence of such a group need only read the detailed first-hand portrayals of ghetto life in Alex Kotlovitz's *There are No Children Here*, Leon Dash's *Rosa Lee*, or Ron Suskind's *A Hope in the Unseen*. These accounts suggest that dysfunctional families, poor schools, and isolation from mainstream institutions are depriving a significant segment of our youth of any prospect of one day joining the middle class.

All of this is by way of a caution: Whatever the broader trends in economic and social mobility, there may be enclaves that get left behind. Moreover, one can argue that it is this subgroup—and their lack of mobility—that should be our main concern. The very existence of such a group threatens our sense of social cohesion and imposes large costs on society. Its nexus with race is particularly disturbing.

WHAT TO DO?

If families and education matter so much, we had best look to them as sources of upward mobility for all Americans—and especially for those stuck at the bottom of the economic ladder. Imagine a world in which everyone graduated from high school with the basic competencies needed by most employers—a world in which no one had a child before they were married and all had a reasonably decent job. Even if these parents held low-wage jobs, and one of them worked less than full-time, they would have an income sufficient to move them above the official poverty line (about $12,000 for a family of three in 1995). The entry-level wage for a male high-school graduate in 1995 was $15,766. If his wife took a half-time job at the minimum wage, they could earn another $5,000 a year. No one should pretend that it is easy to live on $20,000 a year, especially in an urban area. Rent, utilities, and work-related expenses alone can quickly gobble up most of this amount. It would make enormous sense, in my view, to supplement the incomes of such families with an earned income tax credit, subsidized health care, and subsidized child care.

What does not make sense is to insist that the public continue to subsidize families started by young unwed mothers. As of 1990, 45 percent of all first births were to women who were either teenagers, unmarried, or lacking a high-school degree. Add in all those with high-school diplomas that are worthless in the job market, and the picture is even grimmer. There is no public-policy substitute for raising a child in a home with two parents who are adequately educated.

Of course, poorly educated parents are nothing new. In fact, the proportion of mothers who are high-school graduates is higher now than it has ever been. But bear in mind that in the past mothers were not expected to work (in part because far more of them were married), that the economy didn't require people of either sex to have nearly as much education, and that the proportion of children in single-parent families was a fraction of what it is today. Because of increases in divorce and especially out-of-wedlock childbearing, we now have a situation in which three-fifths of all children will spend time in a fatherless family. Almost one-third of all children are born out of wedlock in the United States, and the proportion exceeds one-half in such cities as New York, Chicago, Philadelphia, Detroit, and Washington, D.C. One needn't be an advocate of more traditional family values to be worried about the economic consequences of such social statistics. In fact, the growth of never-married mothers can account for almost all of the growth in the child poverty rate since 1970.

Where does the cycle stop? Urban schools that half a century ago might have provided the children of the poor a way into the middle class are now more likely to lock them into poverty. More than half of fourth and eighth graders in urban public schools fail to meet even minimal standards in reading, math, or science, and more than half of students in big cities will fail to graduate from high school. How can America continue to be the land of opportunity under these circumstances? If families and schools are critical to upward mobility, these children have little chance of success. We have no choice but to address both of these issues if we want to provide opportunities for the next generation.

STRENGTHENING FAMILIES

Despite all the talk about the deterioration of the family, no one knows quite what to do about the problem. Welfare reform, which has not only eliminated AFDC as a permanent source of income for young mothers but also made young fathers more liable to pay child support, may well deter some out-of-wedlock childbearing. The next step should be to make the Earned Income Tax Credit (EITC) more marriage friendly. Today, as a result of the credit, a working single parent with two children can qualify for almost $4,000 a year. But if she marries another low-wage earner, she stands to lose most or all of these benefits. Congress should consider basing the credit on individual, rather than family, earnings. (A requirement that couples split their total earnings before the credit rate was applied would prevent benefits from going to low-wage spouses in middle-income families.) Such a revised EITC would greatly enhance the incentive to marry.

Equally important, we should find top-quality child care for those children whose mothers are required to work under the new welfare law. Indeed, such care might provide them with the positive experiences that they often fail to get within the home. Such intervention, if properly structured to accomplish this goal, can pay rich dividends in terms of later educational attainment and other social outcomes. The research on this point is, by now, clear. Although early gains in IQ may fade, rigorous studies have documented that disadvantaged children who receive a strong preschool experience are more likely to perform well in school.

Some argue that out-of-wedlock childbearing is the result of a lack of jobs for unskilled men. Although I don't think the evidence backs this view, it may have some merit. If so, we should offer jobs to such men in a few communities and see what happens. But we should tie the offer of a job to parental responsibility or give preference to men who are married.

Finally, I am convinced that messages matter. Many liberals argue that young women are having babies out of wedlock because they or their potential spouses are poor and face bleak futures. It is said that such women have no choice but to become unwed mothers. As an after-the-fact explanation, this may be partly true, but it is often accompanied by too ready an acceptance of early, out-of-wedlock childbearing by all concerned. Such fatalistic expectations have a way of becoming self-fulfilling. Just as it is wrong to presume that poor children can't excel in school, so too it is wrong to suggest to young women from disadvantaged backgrounds that early out-of-wedlock childbearing is their only option. The fact remains that education and deferred childbearing, preferably within marriage, are an almost certain route out of poverty. Perhaps if more people were willing to deliver this message more forcefully, it would begin to influence behavior. Though the question needs to be studied more closely, it would appear that the decline in welfare cascloads since 1993 was triggered, in part, by a new message. Moreover, the new emphasis on conservative values may have contributed to the decrease in teen pregnancy and early childbearing since 1991. These new values can explain as much as two-thirds of the decline in sexual activity among males between 1988 and 1995, according to an Urban Institute study.

FIXING URBAN SCHOOLS

We must stem the tide of early, out-of-wedlock births for one simple reason: Even good teachers cannot cope with large numbers of children from poor or dysfunctional homes. And equally important, children who are not doing well in school are more likely to become the next generation of teenage parents. This is a two-front war in which success on one front can pay rich dividends on the other. Lose the battle on one front, and the other is likely to be lost as well.

That many schools, especially those in urban poor neighborhoods, are failing to educate their students is, I think, no longer in dispute. What is contested is how to respond. Some say that the solution lies in providing vouchers to low-income parents, enabling them to send their children to the school of their choice. Others argue that school choice will deprive public schools of good students and adequate resources. They favor putting more money into the public schools. But choice programs have the potential to provide a needed wake-up call to these same schools. Too many people are still defending a system that has shortchanged the children of the poor. Public schools are not about to disappear, and no one should believe that choice programs alone are a sufficient response to the education crisis. We should be equally attentive to the new choice programs and to serious efforts to reform the public schools.

In Chicago, for example, a new leadership team took over the school system in 1995–96 and instituted strong accountability measures with real consequences for schools, students, and teachers. Failure to perform can place a school on probation, lead to the removal of a principal, or necessitate that a student repeat a grade. New supports, such as preschool programs, home visiting, after-school and summer programs, and professional development of teachers, are also emphasized. Early indications are that these efforts are working to improve Chicago's public schools.

A MORE EQUAL CHANCE

I began with a plea that we focus our attention less on the distribution of income and more on the opportunity each of us has to achieve a measure of success, recognizing that there will always be winners and losers but that the process needs to be as fair and open as possible. It can be argued that the process is, to one degree or another, inherently unfair. Children do not have much opportunity. They do not get to pick their parents—or, for that matter, their genetic endowments. It is these deepest of inequalities that have frustrated attempts to provide a greater measure of opportunity. Education is supposed to be the great leveler in our society, but it can just as easily reinforce these initial inequalities.

Thus any attempt to give every child the same chance to succeed must come to terms with the diversity of both early family environments and genetic endowments. In policy terms, this requires favoring the most disadvantaged. Numerous programs from Head Start to extra funding for children in low-income schools have attempted to level the playing field. But even where such efforts have been effective, they have been grossly inadequate to the task of compensating for differences in early environment. Assuming we are not willing to contemplate such radical solutions as removing children from their homes or cloning human beings, we are stuck with a certain amount of unfairness and inequality.

The traditional liberal response to this dilemma has been to redistribute income after the fact. It is technically easy to do but likely to run afoul of public sentiment in this country, including the hopes and dreams of the disadvantaged themselves. They need income; but they also want self-respect. In my view, we must find ways to strengthen families and schools in ways that give children a more equal chance to compete for society's prizes. To do otherwise runs counter to America's deepest and most cherished values.

STUDY QUESTIONS

1. What does Sawhill mean by "equal opportunity"?
2. Why according to Sawhill is equal opportunity a better measure of equality than equality of result?
3. Why would most people prefer to live in a meritocracy, according to Sawhill?
4. Is the United States a meritocracy? Provide evidence for your view?
5. To what extent is an individual fully responsible for her/his economic success or lack of it?
6. According to Sawhill, what is the main determinant in achieving economic success?
7. On Sawhill's interpretation, what does the data show with regard to social and economic mobility during the past five decades? What is the most persistent problem regarding economic and social mobility?
8. Does Sawhill provide plausible solutions to the problem of economic and social mobility?

INTERVENTIONS: ARE WE EQUAL IN OUR CAPACITY TO MAKE OUR OWN DECISIONS?

Libertarians such as Pipes argue that our interest in autonomy gives rise to fundamental rights to property that protect us against government power. Egalitarian liberals grant that our autonomy can be threatened by arbitrary and excessive government power, but argue that ruinous social conditions are an equal or greater threat to autonomy.

Are libertarians denying that poverty, ill health, or poor education inhibit autonomy? Libertarian answers to this question vary but many will argue that in a mobile, competitive society, individuals can overcome the negative effects of ruinous social conditions. Thus, natural differences in the capabilities of individuals as well as poor judgment play a more significant role than social conditions in explaining why some people succeed in carrying out life plans and others do not succeed. Government power is a more significant threat to liberty than oppressive social conditions.

By contrast, egalitarian liberals (represented here by West and Sawhill) question whether people can make their own decisions when poverty, racism, sexism or other destructive social conditions limit their choices and their capacities to act on them. Parenting, education, health, psychological well-being, and security matter a great deal in the development of qualities of character that enable autonomy. When individuals cannot acquire the ability to make competent decisions, their decisions are unlikely to reflect their real interests, and are more likely to reflect the influence of social forces outside their control. Thus, egalitarian liberals argue that individuals who live with crushing poverty, persistent racism, or other ruinous social conditions lack an equal capacity for autonomy. A society that permits such inequities lacks equal respect for individuals' capacity to choose.

The libertarian response to this concern with oppressive socialization is to argue that beneficiaries of government programs to redistribute opportunities experience a debilitating sense of dependence on others, which undermines initiative and fails to build the capacities needed for autonomy. Government attempts to rectify inequalities undermine the competitiveness of free markets because failure is not punished. Thus, attempts to rectify inequalities undermine the ability of competition to encourage the moral virtues required to compete.

The underlying assumption in the libertarian position is that human beings exist as independent agents with an inherent ability to resist socialization processes. Most of our qualities and characteristics are so malleable that we can decide to change them if we want. Thus, self-sufficiency is a condition for which most human beings have the capacity and they need only be protected from government interference in order to exercise it. Egalitarian liberals are less confident that individuals can resist the effects of negative socialization and doubt that economic success or failure are products of individual initiative alone. Thus, egalitarian liberals are more favorably disposed to support policies that support disadvantaged groups. Because individuals are to a significant degree dependent on social influences, self-direction is a more appropriate model of autonomy for many egalitarian liberals.

How easy or difficult is it to change our patterns of emotional and cognitive response, many of which we acquire in childhood and which, for some people, are shaped by hopelessness and despair? Is self-sufficiency an intelligible ideal toward which we should strive? On the other hand, if self-direction is the appropriate model, how do we distinguish between a healthy dependence on social influences and debilitating victimization? (See the Introduction, pp. xix–xxii, for a description of self-sufficiency and self-direction.)

7

The Moral Demands
of Global Justice

Thomas Pogge

Thomas W. Pogge teaches moral and political philosophy at Columbia University. He is the author of *World Poverty and Human Rights: Cosmopolitan Responsibilities and Reforms* (Cambridge: Polity Press 2002). Pogge argues that global inequality is increasing despite the fact that problems of global poverty can be solved without significant costs to wealthy countries. Thus, the problem is a moral failure rather than a technical or political problem. Citizens of wealthy countries and their governments fail to recognize a moral obligation to substantially reduce global poverty.

The retrospectives on the 20th century give ample space to its horrors. Here natural catastrophes are overshadowed by wars and by other human-made disasters: 6 million murdered in the German holocaust, 30 million starved to death in Mao's Great Leap Forward, 11 million wiped out by Stalin, 2 million killed by the Khmer Rouge, a half million hacked to death in Rwanda, and so on. Missing from these retrospectives are the deaths from starvation and preventable diseases—world hunger for short—some 270 million in just the few years since the end of the Cold War. Why are these deaths not mentioned? Are they too humdrum, too ordinary, not shocking enough? Or are they perhaps *too* disturbing—deaths that, unlike the others, are *not* clearly someone else's responsibility?

Let us consider the disturbing thought. Do we bear some responsibility for deaths due to extreme poverty abroad? Confronted with this question, most respond with a firm *No*. But this *No* comes very quickly and with a real reluctance to delve more deeply into the reasons for it. This reluctance is

From Thomas Pogge, "The Moral Demands of Global Justice," in *Dissent*, Fall 2000. Reprinted by permission.

shared by ethicists, whose job it is to think about moral issues and responsibilities. Most of them probably agree with the firm *No* of their compatriots,
but very few have taken the trouble to examine the question carefully
enough to provide good reasons for this answer.

How does one examine such a question? One may begin by recapitulating
the basic facts about world hunger. Of a total of over 6 billion human beings,
more than 2.8 billion are estimated to live on less than $2.15 (1993) per per-
son per day, that is, on annual *per capita* incomes whose purchasing power
is less than that of $1,000 in the U.S. today. Their average shortfall is 43 per-
cent; and 1.2 billion live on less than half (Chen and Ravallion 2001,
283–300).

Such severe poverty has consequences: 799 million human beings are undernourished, 1 billion lack access to safe water, 2.4 billion lack access to basic sanitation, and 876 million adults are illiterate (UNDP 2003, 87, 9, 6). More
than 880 million lack access to basic health services (UNDP 1999, 22). Approximately 1 billion have no adequate shelter and 2 billion no electricity
(UNDP 1998, 49). "Two out of five children in the developing world are
stunted, one in three is underweight and one in ten is wasted" (FAO 1999, 11).
Some 250 million children between 5 and 14 do wage work outside their
household—often under harsh or cruel conditions: as soldiers, prostitutes, or
domestic servants, or in agriculture, construction, textile or carpet production
(ILO, 9, 11, 18). "Worldwide 34,000 children under age five die daily from
hunger and preventable diseases" (USDA, iii). Roughly one third of all human
deaths, some 50,000 daily, are due to poverty-related causes, easily preventable through better nutrition, safe drinking water, vaccines, cheap re-hydra-
tion packs and antibiotics (WHO 2001, annex table 2). (This fraction is so high
because far more than a quarter of all human deaths, and lives, occur in the
poorest quarter due to the much shorter life-expectancy among the poor.)

Many people in the more affluent countries believe that severe global
poverty is rapidly declining. With so much economic and technological
progress, it seems reasonable to assume that a rising tide must be lifting all
boats. Declarations, summits, and conventions devoted to the problem
moreover project a strong image of concerted action and brisk progress. But
the real trend is rather more mixed. There has been significant progress in
formulations and ratifications of relevant documents, in the gathering and
publication of statistical information, and even progress in reducing important aspects of poverty. And yet, in the eleven years following the end of the
Cold War the number of persons subsisting below the $2.15/day (1993)
poverty line has risen by over 10 percent (Chen and Ravallion, 290), and the
number of malnourished has remained about the same.

The trend in international inequality clearly shows the inadequacy of the
rising-tide image: "The income gap between the fifth of the world's people
living in the richest countries and the fifth in the poorest was 74 to 1 in 1997,

up from 60 to 1 in 1990 and 30 to 1 in 1960." Estimates for other years are 72 to 1 in 1992, 44 to 1 in 1973, 35 to 1 in 1950, 11 to 1 in 1913, 7 to 1 in 1870, and 3 to 1 in 1820 (UNDP 1999, 3, 38). A steady tendency toward increasing income inequality has continued unbroken through the end of the colonial period forty years ago. Today, while the bottom 47 percent of humankind live on about $140 (purchasing power of ca. $570) per year on average, 2001 *per capita* GDP was $35,277 in the U.S. and somewhat less, on average, in the other affluent countries (UNDP 2003, 278).

Such enormous inequality casts doubt upon the common view that eradicating world hunger would be prohibitively expensive, that it would truly impoverish us, destroy our culture and lifestyle. Richard Rorty articulates such a view: "the rich parts of the world may be in the position of somebody proposing to share her one loaf of bread with a hundred starving people. Even if she does share, everybody, including herself, will starve anyway." He expresses doubt that we can help the global poor by pointing out that "a politically feasible project of egalitarian redistribution of wealth, requires there to be enough money around to insure that, after the redistribution, the rich will still be able to recognize themselves—will still think their lives worth living" (Rorty 1996, 10, 14). Such apprehension may seem justified in view of the huge number of very poor people: 2.8 billion. But it is in fact grossly exaggerated due to the fact that global income inequality is much larger than Rorty seems to realize. The aggregate income of all these people is only about $384 billion, which is 1.25 percent of the global social product of $31.5 trillion (World Bank 2002, 235). A shift in global income distribution that would *double* their incomes entirely at our expense would still be quite minor. It would reduce the top tenth of incomes by about 1.5 percent—hardly a serious threat to our culture and lifestyle.

This conclusion is reinforced by looking at inequalities in wealth. These are considerably greater than inequalities in income, since well-off households typically have more net worth than annual income while poor households typically have less. The fortunes of the ultra-rich, in particular, have become quite enormous: "The world's 200 richest people more than doubled their net worth in the four years to 1998, to more than $1 trillion. The assets of the top three billionaires are more than the combined GNP of all least developed countries and their 600 million people" (UNDP 1999, 3). "The additional cost of achieving and maintaining universal access to basic education for all, basic health care for all, reproductive health care for all women, adequate food for all and safe water and sanitation for all is . . . less than 4% of the combined wealth of the 225 richest people in the world" (UNDP 1998, 30). Once again, Rorty's apprehension looks vastly overblown.

A third way of putting the cost of eradicating world hunger in perspective relates this cost to the so-called peace dividend. Following the end of the Cold War, military expenditures have declined from 4.7 percent of the global social product in 1985 to 2.9 percent in 1996 (UNDP 1998, 197). This decline has produced a huge annual dividend of currently well over $500 billion— far more than the $288 billion by which the global poor fall short, in aggregate, of the $2.15/day (1993) poverty line.

Many U.S. citizens apparently believe that a large proportion of the federal budget is already being spent on foreign aid. But this is not so: "The U.S. Agency for International Development (USAID) administers America's foreign assistance programs, which account for less than one-half of 1% of the federal budget" (USAID). Moreover, the high-income countries have reduced their official development assistance (ODA) from 0.33 percent of their combined GNPs in 1990 to 0.22 percent in 2001 (UNDP 2003, 290). The U.S. has led the decline by reducing ODA from 0.21 to 0.11 percent of GNP in a time of great prosperity, culminating in enormous budget surpluses (UNDP 2003, 290). Most ODA is allocated for political effect: Only 23 percent goes to the 49 least developed countries (UNDP 2003, 290); and only $3.7 billion is spent on basic social services (millenniumindicators.un.org/unsd/mi/mi_series_results.asp?rowId=592)—less than the 20 percent agreed to at the 1995 World Summit for Social Development. ODA for basic social services—basic education, basic health, population programs, water supply, and sanitation—is then about $4 per year from each citizen of these countries, on average. Citizens of the high-income countries also give aid through non-governmental organizations. Each year, such aid amounts to about $7 billion, or $7.60 per citizen (UNDP 2003, 290). On average, we thus spend about $11.60 annually on eradicating severe poverty, about $3.80 per year for each poor person.

A telling example of prevailing official attitudes toward poverty eradication is afforded by the World Food Summit in Rome, organized by the UN Food and Agriculture Organization in November 1996. Its principal achievement was this pledge by the 186 participating governments: "We, the Heads of State and Government, or our representatives, gathered at the World Food Summit . . . reaffirm the right of everyone to have access to safe and nutritious food, consistent with the right to adequate food and the fundamental right of everyone to be free from hunger. We pledge our political will and our common and national commitment to achieving food security for all and to an on-going effort to eradicate hunger in all countries, with an immediate [!] view to reducing the number of undernourished people to half their present level no later than 2015. We consider it intolerable that more than 800 million people throughout the world, and particularly in developing countries, do not have enough food to meet their basic nutritional needs. This situation is unacceptable . . ." (Rome).

The U.S. government published its own interpretation of this pledge: "the attainment of any 'right to adequate food' or 'fundamental right to be free from hunger' is a goal or aspiration to be realized progressively that does not give rise to any international obligations" ("Interpretive Statement"). It also challenged the FAO's claim (Alexandratos 1995) that fulfilling the pledge would require all developed states combined to increase their ODA in agriculture by $6 billion annually: "As part of the *U.S. Action Plan on Food Security*, USAID commissioned a separate study of the projected cost of meeting the World Food Summit target and a strategy for reaching this goal. The study, completed in mid 1998, focused on a potential framework for ODA investments and estimated that the target could be reached with additional global ODA of $2.6 billion annually, as compared to the FAO's estimate of $6 billion annually" (USDA, appendix A). So the study proposes that the pledge be backed by only $3 rather than $7 annually for each malnourished person. The hunger reduction plan adopted in Rome implicitly envisions well over 200 million deaths from hunger and preventable diseases over the 1996–2015 plan period. One might have thought that even if the FAO's proposed annual increase of $6 billion were to reduce hunger faster than planned, this should be no cause for regret. Halving world hunger in nineteen years, after all, is glacial progress. And $6 billion is not much to ask from the high-income countries, whose combined annual GNP in 1998 was $22,600 billion.

The growing reluctance to spend money on reducing world hunger is associated with the increasingly popular idea that this goal is best achieved through investment rather than aid. Hunger will be erased through globalization and free markets. But this idea is problematic. The freer, globalized markets of recent years have actually not brought a meaningful reduction in poverty and malnutrition. Foreign investment and free markets can be helpful where a minimally adequate infrastructure is in place and the physical and mental development of prospective employees has not been permanently retarded through disease, malnutrition, and illiteracy. But foreign investment will rarely create such conditions, will not help those children who *now* need food, safe water, basic sanitation, basic health services, and primary education. Money spent to meet these needs now would produce an advance that would help attract foreign investment, which could then sustain the advance on its own. If these needs are not met, investment will flow elsewhere, and the enormous gap between rich and poor will continue to grow.

This response—that children must have their basic needs met, must have a decent start—is one we would give unquestioningly in a domestic context. We would find it intolerable if, somewhere in the U.S., infant mortality were 20 percent due to lack of food, safe water, basic sanitation, basic health services, and primary education. Why are similar conditions abroad seen as so much more acceptable? Obviously, the national border around our country plays a significant role in our moral thinking. But what exactly is its supposed moral significance?

One common thought is that the United States is a solidaristic community whose members owe much more to one another than to outsiders. This thought can be relevantly extended in two ways. One could claim that our responsibilities toward foreigners are overridden by our responsibilities toward compatriots. But this claim would be ineffective, because the cost of erasing world hunger is too small to entail any real losses for our compatriots. One percent of the developed countries' GNP—less than half the "peace dividend"—could greatly reduce world hunger within a few years, allowing expenditures to decline significantly thereafter (*cf.* Pogge 2002, ch. 8). This outlay would not prevent us from meeting our responsibilities toward our compatriots, however expansively these may be conceived.

Alternatively, one could claim that we have no responsibilities to provide any aid and support beyond the solidaristic national community we sustain with one another. This claim might be backed by saying that the responsibilities we would otherwise have are, in this case, canceled by the fact that starving foreigners have states and compatriots of their own who ought to provide the needed aid and support. But this argument is unpromising because the global poor do not in fact have states and compatriots willing and able to secure their basic needs and also have not agreed to waive whatever claims they would otherwise have on us. It is more promising to back the claim by saying that responsibilities to provide any aid and support, beyond one's immediate family and beyond emergencies one immediately encounters, arise only through voluntary participation in a solidaristic community. By living in the United States, we have accepted such responsibilities toward our compatriots; but we have not accepted any such responsibilities toward foreigners.

To examine this view, let us reflect on Brazil for a moment and let us assume that most Brazilians do not think of their country as a solidaristic community. There is in fact evidence for this assumption, as Brazil is one of the most unequal societies on earth, with the highest fifth of incomes being 29.7 times the lowest fifth (UNDP 2003, 283—this quintile ratio tends to be between 4 and 10 for countries outside Latin America). Global income inequality is only slightly greater than Brazil's when incomes are scored in terms of purchasing power (though it is vastly greater when we score incomes in terms of exchange rates, as we should to obtain a rough measure of the cost of reducing poverty). The two cases are close in other respects as well: in terms of real *per capita* GNP, poverty incidence, life expectancy, and illiteracy.

Now suppose the rich elite in Brazil maintain that they have no responsibilities with regard to the poor in their country because most Brazilians do not see themselves as members, with the poor, in one solidaristic community. Few Americans would, I think, accept this disclaimer. We are willing to respect other societies even if they do not realize, or even aspire to realize, full justice as we understand it. But we do believe that there are certain minimum conditions that any state—whether its people conceive it as a solidaristic community or not—must meet for it to deserve moral respect. However such a minimal standard of decency might be formulated in detail (*cf.* Rawls 1999), it seems clear that Brazil, given its massive and avoidable poverty, would fail to qualify.

But if the global economic order is at least as bad as Brazil's, must not the same judgment apply to it as well? This thought is suggested by the *Universal Declaration of Human Rights*, which proclaims that "Everyone is entitled to a social and international order in which the rights and freedoms set forth in this Declaration can be fully realized," including the "right to a standard of living adequate for the health and well-being of himself and of his family, including food, clothing, housing and medical care" (§28 and §25). As §28 suggests, the incidence of severe poverty is importantly influenced by the existing social and international order. And such poverty may then entail not merely positive responsibilities for influential Brazilians and for us as potential helpers, but also negative responsibilities for influential Brazilians and for us as supporters of an economic order that reproduces massive starvation and poverty. Instead of merely failing to help the poor, we may be involved in harming them through the imposition of a global economic order under which economic inequality increases so rapidly that the gains from economic progress are huge at the top and minuscule or non-existent at the bottom of the global economic hierarchy (*cf.* Milanovic 2002, 88).

It is hardly surprising that the global order reflects the interests of the wealthy and powerful states. Dependent on our votes and taxes, our government, with its allies, works very hard on shaping the rules for our benefit, as we can see from its response to the World Food Summit, from its successful renegotiation of the Law of the Seas Treaty, and from countless other examples. To be sure, the global poor have their own governments. But almost all of them are too weak to exert any real influence on the organization of the global economy. More importantly, such governments have little incentive to attend to the needs of their poor compatriots, as their continuation in power depends much more on the local elite and on foreign governments and corporations. It is not surprising, then, that developing countries with rich natural resource endowments are especially likely to experience civil wars and undemocratic rule and hence tend to achieve slower (if any) economic growth (Lam and Wantchekon 1999). Their rulers can sell the country's resources, buy arms and soldiers to maintain their rule, and amass personal fortunes. These rulers like the global economic order just the way it is. And the affluent states, too, have no interest in changing the rules so that ownership rights in natural resources cannot be acquired from tyrannical governments. Such a change would reduce the supply and hence increase the price of the resources we need to import.

People can kill one another with bombs and machetes. But economic arrangements are often quite as effective. Millions were killed this way in the Irish potato famine, in Stalin's forced collectivization, in Mao's Great Leap Forward, in contemporary North Korea, as well as in many other spatio-temporally limited human-made disasters. The ongoing catastrophe of world hunger is of the same kind. But it is also different: by being less confined in space and time, even more devastating, and less recognized. It claims a third of all human deaths. But these deaths happen far away to people we never encounter. They happen in social contexts whose dependence on the existing global order we do not understand. And they happen in areas where we assume people have always been desperately poor. It seems unlikely, then, that the citizens and governments of the developed countries will be struck by the problem enough to recognize their responsibility. And so the deaths, with occasional summits, can be expected to continue for quite some time to come.

It is often said that moral reflections on world hunger are worthless, because no one denies that hunger is bad and should not exist. We should instead think about the practical question: how hunger might best be erased. I certainly agree that we should think about this practical question and will speak to it shortly. But I strongly disagree with the first point. The U.S. government has gone far out of its way to deny that the World Food Summit pledge, which calls hunger "intolerable" and "unacceptable," gives rise to any international obligations. This great moral error, shared by most governments and citizens of the developed countries, is the principal obstacle to eradicating world hunger. Without a sense of moral responsibility for the global economic order we are imposing, there will not be the political will to reform this order, nor sufficient readiness by governments and individuals to mitigate its worst effects.

The moral responsibility I assert presupposes that the governments and citizens of the developed countries *can* reduce world hunger through such measures of reform and mitigation. Some writings by professional economists nourish skepticism about this assumption, in three ways: by showing that various methods (*e.g.*, much development aid) have not worked well; by arguing that the effects of individual variables in a highly complex system cannot be reliably measured (the clear benefits of Oxfam projects or Grameen Bank microlending to specific individuals may well be offset by their unknowable indirect effects); and by spirited disagreements about what is to be done (causing laypersons to shrug: "if even economists differ so sharply, then perhaps we better do nothing").

Such skepticism is rejected even by the governments of the affluent states. They have made the World Food Summit pledge and, in the case of the U.S., argued in great detail that they can halve hunger by 2015 even more cheaply than the FAO has estimated. Not even these governments—certainly not above characterizing things they don't want to do as things they cannot do—

have endorsed the view that reducing world hunger is beyond our capacities. To be sure, these governments, mistakenly, recognize no moral responsibility to make a massive effort toward the immediate and rapid reduction of world hunger. But even they are constrained to agree that, if there is such a responsibility, it is not defeated by any evident incapacity to fulfill it.

It is true that much so-called aid has not been effective in eradicating poverty. But this is hardly surprising, given that most has been bilateral development aid focused on buying political support from foreign governments and domestic exporters. Money can be effectively spent, especially on local goods and services: on enabling poor people to buy more and better foodstuffs and shelter, on financing more and better schools and health services, on improving the local infrastructure (safe water, sanitation, electricity, road and rail links). Many governments of developing countries would welcome such funds and would contribute to making them effective, especially if such support were rewarded with continued funding. Yes, there are other poor countries whose rulers are more interested in keeping their poorer compatriots destitute, uneducated, impotent, dependent, and hence exploitable. In such cases, the least we should do is withdraw support from these rulers: by not letting them sell their country's resources to our firms, by not letting them borrow from our banks in their country's name, and by not letting them buy from our firms the arms they need to stay in power. Doing so would make it harder for such rulers to maintain their power without popular support and, most importantly, would greatly reduce the rewards of, and hence incentives toward, the undemocratic acquisition and unresponsive exercise of political power.

A third response to the economists' smokescreen of skepticism goes back to Immanuel Kant, who argues that a morally mandated project may be abandoned not merely because, for all we currently happen to know, it *may* be unachievable, but only if it is "demonstrably impossible" (Kant 1970, 89, *cf.* 173–4). When the income of the top sixth of humankind is seventy times the income of bottom half, when a third of all human deaths are due to poverty-related causes, and when aggregate global income is continuously rising, it would be ludicrous to claim that reducing poverty is demonstrably impossible. We do not perhaps know offhand what is the best way to proceed. But we are not exactly clueless either and would learn much more in the course of making a serious and concerted effort. Clearly, our critical deficiency here is not expertise, but a sense of moral responsibility and, based thereon, the political will to fund basic development and to push reforms in our global economic order.

STUDY QUESTIONS

1. According to Pogge, are we making progress in reducing world hunger and poverty?

2. To what degree has global inequality increased throughout the last half-century?
3. What reasons does Pogge give for thinking that problems of global poverty could be solved without having a serious impact on life in the wealthiest countries?
4. One argument against using American resources to solve the problem of world poverty is that American citizens have obligations only to other Americans. Do you agree with this? Why or why not?
5. What is Pogge's argument for accepting responsibility for world poverty? Do you agree? Why or why not?
6. In your opinion, why do we allow global hunger to persist?

SOURCES (IN ORDER OF FIRST APPEARANCE)

Chen, Shaohua, and Martin Ravallion: "How Did the World's Poorest Fare in the 1990s?," in *Review of Income and Wealth* 47 (2001), 283–300.

UNDP (United Nations Development Program): *Human Development Report 2003* (New York: Oxford University Press, 2003).

UNDP: *Human Development Report 1999* (New York: Oxford University Press, 1999).

UNDP: *Human Development Report 1998* (New York: Oxford University Press, 1998).

FAO (UN Food and Agriculture Organisation): *The State of Food Insecurity in the World 1999* (www.fao.org/news/1999/img/sofi99-e.pdf).

ILO (UN International Labour Organisation): *A Future Without Child Labour* (www.ilo.org/public/english/standards/decl/publ/reports/report3.htm).

USDA (United States Department of Agriculture): *U.S. Action Plan on Food Security* (www.fas.usda.gov/icd/summit/usactplan.pdf).

WHO (World Health Organisation): *The World Health Report 2001* (Geneva: WHO Publications, 2001).

Rorty, Richard: "Who are We? Moral Universalism and Economic Triage," in *Diogenes* 44 (1996), 5–15.

World Bank: *World Development Report 2003* (New York: Oxford University Press, 2002).

USAID. www.info.usaid.gov/pubs/cp98/progprview.htm.

Rome Declaration on World Food Security (www.fao.org/wfs/).

"Interpretive Statement" filed by the US Government in reference to the first paragraph of the Rome Declaration on World Food Security (www.fas.usda.gov:80/icd/summit/interpre.html).

Alexandratos, Nikos, ed.: *World Agriculture: Toward 2010, an FAO Study* (Chichester, UK: J. Wiley & Sons, and Rome: FAO, 1995).

Pogge, Thomas W.: *World Poverty and Human Rights* (Cambridge: Polity Press, 2002).

Rawls, John: *A Law of Peoples* (Cambridge, MA: Harvard University Press, 1999).

Milanovic, Branko: "True World Income Distribution, 1988 and 1993: First Calculation Based on Household Surveys Alone," in *The Economic Journal* 112 (2002), 51–92.

Lam, Ricky, and Leonard Wantchekon: "Dictatorships as a Political Dutch Disease," working paper, www.nyarko.com/wantche1.pdf, 1999.

Kant, Immanuel: *Kant's Political Writings*, edited by Hans Reiss (Cambridge: Cambridge University Press, 1970).

INTERVENTIONS: IS PERSONAL AUTONOMY COMPATIBLE WITH JUSTICE FOR ALL?

The aspect of our moral life in which the tension with personal autonomy is most salient is when an action is based on an obligation. Although a person may choose some of her obligations, many are not the product of our decisions. For instance, a parent has obligations to a child whether or not she chooses to acknowledge them. When we are obligated to others, their interests limit our will. Yet, any reasonable account of autonomy must make room for moral obligations.

I will argue later that moral obligations naturally arise from the relationships that make up our social lives, and as such are not a limitation on our autonomy. However, this suggests that obligations are particularly strong when they involve people with whom we share a relationship. Pogge's call for action to end the injustice of poverty challenges this idea that the proximity of a relationship determines the strength of an obligation. Justice requires that we give each person what they deserve. If we are concerned primarily with those with whom we share a life, don't we weaken claims of justice? If we frame moral issues from the standpoint of the personal point of view—"living life from the inside"—can we explain why we have an obligation to end world hunger?

III

WHERE LOVE MEETS OBLIGATION: THE FAMILY IN TURMOIL

Many commentators have argued that the changes in family structure that have occurred over the last fifty years explain what they perceive as a decline in moral values. According to these social critics, morality requires a set of traditional values handed down from generation to generation, which primarily occurs within families, where self-restraint and responsibility can be most effectively taught. In order to transmit values to children, the presence of both a father and a mother of the appropriate gender is essential, and the mother must provide constant monitoring and nurturing, especially in early childhood. Thus, high rates of divorce, single parenthood, homosexuality, and mothers in the work force have contributed to moral decline as well as more measurable evidence of social decay such as behavioral problems, drug abuse, teenage pregnancy, and high school dropouts. The solution is to develop policies that discourage unconventional family arrangements.

Other commentators argue that the traditional family structure is a site of injustice and ultimately harmful to women and children. In the traditional family structure, the interests of men have priority over the interests of women. Thus, women are often exploited, abused, and rendered utterly dependent, unable to fend for themselves or their children when men abandon them. Children are harmed materially and emotionally when raised in such circumstances. Moreover, social pathologies are not directly caused by unconventional family structure but are instead the product of larger economic and cultural factors that negatively influence children, such as violence in the media and on the street, dysfunctional schools, and economic uncertainty.

Some of the disagreement is over empirical questions about which social scientists disagree. For instance, social scientists disagree on the effect of divorce on children. However, there are important moral issues here as well. Should each of us see ourselves as having the capacity and the right to define family structure as we see fit? Or should we make an effort to tie our judgments about family structure more closely to traditional views of how family relationships should be defined?

8

Philosophical Reflections on the Family at Millennium's Beginning

Jean Bethke Elshtain

Jean Bethke Elshtain is Laura Spelman Professor of Social and Political
Ethics in the Divinity School of the University of Chicago. She is the author
of numerous books including *Just War against Terror: The Burden of
American Power in a Violent World* (2003) and *Jane Addams and the
Dream of American Democracy* (2001). Elshtain argues that evidence of
decline in the well being of children is best explained by the unraveling of
traditional norms governing family structure and interaction. We now view
the family as a peripheral institution in the reproduction of society and see
the presence of two committed, loving parents willing to sacrifice in order
to raise children as an optional life-style choice rather than a moral commitment. The solution to many of our social problems is to return to a more
traditional understanding of what a family is.

The problems of teen pregnancies, deadbeat dads, violent youth, and children in poverty are well known. But we tend to overlook a common denominator behind so many of these phenomena—the spreading collapse of
marriage. With each passing year of the just-completed century, an ever
smaller percentage of people in the United States were married. An even
larger percentage of the nation's children lived in households absent a parent—most often the father. This figure now stands at about one-third of
American children overall.

By education and training, I am a political and civil philosopher. This
means that I tend to what is happening to the social and political fabric of
my own society in particular and other societies in general. The evidence

From Jean Bethke Elshtain, "Philosophical Reflections on the Family at Millennium's End,"
The World and I, March 2000. Reprinted by permission.

comes from the streets, the neighborhoods, the schools, the churches, and our homes: The eloquent and often terrifying testimony of events—violence suffered and perpetrated; children unhappy, ignored, home alone; teen mothers, isolated and hovering in drug-ridden dangerous places; teachers afraid of their students; students afraid of other students; civic leaders gazing at a precipitous decline in involvement and participation in all community activities at all levels. This is one face of America as we enter this new millennium. The evidence is overwhelming, based on hundreds of studies by reputable scholars from dozens of disciplines. Indeed, none but the individual committed to the status quo can cast his eyes over this encroaching wasteland and say, "This is good. Let's have more of it." What do we see when we look around? We see that more and more children are growing up with little or no experience of seeing married life, hence no living examples of what it means for two people to commit themselves to one another over time. More American children every day are growing up with little or no confidence that they could be, or even want to be, in an enduring marital relationship, as the *Marriage Report of the Council on Families in America* argues.[1]

Mind you, I for one have no desire to marry everyone off. I recognize that many people choose not to marry and that they live rich and interesting lives and contribute to their communities in a variety of ways. No, my concern is with how difficult it has been for children to grow up in America. Because, where they are concerned, regularity in human relationships is vital, and such relations go by the names "marriage" and "family."

CULTURAL MESSAGE: ROMANCE AND SEX:YES! MARRIAGE: NO!

Over the past three or four decades, the message American children receive from the wider culture is one that is high on romance and sex but hostile or, at best, indifferent to marriage. It does not seem at all far-fetched to say that during the last century we as a society have been failing in the task of social reproduction. In other words, we have not been imparting to the next generation a set of fundamental norms and beliefs about the meaning and purposes, responsibilities and freedom, of marriage and family life.

This, in turn, has had a debilitating effect on civic life overall. Democratic civic life relies on persons who have been formed in such a way that they are capable of commitment; they understand and accept responsibility; they share a sense of stewardship about their communities; and they appreciate the fact that the creation of decent and relatively stable relationships and societies is a complex and fragile task, not an automatic outcome when human beings share a territorial space or even a bedroom.

Witness the discouraging data: In the decades 1960-1990, the percentage of out-of-wedlock births skyrocketed from 5.3 percent to 30 percent. Although as the century ended there was evidence of a small decline in the rate of out-of-wedlock births—or nonmarital births, in the terminology adopted near the end of 1996—the figures were still quite high, with about three-quarters of births to teens being nonmarital and about 25 percent of the births to women over twenty. The illegitimacy rate among blacks was about 70 percent, and that for whites about 25 percent.

If the children from such single-parent units were doing just fine, perhaps there would be no problem. But they have not been doing so: They have been at far greater risk than children from two-parent households. As well, in those same decades the divorce rate doubled or tripled, depending upon how it is calculated. As a result, the percentage of children living apart from their biological fathers rose from 17 percent to 36 percent, and it is still rising.

Juvenile violent crime also increased in the past three decades. Reports of child neglect and abuse quintupled since 1976. The teen suicide rate tripled. The New York Times and many other publications reported the facts: Children from broken homes have two to three times more behavioral and psychological problems than do children from intact homes.[2] Finally, the poverty rate of young children stood at about 25 percent at the end of the century, the highest since 1969, and family formation, or the failure to form families, has been indicted as a central causal factor in the growth of childhood poverty.[3]

Because all societies have a stake in the creation and sustaining of norms surrounding sexuality, child rearing, and other vital human activities tied to our complex social and embodied identities, all societies have attempted to regularize these activities in some way. No society has ever declared any of this to be a matter of indifference. There are many possible arrangements, of course—some more restrictive, some less. But sometimes, it seems, "less" can become "more." That is, as a general laissez-faire attitude toward social arrangements has spread, it has generated many different varieties of social troubles. Or so our recent history suggests. Ironically, the growth in "self-expression" and "individualism" appears to go hand-in-hand with a growth in fearfulness, destructive forms of dependency, and even greater social conformism as the primary reference group for the young becomes an age-specific cohort, with adults scarcely in the picture.

There are big conceptual and historical issues here. There are also simple, humble truths. The humble truth is that every child needs and deserves the love and provision of caring adults in a relationship that perdures. The committed, two-married-parent family is the best environment we know anything about in which to rear children. Because it is the main teacher of the

next generation—and a protector and defender of our love of, and commitment to, pluralism—it is also an irreplaceable foundation for long-term civic
vitality, endurance, and flexibility.

A British observer, summarizing the data for his own society, reports that
"every form of psychosocial disorder among young people—crime, suicide, depression, eating problems, vandalism, alcohol and drug abuse—can be linked
to the modern-day cult of juvenile freedom, to their spending power, their
moral and social independence from their parents, and their entire lifestyle of
music, clothes, sex and whatever. In short, the problem is a colossal and
chronic breakdown in parenting. By no means does this only apply to Britain."[4]

What we seem to have lost along the way is an earlier conceptual richness
that recognized, as the *Marriage in America Report* argues, that marriage
contained, or encompassed, at least five basic dimensions. It was viewed as,
in some sense, a natural institution, flowing from basic bodily imperatives. It
was a sacramental institution, surrounded by rituals and sacral norms. It was
an economic institution, an arena of both production and consumption, of
human fabrication and laboring. It was a social institution, helping to create
cultural forms that encouraged certain kinds of behavior and discouraged
others. It was a legal entity, protected and regulated by a complex body of
public and private law.

In each of these arenas, the family has sustained a series of body blows
that have had the effect, over time, not so much of transforming the family
with each of these five interlocked imperatives in mind but of deinstitution-
alizing the family by removing many previous imperatives and norms and
putting nothing in their place. Let me reiterate: If what we were currently
seeing were a growth in child well-being, there would be little reason to
raise the alarm. But that is not what we see. It is arguably also the case that
the seductive but elusive chimera, "adult happiness," has not been well
served either, but that is not my primary concern.

FUNCTIONALIST SOCIOLOGY

Let's take a brief look, in the form of a review and overview, of how scholars of the family themselves have played a role—for some unwitting, for others quite knowing—in these developments. The dominant conceptual
framework within which the family was studied in the American academy, at
least from mid-twentieth century on, has been a school of sociology called
functionalism. For the functionalist, the family is a structure that performs
certain functions. To be sure, the family is a universal institution. No society
has yet been discovered in which an entity that could be either identified or
labeled "family" did not exist. For the functionalist, the important question is
what functions the family performs for the wider society.

But there have been serious drawbacks to this approach. For one thing, it has tended to promote a historical approach to the family. For another, functionalists were (and are!) rather flatfooted when it comes to consideration of the sacramental and the biological, or embodied, dimensions of human life, focusing almost exclusively on "socialization" and on "systems maintenance." This has meant, as well, that the family's role in civic life—in the creation of citizens—has also been ignored, as functionalists have viewed men and women in and through the language of roles almost exclusively.

The central claim of functionalists has been that "whenever a country becomes modern, industrial, urban, family organization shifts from large kinship groups to a more isolated nuclear or conjugal pattern."[5] This assumption received its most elaborate theoretical formulation in the works of Talcott Parsons. Parsons claimed that the nuclear family was a product of the economic and social forces of the past several hundred years. He posited an alteration in family structure along with changes in family function and viewed this alteration as the ineluctable result of forces impinging on the family from the outside. The assumption was that the basic nuclear family configuration (mother, father, children) did not exist before the forces of modernization brought it into being.[6]

The functionalist model held that the extended family was the ideal typical family prior to industrialization. In this schema, the extended family placed undue restraint on many things, including the creation of a mobile labor force. Because a mobile labor force is necessary to the maintenance and stability of modern society, family structure was altered to meet the new demands of the "macro-order." The picture of a tidy fit between industrialization and the nuclear family became nigh irresistible. Notice that there is no room in this model for families to resist change or to serve as catalysts for change. Families were seen as entities shedding one "function" after another as the macro-order mutated. The family, having lost many functions, was then forced to become "a more specialized agency," in Parsons's terms. Indeed, he claimed that it was "important that socializing agents should not themselves be too completely immersed in family ties," as a too strong commitment to the family would handicap such persons in their ability to "fit" with the needs and demands of a mobile, opportunistic society.[7] Women got assigned an "expressive" role; men, an "instrumental-adaptive" role.

Having construed the family within functionalist terms, scholars have deprived themselves of any normative stance from which to evaluate what was, in fact, happening to and with families. So long as the abstract "needs" of the overall social order were served, then, according to this view, all must be well (more or less) with families. The importance of parenting to the well-being of real flesh and blood children—rather than the abstract needs of an abstractly construed "social order"—was slighted or ignored altogether. It was easy to accept any changes that appeared in family norms, including the rise in divorce, as just the latest variation in the family's endless mutability given the demands of social life. Mothers and fathers fell out of the picture as role players came to dominate. This led, in turn, to the notion that so long as a "role" was being served, it scarcely mattered who occupied the role. Indeed, I heard one family sociologist (at a feminist conference in the mid-1970s) argue that "antibiotics and birth control made mothering unnecessary." She advocated the total replacement of mothers by professional child rearers in order that women, too, could be part of the mobile labor force required by industrial capitalism.

Because the functionalist schema extended to internal family relations as well, and because it tended to celebrate greater "role differentiation" as an inevitable thing (and inevitability within functionalism tends, implicitly, to be equated with "what is good"), academic scholars tended to be unabashed celebrants of the "role divergence" that comes with a rapidly changing social order. The story went like this: The family performs pared-down functions. It turns out that many other institutions could perform these functions as well. It further happens that we don't really need "mothers" and "fathers" so long as various persons or institutions are assigned "nurturant" and "socialization" tasks. My summary no doubt overstates things, but not by much.

To be sure, there were critics, including the so-called Cambridge School of historic demographers, who challenged the abstractedness of the functionalist formula. They argued that, in fact, the basic mother-father-children configuration had always been the pattern, certainly in Western societies, with variations on that mode. The "nuclear family" was not a recent invention, coming into being only with industrialization.[8] The demographic evidence indicated that a basic nuclear or conjugal household had long pertained and that, even in preindustrial epochs, marriage meant the formation of a new household, often with members of the couple's households of origin figuring as central or adjunct members, so to speak.

AN ALTERNATIVE TO FUNCTIONALISM

Of course, calling into question the dominant functionalist model means one is obliged to offer another set of categories and explanatory features, especially if one hopes to make the case that the family is in trouble—that what we are witnessing is, in fact, family decline. How do we know? Here the focus must shift to the well-being of children, and on that score, as I have already indicated, things do not look good. There are ways in which a wider order may be served, particularly in its current consumption-driven, expressivist forms in the United States, even as individuals are ill served and the overall society itself, over time, reels from the changes that are taking place, although it may come to realize that too late.

My claim is that our societal experiment in loosening the ties that bind has failed: that it has failed our children, first and foremost, but that also, in ways we are only just beginning to recognize, it has failed adults understood as moral agents and responsible citizens, not just as a "mobile labor force."

This is the harsh truth of the matter: Americans at the end of the twentieth century suffer from the effects of a dramatic decline in the formation of social bonds, networks, and trust coupled with a diminution in investment in children. Children have borne the brunt of decades of negative social trends whose results are just now coming into clear focus. Standing out in harsh relief, family breakdown (1) generates unparented children who attend schools that increasingly resemble detention homes rather than centers of enduring training, discipline, and education, and (2) contributes to out-of-wedlock births and adolescent violence that, so far as we know, is now at unprecedented levels.

Here a reminder from the perspective of political and civil philosophy is in order as a way to reaffirm the civic dimensions of this question. Historically democratic theorists have either taken for granted a backdrop of vibrant informal and formal civic associations or, as in the case of Alexis de Tocqueville in *Democracy in America*, have articulated explicitly the relationship between democracy and the everyday actions and spirit of a people.

Democracy requires laws, constitutions, and authoritative institutions, as I argue in my book *Democracy on Trial*, but it also requires what might be called democratic dispositions.[9] These include a preparedness to work with others for shared ends; a combination of often strong convictions coupled with a readiness to compromise in the recognition that one can't always get everything one wants; a sense of individuality; and a commitment to civic goods that are not the possession of one person or one small group alone. The world that nourished and sustained such democratic dispositions was a thickly interwoven social fabric—a web of mediating institutions, of which the family was one. (Note the very different model implied here: rather than the family as a subsystem playing functions for a wider system—a series of boxes with connecting lines, with some dominating over others—the implied picture is one of a web of interlaced institutions, a social ecology.)

In his great book Tocqueville warned of a world different from the democracy he surveyed. He urged Americans to take to heart a possible corruption of their way of life. His worst fear was that narrowly self-involved individualists, disarticulated from the saving constraints and nurture of the overlapping associations of social life, would require, even come to demand, more control from above to muffle at least somewhat the disintegrative effects of what he called a bad form of "egoism." He saw that only small-scale civic bodies enabled citizens to cultivate the democratic virtues and play an active role in the democratic community.

UNRAVELING THE INSTITUTIONS OF CIVIL SOCIETY

The tale I am tracing argues that the deinstitutionalization of the family is part and parcel of a wider unraveling of the institutions of civil society tied, in turn, to a dramatic upsurge in all forms of social mistrust, generalized fearfulness, and cynicism. Recent studies show that Americans, without regard to race, cite very similar social problems: fear of crime, concern about poor education, the decline of home and family. Indeed, if anything, African Americans are more insistent that their society faces a crisis in values, beginning with the family.

What, then, is to be done as we enter this new millennium? Sociologist Robert Bellah reports that Americans today brighten to tales of community, especially if the talk is soothing and doesn't appear to demand much. Yet when discussion turns to institutions and the need to sustain and support authoritative civic institutions, attention withers and a certain sourness arises. This bodes ill for liberal democratic society, a political regime that requires robust yet resilient institutions that embody and reflect the urgencies of democratic passions and interests. As our mediating institutions, from the Parent Teachers Association to political parties, disappear or are stripped of legitimacy, a political wilderness spreads. People roam the prairie fixing on objects or policies or persons to excoriate or to celebrate, at least for a time, until some other enthusiasm or scandal sweeps over them. If we lose the sturdiness and patience necessary to sustain a civil society over the long haul, then liberal democracy is in trouble.

This is why the family matters. This is why conformist insouciance concerning what is happening to the family rings increasingly hollow. This is why the functionalist perspective is not up to the conceptual task, given its inability to account for change as anything other than a kind of lock-step transmutation of certain structures to keep up with either the functions they are deprived of or new job descriptions they are assigned by the "macro-order." What we require here at millennium's beginning is a way to reweave the threads of community, to restore our faltering faith in cultural forms themselves.

The speed and glitz of late modernity—at least in the consumerist West—helps to stoke the fires of great impatience. Americans are especially known for being an impatient people. We want things to happen right away. We want problems to be solved overnight. But that isn't going to happen, not when we are faced with problems of such social, economic, sacramental, legal, political, and yes, embodied power and force. Twenty-first-century moderns are dealing with the wreckage that mounted because, in the words of Vaclav Havel of the Czech Republic, we have forgotten that we are not God.

Although the family is the locus of private life, it is also critical to public life—to the life of the community and civic associations. Here the testimony of parents and experts converges. When parents are asked to tell their own version of our current discontents, they lament the fact that it is harder to do a decent job raising children in a culture that is unfriendly to families and family attachments. The overwhelming majority of Americans, 80–85 percent, believe that being a parent is much more difficult than it used to be. Pessimism about the decline of family norms is on the rise among all groups, especially among women and African-American and Hispanic citizens.

The family of which I speak is not an isolated unit but very much a social institution, nested in a wider surrounding, that either helps to sustain parental commitment and accomplishment or puts negative pressure on mothers and fathers. That pressure obviously takes many forms. I have articulated just a few. Being a parent is more than playing a role. Being a parent is more than a "lifestyle choice." It is an ethical vocation. We, as a society—and this I would urge on all societies more generally—should, insofar as is possible, lighten the burdens and smooth the paths for parents in order that the complex joys of family life might rise to the surface and in order that the undeniable burdens of family responsibility might be more openheartedly borne.

INEXORABLE QUESTIONS

Children lost to society may be a growing phenomenon, but it is one we must name for what it is: a loss, a crying shame. Protecting, preserving, and strengthening family autonomy and the well-being of mothers and fathers is a way of affirming our commitment to the individual and to democratic social life. We have, it appears, lost the recognition that the rights of persons are fundamentally social. What is at stake in the family debate, and in our response to it as we enter this new millennium, is nothing less than our capacity for human sociality and community.

Here are a few concluding questions for further consideration; indeed, they are inexorable questions, given my analysis:

1. What are the root causes of family disintegration? What are the effects of this deinstitutionalization?
2. Why is concern with the family a civic and ethical issue?
3. What does the family (mothers and fathers, brothers and sisters, grandparents, uncles, aunts, cousins, etc.) do that no other human institution can?
4. What is the role or responsibility of individuals, communities, business, and government in dealing with family issues?
5. How can we stem the tide of out-of-wedlock births, teenage violence, and family breakdown without enhancing states' avowedly coercive apparatuses?

These are serious issues. If we are not up to the task, this twenty-first century will be a tale of further coarsening of social life and deepening pressure on democratic society to enhance its coercive powers to save us from ourselves. If we hope to forestall this unhappy prospect, we must tend to our social ecology before it is too late. The family—alas!—now belongs on the list of endangered species.

STUDY QUESTIONS

1. What does Elshtain mean by the claim that the family as an institution is in decline?
2. Elshtain argues that a variety of social problems are best explained by the decline in the family as an institution. What evidence does she provide for this claim?
3. What social trends have contributed to the decline in the family, according to Elshtain?
4. Briefly explain how academic sociology has contributed to this decline, on Elsthtain's view.
5. Why does the decline in the institutions of civil society, such as the family, threaten democracy?
6. According to Elshtain, how should we think and act differently in order to revitalize the family?

NOTES

1. *Marriage Report of the Council on Families in America* (New York: Institute for American Values, March 1995).
2. Susan Chira, "Struggling to Find Stability When Divorce Is a Pattern," *New York Times*, 19 March 1995, 17.
3. This data is summarized in the *Marriage Report*.
4. Clifford Longley, "Valuing the Family," *Tablet* (June 10, 1995) 735.
5. Arlene Skolnick, "Families Can Be Unhealthy for Children and Other Living Things," *Psychology Today* 5:3 (August 1971), 18-22.
6. See Talcott Parsons, "The Family in Urban Industrial America," in *Sociology of the Family*, ed. Michael Anderson (Baltimore: Penguin Books, 1971), 43-62.
7. Parsons, "Family," 59
8. Peter Laslett, "The Comparative History of Household and Family," *Journal of Social History* 4:1 (Fall 1970), 74-87.
9. Jean Bethke Elshtain, *Democracy on Trial* (New York: Basic Books, 1995).

9

Reconcilable Differences: What It Would Take for Marriage and Feminism to Say "I Do."

Janet C. Gornick

> Janet C. Gornick is an associate professor of political science at the Graduate Center and Baruch College at the City University of New York. She is the author of numerous articles on the effects of social policy on women's status in the labor market and on the economic well-being of children. Gornick discusses the variety of ways family structure imposes obstacles on women, preventing them from achieving autonomy. Whether the issue is career choice or the division of labor within families, women are forced to place less value on autonomy than men.

> In the true marriage relation the independence of the husband and
> wife is equal, their dependence mutual and their obligations reciprocal.

> —Lucretia Mott (1793–1880)

Feminists have long been queasy about marriage, but our queasiness is not about marriage per se; it concerns the way marriage has been practiced. The religious right paints feminists as opposed to marriage and all that goes with it: heterosexuality, men, family, love, caring, and children. Campaigning against the Equal Rights Amendment in the 1970s, Phyllis Schlafly flatly warned that "feminists hate men, marriage, and children." Twenty years later, Pat Robertson advised would-be supporters in a fundraising letter: "The feminist agenda is not about equal rights for women. It is about a socialist, anti-family political movement that encourages women to leave their husbands, kill their children . . . and become lesbians."

Clearly, the right misrepresents feminists' struggle with marriage, but many moderates and even some progressives have misunderstood feminist concerns. What have American feminists really said about marriage? During the first wave of the American women's movement, which intensified during the 1840s and culminated with the achievement of suffrage in 1920, feminists battled for egalitarian marriage as passionately as they fought for voting rights. In 1848—in the Declaration of Sentiments adopted at the First Women's Rights Convention at Seneca Falls, New York—Mary Ann McClintock and Elizabeth Cady Stanton wrote:

> The history of mankind is a history of repeated injuries and usurpations on the part of man toward woman. . . . He has made her, if married, in the eye of the law, civilly dead. He has taken from her all right in property, even to the wages she earns. . . . In the covenant of marriage, . . . the law gives him power to deprive her of her liberty and to administer chastisement.

For the most part, nineteenth-century feminists did not oppose marriage itself. Rather, they fought tirelessly for the legal rights of wives, gradually winning statutory reforms that granted married women property rights.

A second wave of American feminism emerged in the 1960s, catalyzed in part by Betty Friedan's 1963 book *The Feminine Mystique*, which sparked a nationwide soul-search about the emptiness of housewifery. "It was a strange stirring, a sense of dissatisfaction, a yearning," Friedan wrote. "As [each suburban housewife] made the beds, shopped for groceries, matched slip cover materials, ate peanut butter sandwiches with her children, chauffeured Cub Scouts and Brownies . . . she was afraid to ask of herself the silent question—'Is this all?'" Friedan's book pulled countless wives into the women's movement and dovetailed with activist efforts aimed at breaking down employment barriers.

While the legal constraints that galvanized their predecessors a century earlier were mostly gone, the new women's liberationists found that marriage, de facto, still served many women poorly, especially in conjunction with motherhood. Sexual divisions of labor, locked in by the social norms of marriage, yielded gender inequality both in the labor market and in the home, saddling women with the lion's share of housework. Those divisions of labor institutionalized wives' economic dependence on their husbands; in the worst scenarios, that dependence placed women in outright danger. Furthermore, feminists argued, the centrality of marriage in the dreams and expectations of girls and young women crowded out long-term aspirations for education, employment, and civic and political engagement.

Those were the central feminist concerns about marriage nearly four decades ago, and they are still the central feminist concerns today. Pegging feminists as coldhearted haters of heterosexuality, love, care, and commitment has always been a bum rap. Were marriages between women and men to become truly egalitarian—especially in economic terms—most contemporary feminists would rejoice. Were same-sex couples invited to participate, feminism and marriage could announce a full truce.

During the 1990s, a new "marriage war" broke out, one that is now front-page news. This time, conservatives fired the first shot when they inserted marriage-promotion policies into welfare reform. Feminists tend to resist these schemes because the assumptions that underlie them are largely nonsense. Basically, conservatives argue that if low-income women could be persuaded to marry, they would join the ranks of the economically secure. Indeed, that might be true if poor women in the South Bronx could marry stockbrokers in Westchester. But poor women's options are usually much less promising, and ample social-science research confirms that marriage-promotion policies per se are unlikely to reduce poverty. I leave the critique of marriage promotion as welfare policy to others in this issue of the *Prospect* in order to pursue here the challenge of egalitarian marriage.

UNEQUAL MARRIAGE: THE PRICE WOMEN PAY

Today, a small minority of couples consist of an exclusive male breadwinner and a full-time female homemaker; in most marriages, husband and wife are both employed. However, the labor-force attachment of husbands remains considerably stronger, especially in families with children; very few men are on a career-sacrificing "daddy track." Married mothers often withdraw from paid work when their children are young; many more work part-time; and a substantial share forgo remunerative jobs that require "24-7" commitment, nighttime meetings, or travel. Few married fathers make such accommodations to family. Not surprisingly, despite progress in women's employment, men remain the primary breadwinners. As of 1997, among American married couples with children under age six, fathers took home three times the earnings of mothers. And studies confirm that wives, even wives employed full-time, still devote substantially more time than their husbands do to unpaid work—both caregiving and housework.

Certainly, children need and deserve their parents' time. It's appropriate that parents weaken labor-market ties when their children are young. The trouble, however, is that marital divisions of labor shape up along gender lines, there are hazards associated with being the non-earner or lower earner, and those hazards are very unequally distributed.

Non-earners (and lower earners) in intact couples lack bargaining power both in the economy and in the marriage. And the lower-earning partner is financially vulnerable in the event of marital dissolution, despite divorce and child-support laws intended to protect them. In addition, weak labor-market ties often mean tenuous civic and political ties, which translate into compromised power both inside and outside the home. In his 2000 book *Bowling Alone*, Robert D. Putnam contradicts the old picture of housewives as pillars of local civil society and links women's connections to employment to their participation in public forms of civic engagement.

Another problem: Huge numbers of married women are plain exhausted, battling worse "time poverty" than their husbands, particularly if they have young children and are also in paid employment. And where are the fruits of wives' unpaid work? One place is in their husbands' wages. A recent study reported in *Business Week* found that wives' unpaid work raises married men's hourly wages by about 12 percent—a "marriage premium" for men that is explained by the "likelihood that wives shoulder household tasks." Women, meanwhile, suffer reduced earnings, not because of marriage per se, but owing to the presence of children. And nearly two-thirds of married women have children. As Ann Crittenden establishes in *The Price of Motherhood*, because of their family responsibilities women in effect pay a hefty "mommy tax" on their earnings—a tax not incurred by their children's daddies.

In their much-argued-about book *The Case for Marriage: Why Married People are Happier, Healthier, and Better Off Financially*, Linda Waite and Maggie Gallagher dismiss most of these concerns. Wives, they argue, are simply better off financially because they have access to their husbands' (increased) income as well as their own (albeit diminished) income; the two together add up to more than she would have had living alone or cohabiting. As for wives' economic dependency on their husbands, Waite and Gallagher are largely unmoved. (I suspected that when, on page 1, they characterized the women's movement as criticizing "marriage per se, which the more flamboyant feminists denounced as, . . . worst of all, 'tied up with a sense of dependency.'") For the most part, these writers view the underlying economic inequality as the result of women's choices—"married moms earn less because they choose to work less"—but they don't seriously consider whether those supposed free choices are constrained by the absence of good alternatives that is inherent in archaic notions about gender, inflexible employment practices, and unsupportive public policies. In the end, they argue that making divorce more difficult and enacting divorce laws that repay women for the sacrificed labor-market attachment can indemnify wives against any losses that they incur. Fairer divorce laws are fine—but why wait for marriages to end? For all their advocacy of marriage, Waite and Gallagher leave untouched the underlying inequities that make marriage costly for so many women.

TOWARD EGALITARIAN MARRIAGE

Among feminists, there are two broad views about greater equity within marriage. "Difference feminists" argue that women's unique characteristics, such as their stronger ties to children, should be celebrated and rewarded. From this perspective, gender equity would be achieved by making parenting a less-unequal sacrifice; essentially, wives would be repaid for the losses that they incur as individuals. "Sameness feminists," by contrast, look toward a greater convergence in gender roles—a rearrangement of marital divisions of labor so that on average wives and husbands, in Francine Deutsch's phrase, would "halve it all."

The latter approach seems more promising. Reliably indemnifying women against losses caused by their greater role in family caregiving is improbable because it is so easy for husbands, employers, and even governments to free-ride on women's unpaid work. And any solution that continues gendered divisions of labor leaves in place problematic power imbalances, both public and private.

Across Europe, feminists have taken seriously this idea of greater convergence of roles in the workplace and the home. In her recent book *Restructuring Gender Relations and Employment: The Decline of the Male Breadwinner*, British sociologist Rosemary Crompton lays out the contours of what she calls a "dual-earner/dual-career" society. This is a society in which women and men engage symmetrically in market work and in caregiving work—a society that incorporates time to care for family members. Wives would not simply become "like husbands are now"; both wives and husbands would end up with substantial time for caregiving at home.

On the whole, what would a shift to gender-egalitarian time allocations entail in the United States? Imagine that mothers and fathers, on average, spend equal time in paid work. The accompanying table summarizes how much time married mothers and fathers in the United States spend working for pay each week (parents who are not employed—mostly women—are included in these averages). The far-right column lists the number of hours that each parent would work weekly if the couple's combined hours on the job were shared equally.

Average Weekly Hours Spent by Married Parents in Employment

Age of Youngest Child	Hours Worked by Mother	Hours Worked by Father	Avg. Hrs. If Total Equalized
Under 3 yrs.	23	44	33.5
3–5	25	44	34.5
6–12	28	44	36.0
13–17	31	44	37.5

Source: U.S. Current Population Survey data for 1999

This table tells us three noteworthy things about marital arrangements in this country. First, married mothers' time in paid work is sensitive to the ages of their children; their hours on the job rise as their children spend more hours outside the home and need less parental time. Second, married fathers' time at work, in contrast, is absolutely constant—perhaps not surprisingly, given that few are primary caregivers. Third, the average time that married mothers spend in employment lags behind that of their husbands, and by a considerable margin.

An egalitarian solution would entail both parents working a slightly-shorter-than-standard workweek and sharing caregiving in the home. In principle this might seem appealing to men, who often say they are sick of employment pressures, want more balance in their lives, and hope to be better fathers than their own fathers were. But for this solution to be attractive to both sexes, workplace practices have to change so that neither spouse suffers a setback as the result of caring for children. And social policy also has to change—starting with, for example, the enactment of generous paid family leave for both fathers and mothers.

At present, the idea that men as a group might shift substantial time from paid work to caregiving is remarkably controversial in the United States. But unless we settle for a society in which families "outsource" unacceptably high levels of family caregiving, a reduction in men's working time is a prerequisite for a shift toward an egalitarian division of labor both at home and at work. Mainstream advocates of "work/family balance" and "family-friendly programs" rarely suggest that men lessen their working time. But truly egalitarian marriage rests on such a shift.

This scenario of change raises at least two fundamental issues. Do women and men want to share earning and caring in a more egalitarian way? And would couples that share and share alike incur joint costs?

Conservatives—and even many progressives—often argue that wives simply want to be at home more than their husbands do; some claim intrinsic differences, while others cite the effect of social norms. There is no question that current work-and-family arrangements reflect the individual and joint decisions of women and men. But those decisions are made in a world with gender-specific constraints and opportunities. Given today's economic and social realities, it's impossible to know whether women's and men's current choices reflect enduring preferences or are, instead, accommodations influenced by inflexible working arrangements, limited options for nonparental child care, and career penalties for allocating time to parenting. The meaningful question is not "What do women and men want now?" but, rather, "What would they prefer in a much changed world—one with expectations not based on gender, with flexible employers, and with supportive policies in place?" The answer to that question is classically counterfactual; in today's socially constructed and highly constrained world, it can't be answered.

An often-raised concern is that there are gains to specialization, so that equal sharing might lower families' total earnings. If both spouses, for example, rejected 50-plus-hour-a-week employment, the couple might be forced to rule out certain highly remunerative occupations altogether. But this too remains an open question; there is remarkably little empirical research on the economic impact of divisions of labor shaped by gender. It's possible, for instance, that having to fit into gender-role expectations reduces parents' productivity, and perhaps that of their children when they reach adulthood. Conversely, some degree of economic loss might be more than offset by non-monetary benefits—such as distributional justice, for starters. And benefits from equal sharing might accrue to society more broadly. The rise of egalitarian marriage and the strengthening of fatherhood could produce healthier children who are enriched by the balance in their parents' lives and by more contact with their fathers. It could also help stem ongoing declines in marriage and childbearing rates and produce more reliable parenting of children generally. Scholars of the family understand that many women, in particular, forgo family after assessing the dismal prospects for combining work and family in a satisfying way.

SUPPORTIVE PUBLIC POLICY

How might we get from here to there? As European feminists painted portraits of the dual-earner/dual-caret society, they also envisioned a change process. Clearly, private changes in gender relations and shifts in employment practices are part of the story; but the state also plays a crucial role, both in shaping social policy and in regulating labor markets.

Couples' capacity to choose egalitarian arrangements would be facilitated by a package of government policies, many of which are in place across the European welfare states. A supportive policy package would have at least four aims: to enable and support the employment of mothers with young children; to provide incentives for men to engage in caregiving at home; to support the development of high-quality reduced-hour work for both mothers and fathers; and to provide income and tax supports for families that would ease the need to maximize market hours while providing incentives for more-equal divisions of labor.

First, paid maternity leave and decent child care would go a long way toward supporting the employment of mothers with young children. Women begin to incur the mommy tax shortly after they have their first child, especially if they're not entitled to paid maternity leave—and most American women are not. All of the Western European nations and many developing countries grant mothers paid maternity leave financed by social insurance funds. Public-maternity-leave schemes have been found to increase mothers' postnatal employment rates, increase the probability that mothers return to the same employer, and lessen the wage penalty associated with time away.

In addition, high-quality, affordable child care enables mothers to work for pay. As with leave, Americans get incredibly little child-care support from government. In the United States, about 5 percent of children under age three are in publicly provided or financed child care, compared with one-quarter in France, one-third in Belgium and Sweden, and fully half in Denmark. Not surprisingly, in all of those countries, married mothers with young children take home larger shares of parental earnings than do American mothers.

Second, paid family leave for fathers, especially if designed with incentives so that fathers actually use the leave, creates a way for men to take off time from employment, temporarily, to provide care at home. Fathers in several European countries are entitled to paternity leave immediately following a birth or adoption and, more consequentially, to paid-parental-leave benefits that can be used throughout the early years of their children's lives. Furthermore, policy makers in Europe have learned that parental-leave benefits that can't be transferred to female partners and that include high wage-replacement rates encourage fathers to take the leave to which they're entitled.

In addition, several European governments are running public-education campaigns that urge men to do more at home, either via family leave or more broadly. While the jury is still out on their effectiveness, even the Swiss government is going this route; an ongoing campaign in Switzerland—"Fair Play at Home"—is aimed at "nudging married men" to share the work at home. Despite all the lip service conservatives pay to the value of marriage, American social policy does almost nothing to encourage fathers in intact families to contribute more at home.

Third, Americans log the longest employment hours in the world. As University of Pennsylvania sociologist Jerry Jacobs observes, long hours on the job and gender equality work at cross-purposes; that is especially true in labor markets that lack options for high-quality, reduced-hour employment. Government policies aimed at shortening standard working time—either directly or via incentives placed on employers—could go a long way toward enabling men to spend more time at home. Several of the European welfare states provide models for working-time regulations designed explicitly to support gender-egalitarian families. Working-time policies (such as maximum hours) can shorten overall hours—a number of countries are aiming to set a new standard of 37.5 hours per week—and "right to time off" policies guarantee parents the right to work part-time while their children are young. (The United States neither limits total hours nor provides rights to time off.)

Further, labor-market regulations throughout the European Union protect workers who work less than full-time by requiring employers to provide equal pay and prorated benefits. So in a more egalitarian world, each spouse might log hours in paid work that fall into a new range—more than standard part-time hours but fewer than standard full-time hours. Public policies can encourage the growth of reduced-hour employment and shore up its rewards.

Finally, income supports and tax reforms would help. Some form of universal child benefit, via transfers or refundable tax credits, could replace some or all of the earnings that couples might sacrifice if husbands lessen their time in employment and wives' increases don't make up the difference. For low-income couples, in particular, cash benefits could relax the necessity to maximize (his) hours in the labor market, no matter how high the personal cost. (Among married couples, average gender differences in employment hours are approximately the same at every point on the income spectrum.) Compared with nearly every country in Europe, the United States spends very little on public income supports for couples with children, even including the Earned Income Tax Credit. And a shift to purely individual-income taxation would encourage a more equal sharing of employment by couples. Joint taxation increases the de facto marginal tax rate on the first dollar earned by the "secondary earner," and that sets up a disincentive for wives' labor-force participation. Individual-income taxation has been implemented in several countries in Europe; it is a major factor underlying Sweden's high female-employment rate. In contrast, the U.S. tax code imposes the same income-tax burden on one- and two-earner couples. Given that employment has fixed costs, this formula disadvantages two-earner couples.

STUDY QUESTIONS

1. For Gornick, what is the primary source of inequality in contemporary marriages?
2. Why does Gornick think that differences in marriage roles and workplace attachments add up to unjust inequalities rather than reasonable differences in social roles between men and women?
3. Why, on Gornick's view, is the subordinate position of women within the family not a position that women have chosen freely? Do you agree with her on this point? Why or why not?
4. What is the solution to inequalities within marriage, according to Gornick?
5. Gornick mentions a variety of policy changes that, if implemented, might rectify inequalities in the family. In your opinion, what is the main obstacle to implementing these changes?

10

Why Marriage?

Jane Smiley

Jane Smiley is a well-known novelist and essayist. Her books include *Good Faith, Horse Heaven*, and *A Thousand Acres*. In this personal essay, Smiley argues that capitalism treats desire as an end in itself and encourages both men and women to act on their desires. Such a way of life has eroded the traditional functions of marriage and renders traditional norms governing marriage irrelevant. The function of marriage today is to teach and encourage forms of intimacy that resist the commodification of life advanced by capitalism. Only the sense of agency which arises from genuine self-knowledge and active concern for others sustains the capacity for intimacy, which can be realized in non-traditional relationships.

FAMILY DINNER

My guinea-pig child, now twenty-one, was home from her senior year in college for Christmas vacation. This child was not by temperament suited to be the unbuffered firstborn of a literary, freethinking mother and an anxiety-prone father, the child of divorce, joint custody, and stepparenting. Her whole life she was a girl who liked things steady and predictable. Thus it came as a surprise to me when she disclosed her ideal family, the one she aims to have when she is the matriarch. The word she used was "welcoming." Should you want to be in her family, whoever you are, well, she is going to be happy to have you. Her house will have plenty of beds and plenty of dishes and plenty of congenial people sitting around discussing issues like women's health care and the third wave of feminism. I liked it. It sounded quite like the home she has grown up in, of which I have been the matriarch.

The last night before my daughter went back to college, we had another one of those family dinners—you know, me, my boyfriend, his daughter and son by his second wife, my daughters by my second husband, and my seven-year-old son by my third husband. The topic of conversation was how my son came to walk home from school—more than a mile up a steep, winding road on a very warm day. "What did you do when cars went by?" I asked.

"I stepped to the side of the road!" he answered. He was laughing at the success of his exploit. Not only had he been a very bold boy who had accomplished something he had been wanting to do; he had been impressively disobedient. We all laughed, and my boyfriend and I squeezed each other's hands, pleased and seduced by that happy-family idea, everyone safe and well-fed, getting along, taken care of.

But we are not married, and we have no plans to blend our families. I come to the theory and practice of marriage at the start of the new millennium with a decidedly checkered past and an outsider's view. But, I admit, I'm still paying attention, implicated, at least, by the fact that my children assume they will get married. I see the same thing as many others do—the breakdown of the traditional family—but I don't see this as a dark and fearsome eventuality, rather as something interesting to observe, something that I have endured, survived, and actually benefited from, something that will certainly be part of the material from which my children build their lives.

CHILDREN

Capitalism has an excellent reputation, among fans of the free market, for disseminating goods and information and molding the lives of consumers in the ways that best serve both the system and individuals. If this is indeed the case, then late capitalism has evidently decided that what is best for us and our children is serial monogamy, frequent changes of employment, and a high degree of instability. It has decided that, on balance, it is better for all adults to work rather than for one designated gender to stay home with the children. It has decided that most children will spend at least part of their early childhoods in the care of people outside their families who are hired to care for them, often in institutional settings rather than at home. It has decided that the inherent instability of marriage is to be promoted rather than suppressed. It has decided that the individual's relationship to society will be less and less mediated through the family and more and more experienced directly. Fans of the free market would say—should say, if they dared—that we should embrace rather than resist what capitalism has decided.

Which is not to say that when, sixteen years ago, I parted from the father of my two daughters I wasn't traumatized. The choice of staying or leaving presented itself to me as a choice between suicide and mass murder. For years afterward, I secretly scrutinized the girls for signs of psychological damage, and I read, with sinking heart, every article in the news about the negative impact of divorce upon children. It wasn't until my son came along, the child of my next marriage, that I appreciated this gloriously cruel fact of life: had I not divorced my daughters' father, I would never have borne my son, and how could I do without any of the three of them?

My daughters are twenty-one and seventeen now, and they have spent many years contemplating their own family and the families of their friends, of course comparing and choosing and wishing. They have a network of siblings: a stepsister and stepbrother nearly their own age from their father's second marriage, a foster brother, also from that marriage, and a half brother, my son. Their stepsiblings have stepsiblings of their own, to which my daughters feel somewhat related. All eight of these kids elect to maintain family ties with one another, ties that bind them more closely to one another than to their various stepparents. My daughters like the looseness of this; in fact, most of the time they like the general looseness of our family and compare it favorably with the tightness, and even suspiciousness, of their friends' traditional families, which seem a little suffocating. Both girls have had crushes on the families of friends, tried in some sense to be in those families, but in the end have found those families a little hidebound, a little boring. And I have experienced the input of the stepparents and the stepsiblings as productive and enlightening. What I thought of as mass murder turned out to be freedom—freedom from the particular family pathology that the girls' father and I were monogamously building in our four-bedroom house on that corner lot in that state I now think of as Monogamy Central.

MEN

Let's say that there is only one thing we know about men: that they feel a tension between monogamy and promiscuity. Let's further say that the balance of that tension is different in different men, and that possibly the balance is inherited, and that it changes as the men age, sometimes from monogamy toward promiscuity and sometimes from promiscuity toward monogamy. If we accept as fact only this one thing about men, then any one marriage would be more or less likely to be unstable, while at the same time marriage as an institution would be a valuable social check upon the chaos of promiscuity. Men themselves would have a stake in promoting stability for others while trying to find some wiggle room for themselves.

One thing that seems to be evident from history is that marriage as a property relationship is more stable than marriage as a personal relationship. It is not until women emerge from property status that the tension between monogamy and promiscuity is really a problem. It is women with voices and a certain amount of power who force men to choose between possible types of relationships. We can easily imagine a man having a mother, a housekeeper, a wife who has produced his legitimate children, a concubine, a sister, and even a female friend, all living under the same roof. The trouble is, we can't imagine him in America. In America custom requires that the mother and sister live elsewhere and all of the others be rolled into one, the wife. Wives require it, too. When courtship was about joining properties, then it could be short. Now that marriage is about being everything to one another, courtship takes a long time and can break down at any point. It is difficult to find a mate who is equally good at every function, and it is also difficult to know oneself well enough to know which function you care about more than the others. And then, of course, as the marriage project moves through its stages—householding, child rearing, professional success, aging—the functions you once cared about change or evolve. The great lover who can't manage to get a dirty dish into the dishwasher becomes more annoying than exciting, the wonderful friend who is infertile is a figure of tragedy, the terrific mother who harps about responsibility comes to seem like a nag.

And that tension between monogamy and promiscuity remains, now transformed into a dilemma of character. The trouble with serial monogamy, which I define as being faithfully married to one person until you can't stand it anymore, and then being faithfully married to another person who fits the new standard better, is that each transition in the series comes as a personal defeat. Serial infidelity is even worse, a strange combination of victory and defeat every time the husband cheats on his wife, until he is numb not only to the moral attractions of monogamy but also to the erotic attractions of promiscuity. Everything he said, every promise he made, every way that he knew himself—all were wrong.

Capitalism doesn't decide between the two simultaneous male drives toward promiscuity and monogamy but promotes both of them frenetically, knowing, like stockbrokers, that there is more money to be made by churning a portfolio than by holding on to it. It is for the men themselves to decide how expensive a great deal of change is, and whether the expense, in the end, is worth it. As late capitalism becomes later capitalism, the pressure toward individual change can only increase, since change generates wealth and circulates it too.

But change also promotes learning and flexibility, at least for some (and no one ever said that capitalism was merciful). Those who can and do learn often not only find mates who suit them but also find out how to value and cherish those mates. They begin to master the idea of relating, sharing, forgiving, taking responsibility. They begin to understand the relative merits of monogamy and promiscuity, even to forge new modes of relating that transcend the apparent split between the two. Whether they can fit these new modes into marriage remains, however, to be seen.

FIDELITY

Infidelity in marriage is a form of inattention. The spouse becomes less interesting than someone new, and the unfaithful party either isn't around much or seems distracted when he or she is. Some years ago, for example, a friend of mine had a breast biopsy. Her husband took her to the clinic on Thursday, stayed with her, brought her home, and tended to her that afternoon and evening. The next morning, when she was to go back for a checkup, he coolly suggested that their sixteen-year-old daughter could handle it and that the wife would be fine for the rest of the day by herself. It later turned out that he had prior plans to spend the day with his twenty-five-year-old girlfriend and didn't want to change them. In the course of their bitter divorce, this callousness seemed particularly monstrous, the wife sitting home alone in pain and fear while the husband was cavorting with a woman twenty-five years his junior. Yes, he was a lout, and no doubt covertly rather than honestly expressing resentment and anger toward his wife that he might have set aside for the time being. But what if he had been able to treat both women with love and compassion and patience and tenderness? What if when he was with the wife he had been fully with her, and when he was with the girlfriend he had been fully with her? Would each have been satisfied? Could he, could anyone, have done that?

When I began seeing my current boyfriend, he had another girlfriend, who was seeing another guy. Since the very thing that broke up my last marriage was my former husband's infidelity, it seemed to me that I was putting myself right back into danger, and so for a long time we refrained from identifying our relationship even as a "relationship." We were friends, then "all-inclusive friends." A turning point came about six months in, when the other girlfriend broke up with her other boyfriend and said to Jack, "Well, I guess it's just you and me again," and he said to her, "Well, you, me, and Jane." Within a few weeks, she had another boyfriend. Sometimes we would have dinner together, all four of us, but our dinners were, to say the least, volatile. Even so, all of the relationships, mine with him, his with her, hers with the other guy, endured, and not without pain and jealousy on the part of every single one of us. But we had a principle. We were not married, and, further, we didn't wish to take marriage as our paradigm. Couples in America begin taking marriage as their paradigm almost as soon as they begin dating: going steady, exchanging rings, or whatever. It takes real conviction and unusual stubbornness to flout the paradigm, and I, for one, needed help to do so. More than anything, I wanted another marriage to close over my head like the surface of a vast sea, preventing the acquisition of any real understanding of myself, my sexuality, and my ways of relating to men. The other girlfriend and her very central place in the life of the man I loved prevented that, and her own refusal to allow her sexual freedom to be restricted offered a model of an alternative.

Some men and women have the knack of being so delightfully present that time with them is worthwhile in and of itself, whether or not any promises about exclusiveness have been made. There are people in whom freedom is the very essence of their appeal, and those who love them have to make the choice: Is the desire to possess, in and of itself, more worth pursuing than the relationship with that delightful person, and if so, why? Or is that relationship, whatever it entails, the valuable thing?

To be forced to ponder these questions is to be forced to ask yourself about your own freedom and autonomy, your own ability to be present with your friend or spouse when he is present with you as well as your ability to be present with yourself when he is not with you.

One thing I have discovered is that I always mistook longing for love. If I felt enough longing, then that was the sure sign that this was love. The trouble was that I could feel unassuageable longing for my friend when he was right there, right in my arms, talking right to me. If I got rid of the longing, then I didn't recognize what was left as love, and in fact it took me a long time to recognize love when I felt it or saw it. Not getting married was the education in learning not to be oblivious, but instead honest and observant.

Fidelity, more than anything else, is the signifier of marriage. To forswear fidelity is to open yourself up to other ideas, other thoughts, about what love is, what desire is, what happiness is, and what commitment is.

FEMINISM

It was inevitable that women would rise out of property status. Capitalism wants every consumer, and ultimately distinctions among consumers according to gender, age, geographical location, or ethnic background must break down as the market inevitably extends itself. The power to sell or buy inevitably carries with it a sense of autonomy and a feeling of freedom, no matter how temporary. Since marriage began as a property relationship, its foundations are challenged by the transformation of the property into personhood. In William Shakespeare's *Winter's Tale*, Leontes's right to kill his wife in a jealous rage is not challenged by law, nor is his right to kill his daughter. He can only be worked on in private, by the nag Paulina, who torments his conscience for sixteen years. Leontes's transformation comes as a result of his recognition of the divine nature of Hermione. She was never his property to begin with. True marriage, or remarriage, begins with the revelation that union between male and female is a divine reconciliation between equals. And it is not a coincidence that Perdita, lost and found, is a daughter rather than a son. Shakespeare perfectly understands the confusion of power and property considerations that would surround the figure of a sixteen-year-old son but are absent with a daughter. Perdita returns as a miraculous gift rather than a possessed female, and Leontes is redeemed.

Personhood and autonomy require the individual to take care of him- or herself, and both the civil rights and feminist movements have been largely about blacks and women gaining access to the education and capital necessary to do so. This does not mean that cataclysms such as the Civil War and World War II didn't cause both men and women to wonder whether property relationships were safer after all. But the reaction to each setback has been increasingly violent—the wave of feminism that began in the seventies as a reaction to post–World War II cocooning has been quite strong and almost universal. The rise of women, in my opinion, is a done deal. Even a huge cataclysm doesn't seem to me capable of returning women to property status.

Let's say that one thing is true about women: they know who their children are. The tension they feel is the tension between the claims of the self and the claims of the child, and once again the balance varies among individuals and over the course of a lifetime. The high fertility level of women suggests that nature favors culling rather than preselection as the mode of limiting the human population. In this, nature is like the free market, which is never merciful nor safe in the short term or to the individual. Free-market capitalism is very much like a large, vital ecosystem that balances itself over time by getting rid of this or that individual or group. As we proliferate, our value as units declines, and we have to enhance our value relative to others by offering a scarce talent or skill, or else combining with others to share both the work and the wealth. Feminism has explored these ideas—sisterhood and entrepreneurship—both theoretically and practically.

The obvious course is to combine with men, the fathers of our children, as a way of avoiding the heartbreak of natural culling, but the success of feminism as an outgrowth of the free market requires the reconstitution of the marriage bond so that both men and women benefit from it. At the turn of the millennium, that is where we find ourselves.

SEX

Marriage as a property relationship organized sex very clearly. The transfer of property from one family to another, and then from one generation to another, gave primacy to the reproductive function of sex, making generally accepted status distinctions among all offspring produced by both members of the couple. Reproductive choice is one of the products of free-market capitalism that actually has been as revolutionary as advertised, and undoubtedly could have destroyed marriage as a property relationship all by itself, because the effect of reproductive choice is to promote desire as an end, and endless desire as the ultimate goal.

More optimistic philosophers of capitalism view desire as a form of greed, perhaps the highest form of greed, and therefore the most profitable. Pessimistic philosophers of capitalism have other ideas: a form of infantilism (Freud), a biological urge, a sin, a weakness, a failure of will. People who get married tend to view it as a promise. The way someone defines desire determines its result. Defining it as hunger for something wanting, for example, dictates that it must be sated, especially in marriage; the best you can hope for is that tricks and brief deprivations will put off satiation temporarily. Some Hollywood movies, such as *Casablanca,* define it as a brief consummation preceded and followed by years of deprivation: the briefer the consummation, the more total the deprivation, the more perfect the experience of desire. Humphrey Bogart's last line to Claude Rains is spoken with relief: romantic deprivation is exactly what he has wanted all along. The alternative scenario, as in, for example, *The Big Sleep*, is that the couple will experience danger and potential deprivation, and their level of desire will thereby be enhanced beyond the power of permanent commitment to drain it off completely. The logical end of this line of thinking is *Bonnie and Clyde* or *Natural Born Killers*, the rapid alternation of sex and the threat of death climaxing in a shootout or the electric chair.

In fact, for market capitalism, sex is like everything else—something to want when you don't have it and to not want when you do have it. This poses a problem for marriage based on personal relationship, especially since the fluctuating desires of two people need to be taken into account, and it is easy for either or both parties to interpret strong desire as pressing need.

The solution to the difficulties of marital sex offered by free-market capitalism is a lifetime of courtship, which, like all courtship, carries a high degree of cruelty. Not long ago I was at the beauty parlor, eavesdropping on a seventy-year-old woman who, when the hairdresser asked if she had a boyfriend, said, "Don't you know? At my age they say, 'If he's younger than you, he's after your purse, if he's older than you, he's after a nurse.'" We all laughed, because we ruefully agreed. And yet courtship after fifty is illuminating in several ways. One of these grows out of the fact that the path from erection to ejaculation is neither as short nor as direct as it once was, thereby inviting both partners, but especially the man, to explore other, some cultures would say higher, modes of pleasure. Another grows out of the uncoupling of roles—neither partner is in the throes of choosing a career, defining an identity, or deciding whether and how to have children; the hopes and fears that impinge upon sexuality in one's twenties and thirties have become regrets or achievements, but at any rate are decided. Sexuality itself is less mysterious, more available for experimentation. Does endless desire result from relaxation?

Comedian Chris Rock has said, "A man is only as faithful as his options," and to that, greed, serial monogamy, and promiscuity would say, "Amen!" Lifetime courtship is an option, though, not a requirement. Marital sex after fifty presents the same opportunities as extramarital sex, if the partners can deflect the definitions of desire that the market offers and shuck off perceived injuries of their common past.

INTIMACY

We marry to make ourselves happy. In this we have the approval of both free-market capitalism and the signers of the Declaration of Independence, who chose "the pursuit of happiness" rather than "property" as the appropriate corollary to life and liberty. Nevertheless, when we marry we mostly don't know what will make us happy. Happiness is a multiple-choice test: steady companionship? lots of stuff? a nice place to live? children? plenty of sex? good health? freedom to do what we want? The free market offers one suggestion after another, and serial monogamy as well as serial infidelity can be seen as a method of sampling all the wares, all the theories about happiness. Usually, once most of the goods have been sampled and found wanting, we try the services—psychotherapy, self-improvement, creative self-expression—and, to some extent, these seem to work better.

Capitalism has ordained diversity. Just as the starling and the Japanese beetle and syphilis and AIDS have spread from their original habitats, so, too, have we been given a wide choice of potential mates. I was Protestant-agnostic from St. Louis. My first husband was Irish-Catholic from Wyoming. My second husband was Hungarian-Catholic from the Bronx. My third husband was Nordic-Baptist from Iowa. In every case, the things we knew unconsciously about how a family is constituted and what various verbal and physical signals meant sometimes agreed and sometimes disagreed. We often found ourselves in unknown territory, misinterpreting, miscommunicating, and feeling very alone. Add to this the inherent communication differences between men and women, and intimacy seems like an unlikely outcome. The preference of many of our parents, stated years ago, that we marry within our faith and within our neighborhood, seems, in retrospect, a practical alternative.

The solution that capitalism offers is bargaining, and, indeed, we are often advised to become good negotiators in our relationships; that is, to communicate specifically and explicitly, to be fair in divvying up responsibilities, and to understand that relationships are like contracts. Bargaining offers some advantages compared with the hierarchy of a property arrangement. For one thing, a bargain implies equality between the bargainers. For another, it invites the investigation and expression of things that might otherwise go assumed; for example, what constitutes a normal family. But bargaining also implies a zero-sum situation—that domestic life is a life of limits and real or potential deprivation. Bargaining in the home shares the limitations of bargaining in the marketplace. Advantage can be gained by being dishonest or secretive or by withholding a desired object. Bargaining and negotiation refine the letter of the agreement, encouraging the temptation to catch the other partner out in reneging on the agreement, and it also rewards the partners for soliciting third parties in deciding whether the agreement has been violated. A bargain can never truly be fair, and so it focuses the minds of the bargainers on inequities and betrayals.

The first requirement of intimacy is honesty. Honesty between spouses is supremely difficult unless each spouse feels him- or herself to be complete, because bargaining is about negotiating needs; that is, compensations for incompleteness. If the only reason to marry is to be happy, and happiness can result only from intimacy, then serial monogamy is the natural result of a strategy of bargaining as a way of divvying up marital responsibilities.

Codependency is an interesting late-capitalist pathology that illuminates both intimacy and bargaining. The codependent is said to be someone who gives up an explicit bargain in favor of an implicit bargain. Instead of you taking care of me and me taking care of the children, say, you bringing home the money and me taking care of the house, our bargain is, allegedly, that you act like my drunken father and I feel a sense of familiarity. Except that the codependent partners often don't consciously feel that such is the bargain they have made. Rather, they feel that they have committed themselves to each other, but problems of addiction, finances, illness, and temperament have made the commitment a troubled one. The instinct of the couple is to try harder to sustain the commitment, but their psychological advisers view this as the very sign that pathology is at work. If bargaining is the model, then they are right—good bargaining always strives for explicitness and fairness. If intimacy is the model, then something else is going on. Psychological professionals always say that codependents are avoiding intimacy, but, in fact, the partners actually have achieved a high level of intimacy, because they have confronted the inconveniences of each other and have chosen to accept them, at least intermittently, rather than avoid them. The problem is not intimacy, per se, but each partner's sense of self. If the depredations of each partner had no negative effect upon the couple's circumstances or upon the other partner's feelings of strength, happiness, and well-being, then the relationship would not be pathological but potentially transformative, rather like what happens when one spouse contracts a serious illness that puts both spouses to the test and brings them to new and deeper levels of intimacy.

The first, last, and most important requirement of recovery from addiction is absolute honesty, the first, last, and most important requirement of intimacy, but, in the pantheon of self-serving virtues required by free-market capitalism, it is nowhere to be found.

MONEY

Divorce laws in the state of California, where I live, are absolute. Whatever property accrues to the partners in a marriage accrues to both and shall be divided equally by both, no matter who accrued it, who left, who broke the contract. The moral construction of the marriage bond has no legal weight, and very little bargaining is allowed. Perhaps these laws were intended to retard marital breakdown. In a model where the husband accrues the money, then discards the wife and children for a younger woman, possibly he might be given pause by the idea that it's cheaper to keep her. If the model is different, and, for example, the money was accrued by the wife, who bore the children and kept to the contract but the husband left her anyway for a younger woman, giving in to his inherent drive toward promiscuity, then the outcome is the same—halving of the property. In such a case, the departing male has no reason to maintain the marriage and every reason to leave it. He who came in with nothing leaves with quite a bit—an excellent deal and a nice bit of income redistribution. In the divorce culture, laws like those in the state of California serve as a disincentive to marriage, especially between people of disparate incomes. Serial monogamy turns out to be a way periodically to halve your assets.

The free market, especially in the last thirty years, has decreed that disparate incomes shall be the norm. Those who have also have lawyers advising them on how to protect what they have against the intimate enemy, the potential future spouse, using the family trust, the prenuptial agreement. When I told my lawyer that my boyfriend was going to remodel my house, she advised me to get a strict estimate and regular billings, then to keep a record of the checks I paid him with so that if we broke up he couldn't claim equity in the house and force me to sell it. In California, apparently, any type of affectional relationship is dangerous. Of course, the logical end to all of this is: every man a monad, and every woman, too.

And yet, as the baby-boom generation ages, the problem that faces Social Security faces individuals and families too. Who provides? When marriage was a property relationship and assets were concentrated in the hands of patriarchs, the answer was clear. In our day, with assets circulating at an accelerated pace through an economy more and more in flux, customs regulating who pays and who is paid for have little time to take hold, while the selfishness and greed that are the default options of the system gain currency, as they did all through the 1980s.

Who pays for the children? Who pays for the men and women without defined benefit pension plans, IRAs, and Keogh plans? Who pays for the unlucky and the unwise? Greed and selfishness always say, not me!

WHY ARE YOU MARRIED?

I know quite a few people who support children not their own. I know some people who support children not even belonging to their spouses or mates. Why they would do so goes unanswered by both economics and sociobiology, and is explained only by invoking love or the common good. And free-market capitalism is a poor teacher when it comes to understanding love or the common good. Traditional marriage and family life don't have much more to say than self-interest does on these topics. Where blood is undiluted by divorce, stepparents, stepchildren, and stepcousins, it does tend to be thicker than water, in accordance with the sociobiological model.

But most of us at the turn of the millennium live in the fluid middle ground between the solitary *Homo economicus*, protecting his assets, and the tribe that uses degrees of blood kinship to define who is one of us and who is not. Our circle of relationships is chosen from those with whom we feel an affinity, and for such relationships as these, free-market capitalism offers no answers to the questions about who provides, what constitutes a commitment or an obligation or a responsibility, even what constitutes a relationship. The free market has shown us how our lives will look but not in what spirit they are to be lived.

If we return to *The Winter's Tale*, we see that Leontes's original sin was the sin of jealousy; that is, the sin of trying to corner the market on another person's inner life. The history of speculation shows us that trying to corner the market is always an act of hubris that leads to bankruptcy. The flow of another's feelings is not unlike the flow of a particular asset through the economy. Stopping the flow or attempting to contain it is a misapprehension of what feelings and assets are, which are inherently dynamic, without meaning or value in themselves but gaining meaning and value from their relationship to other feelings, other assets. Leontes's sin and punishment are ones he imposes upon himself, by misinterpreting a personal relationship as a property relationship and discovering that the lost "property" is, indeed, irreplaceable. His misapprehension runs so deep that he can be saved only by what he interprets as a miracle; the recognition of the holy in another person is the one thing that counteracts the idea that another person is merely an object to be exploited.

If marriage or partnership is for anything in this day and age, then it is for this: learning by experience how to express love. Compassion, tenderness, patience, responsibility, kindness, and honesty are actions that elicit similar responses from others. These are not bargaining chips; when they are used that way they lose their essence as well as their ability to elicit anything from others but suspicion. Moreover, compassion, tenderness, patience, responsibility, kindness, and honesty increase the happiness of the compassionate, tender, patient, responsible, kind, and honest man or woman, no matter what the response of others is, because they remind him or her of his or her own agency. To live in accordance with these qualities is to live by choice and awareness rather than by obliviousness and reactiveness. Who better to practice them with than someone whom you already love and who loves you, with whom you have agreed to seek happiness?

The social redemption of marriage in our time is precisely in intimacy as a countervailing force against the chaotic isolation promoted by free-market capitalism. If we can share with our spouses and understand that we both benefit, then we can share with our children and understand the same thing, and after that we can share with other children, and with our friends, with our communities, and with the larger community that is all around us, now rendered less fearsome by our own choice to approach it with a sense of connection. We can build up a network that reminds us over and over that connection is the very stuff of life, liberty, and the pursuit of happiness.

STUDY QUESTIONS

1. Smiley claims that she has benefited from the erosion of traditional norms governing family structure. How has she benefited?
2. Smiley points to a variety of tensions in modern life that undermine traditional family norms. Briefly describe these tensions.
3. How has capitalism promoted instability in family norms, according to Smiley? Are her explanations plausible? Explain.
4. How has the instability in Smiley's romantic life encouraged self-understanding?
5. According to Smiley, what is the purpose of marriage in contemporary life? How have Smiley's decisions regarding family life helped her accomplish this purpose?

INTERVENTIONS: NEGOTIATING
DEPENDENCE AND INDEPENDENCE

As Elshtain argues, traditions provide social life with stability. A person who adopts traditional family values as a set of guiding norms commits herself to a certain continuity in life, and thus cannot think that tomorrow or the next day it may be an open question what the norms of family life are to be. Although some degree of independent judgment may be compatible with traditional beliefs, there are limits to this independence if one is to live in continuity with the tradition.

Thus, if we define autonomy as self-sufficiency, traditional family values will be incompatible with autonomy. A self-sufficient person values independent judgment more highly than anything else, and reserves for herself alone the authority to judge. For such a person, traditions, moral authorities, and social norms will always be vulnerable to modification or rejection simply because, for a self-sufficient person, nothing is immune to criticism, and that increases the likelihood that some traditions will be too constraining. When Elshtain writes that marriage has been deinstitutionalized, she is in part objecting to the fact that many people no longer feel bound by traditional marriage norms, preferring instead to exercise individual choice on family matters.

Many people achieve self-sufficiency in some aspects of their lives, but as a comprehensive ideal of how to live, it is likely to be unavailable to most of us. It is extraordinarily difficult to live while leaving one's values and attachments persistently open to reassessment. How much instability in life is desirable? Is the ability to make independent judgments worth the cost of fragmented relationships, insecurity, and emotional turmoil? Self-sufficiency implausibly implies that anyone who relies on authority or tradition lacks autonomy, at least in those areas of life where authority is at issue. That would appear to render nonautonomous many people who are self-controlled, thoughtful, and effective, despite relying on traditional beliefs. Thus, self-sufficiency seems to set the bar for achieving autonomy too high, requiring more independence than is possible or desirable for most human beings.

However, autonomy defined as self-direction may be more accommodating to the authority of traditional values. In order to determine whether someone who leads a life that conforms to traditional beliefs can be self-directed we need a richer account of self-direction than I have given thus far.

As I wrote in the introduction, a person is self-directed if her desires are consistent with her deeper values and commitments, she critically assesses her desires and values, and she approves of them. There is much debate among philosophers regarding what should be included in the critical assessment condition. The following criteria represent a summary of this debate. Let's hypothesize that a desire is autonomous if the person who has it:

1. is aware of the desire's existence;
2. is self-aware enough to understand how she came to have the desire (e.g., through socialization, advertising, mother's advice, etc.), or, if she is unaware of its development, would not resist developing it were she aware of it;
3. assesses the desire in light of deeper values and commitments and experiences no serious conflict between them;
4. wishes the desire to be effective;
5. exhibits normal cognitive competence;[1] and
6. is not prevented from engaging in self-reflection.

Many people who adopt traditional family arrangements satisfy conditions 1–6. Thus, a self-directed person can be deeply committed to traditional values without sacrificing autonomy. As long as one is fully aware that one is allowing the authority of tradition to govern one's life, and wholeheartedly endorses this influence, the conditions of self-direction are satisfied.

However, it is important to note that this account of autonomy focuses on the psychological conditions of autonomy while ignoring external factors, such as legal regulations or social norms, that prevent a person who satisfies 1–6 from acting autonomously. For instance, gays and lesbians who value traditional family arrangements (aside from the requirement that marriage partners be of different genders) are incapable of acting on those desires, under current law. Thus, although they may satisfy the conditions of self-direction, it is implausible to claim they have autonomy with respect to their desires for marriage. In this regard, the self-sufficiency model is superior to self-direction because it requires that we achieve a real, substantive independence from the influence of external factors.

Gornick gives us similar reasons for thinking the self-direction model of autonomy is incomplete. Gornick argues that traditional norms regarding the role of women in the family are so powerful and pervasive that they crowd out other aspirations women might have. Furthermore, women who give up career aspirations or who frantically try to balance work and family life, though never quite succeeding at either, may have made their decisions thoughtfully and wholeheartedly, but they often do so in the absence of good alternatives. The upshot of Gornick's essay is that, given the history of patriarchy that has defined the structure of marriage, it is implausible to consider women in traditional family arrangements autonomous.

When Gornick writes, "The meaningful question is not 'What do women and men want now?' but, rather, 'What would they prefer in a much changed world—one with expectations not based on gender, with flexible employers, and with supportive policies in place?'" she is raising the issue of oppressive socialization. Our beliefs and desires are often the product of socialization so deeply embedded in patterns of thought and behavior that we can no longer see alternatives. Even thoughtful self-reflection is not sufficient to guarantee autonomy, if the options available in one's circumstances are too limited. If Gornick is right about the constraints of traditional family arrangements, then many women in traditional family arrangements lack autonomy even though they satisfy the conditions for self-direction listed above.

In addition to ignoring external impediments to autonomy, self-direction does not require enough experiential insight regarding basic values. Although in the self-direction model we have to think about where our values came from and endorse that process, there is no requirement that we compare our values with those of others who may think differently, or be aware of alternatives that can serve as a point of comparison. Self-direction sets the bar for achieving autonomy too low, requiring thoughtfulness but ignoring the degree to which circumstances prevent us from seeing real alternatives that would enhance autonomy. Similar impediments to autonomy exist for the victims of nihilism that Cornel West discusses in chapter 4.

However, as we have seen, self-sufficiency sets the bar for achieving autonomy too high, requiring more independence and instability than is possible or desirable. This dilemma describes the condition of many individuals torn between adopting the constraints of traditional ways of life and revising their beliefs and desires to adapt to a rapidly changing society, in the process sacrificing something about which they deeply care.

Yet, individuals who confront such dilemmas are not helpless. How do people, when faced with the burden of commitments under social circumstances difficult to escape, gain a sense of autonomy? Jane Smiley describes her own experience of negotiating conflicts over dependence and independence, social conventions and desire, traditions and moral freedom. The first thing to notice about Smiley's deliberative process is that although some components of her system of beliefs and values are revisable, others remain stable, fixed centers around which she organizes her life. Marriage gradually becomes unimportant to her, but she never compromises the search for genuine intimacy or her love for her children, and remains committed to what she calls serial monogamy.

Thus, she does not seek a life of independence from the commitments that relationships impose on us. The search for genuine intimacy is her goal throughout. Yet, she is willing to give up some relationships to strengthen others. This capacity to sort out which of one's beliefs and commitments are revisable and which are not requires imagination—the ability to imagine oneself otherwise, to play around with new identities in one's mind—as a central component in the deliberative process. Imagination enables us to remove ourselves from habitual ways of thinking and envisage new possibilities. Thus, Smiley's personal essay illustrates the importance of imagination in the deliberative process, suggesting that we add the capacity to imagine oneself otherwise to our list of conditions for self-direction.

But Smiley's capacity to achieve autonomy with regard to her married life involves one other capacity I have not yet mentioned—the self-confidence to implement her decisions once she makes them. In the end, only by changing the actual social relationships that obtain in her life is she able to sustain control over her life, and this involves the tragedy of divorce and the flouting of social norms regarding marriage. Smiley is able to achieve the integration between immediate desires and deeper values required to lead a self-directed life only by adopting a style of life that seems, on the surface, to implement the requirements of self-sufficiency. She clearly values a pattern of life that seeks to maximize personal control over her situation by actively cultivating the competence to question her commitments and revising her values when she judges them to be unworthy of allegiance. However, she does not seek the wholesale rejection of social norms or the kind of independence from commitments and external influence that defines self-sufficiency. Instead, she attempts to hold on to as much of traditional marriage as possible. The quality of her relationships matters most to her and is an aim that she never compromises. This suggests that questioning commitments, flouting social norms, and revising values need not be driven by a desire for self-sufficiency but can be driven by a deep desire for relationships and commitments.

Thus, neither self-sufficiency nor self-direction quite captures the process through which Smiley achieves control over her life. This suggests that we need an alternative account of autonomy that requires greater capacity to revise values than self-direction does, but is compatible with strong, enduring commitments, unlike self-sufficiency.

NOTE

1. Many philosophers would replace 5 with the requirement that self-directed persons must respond to objective reasons. They must be willing to abandon beliefs or desires when offered, from an objective point of view, good reasons to do so. However, this condition may be too strong for a workable conception of autonomy because it assumes that our value systems, beliefs, and desires are subject to change when we consider them impartially. This may be an unwarranted assumption, especially when emotions are involved, as in issues of family relationships. We often cannot suspend or substantially modify family relationships even when we have good reasons to do so. As I will argue in a later chapter, such a strong condition is closer to self-sufficiency than self-direction.

IV

COPING WITH
HI-TECH COWBOYS

Technological advance has always profoundly affected the human condition. However, recent advances in communication technology and biotechnology promise to transform human nature itself. Disagreements over cloning, genetic research, and information privacy are the leading edge of a vigorous cultural debate over the meaning of technology, and its benefits, risks, and burdens.

Technology promotes the new and the different while uprooting established institutions and the norms that provide stability to life. Communication and transportation technologies enable us to traverse great distances almost instantaneously. But such efficient mobility may loosen our attachments to the people and places that make up our immediate surroundings, threatening our sense of community, which requires long-term relationships with emotional depth. Information technology makes vast quantities of data available, enhancing the search for knowledge, but threatens our privacy when we lose control of our own information.

Biotechnology promises the alleviation of great suffering through the pharmacological manipulation of mood, genetic enhancement of physical and mental capacities, and techniques for preventing disease and extending human life span. However, it also gives us the power to manipulate human genetic structure and intervene in the process of evolution with uncertain results. Much of our current technology burdens future generations with depleted resources and ravaged ecosystems.

How much should we intervene in the processes of life to satisfy our desires? Many reject such intervention as arrogant hubris; others believe that technological development is the natural product of our intelligence on which our flourishing depends. There are fundamental moral values at stake with these questions. Perhaps we have a moral obligation to develop technology that will diminish suffering and save lives. However, some people argue that in the process we will sacrifice that which makes human life meaningful—communal attachments with emotional depth and the experience of human dignity, which genetic engineering threatens by transforming human beings into manufactured commodities.

11

The Age of Genetic Technology Arrives

Leon Kass

Leon R. Kass, M.D., Ph.D., is Addie Clark Harding Professor in the Committee on Social Thought and the College at the University of Chicago and Hertog Fellow in Social Thought at the American Enterprise Institute. Dr. Kass is the author of numerous books, including *The Ethics of Human Cloning* (1998, with James Q. Wilson); *Wing to Wing, Oar to Oar: Readings on Courting and Marrying* (2000, with Amy A. Kass); *Life, Liberty, and the Defense of Dignity: The Challenge for Bioethics* (2002); and *The Beginning of Wisdom: Reading Genesis* (2003). Kass argues that genetic engineering technology gives us the power not only to cure disease, but also to shape the biological dispositions of future generations. Thus, we undermine the autonomy of future generations while fundamentally transforming human nature and our conception of human dignity. Furthermore, the materialist philosophy that underwrites biological science eviscerates traditional moral and religious values without replacing them with a comprehensive moral framework. Thus, we lack the moral standards that must govern this awesome power.

As one contemplates the current and projected state of genetic knowledge and technology, one is astonished by how far we have come in the less than fifty years since Watson and Crick first announced the structure of DNA. True, soon after that discovery, scientists began seriously to discuss the futuristic prospects of gene therapy for genetic disease and of genetic engineering more generally. But no one then imagined how rapidly genetic technology would emerge. The Human Genome Project, disclosing the DNA

From Leon Kass, *Life, Liberty, and the Defense of Dignity: The Challenge for Bioethics*, Encounter Books, 2002. Reprinted by permission.

sequences of all thirty thousand human genes, is all but completed. And even without comprehensive genomic knowledge, biotech business is booming. According to a recent report by the research director for Glaxo Smith Kline, enough sequencing data are already available to keep his researchers busy for the next twenty years, developing early-detection screening techniques, rationally designed vaccines, genetically engineered changes in malignant tumors leading to enhanced immune response, and, ultimately, precise gene therapy for specific genetic diseases. The age of genetic technology has arrived.

Genetic technology comes into existence as part of the large humanitarian project to cure disease, prolong life, and alleviate suffering. As such, it occupies the moral high ground of compassionate healing. Who would not welcome personal genetic profiling that would enable doctors to customize the most effective and safest drug treatments for individuals with hypertension or rheumatoid arthritis? Who would not welcome genetic therapy to correct the defects that lead to sickle cell anemia, Huntington's disease, and breast cancer, or to protect against the immune deficiency caused by the AIDS virus?

And yet genetic technology has also aroused considerable public concern, for it strikes most people as different from other biomedical technologies. Even people duly impressed by the astonishing genetic achievements of the last decades and eager for the medical benefits are nonetheless ambivalent about these new developments. For they sense that genetic technology, while in some respects continuous with the traditional medical project of compassionate healing, also represents something radically new and disquieting. Often hard-pressed to articulate the precise basis of their disquiet, they talk rather in general terms about the dangers of eugenics or the fear of "tampering with human genes" or, for that matter, "playing God."

Enthusiasts for genetic technology, made confident by their expertise and by their growing prestige and power, are often impatient with the public's unease. Much of it they attribute to ignorance of science: "If the public only knew what we know, it would see things our way and give up its irrational fears." For the rest, they blame outmoded moral and religious notions, ideas that scientists insist no longer hold water and only serve to obstruct scientific progress.

In my own view, the scientists' attempt to cast the debate as a battle of beneficial and knowledgeable cleverness versus ignorant and superstitious anxiety should be resisted. For the public is right to be ambivalent about genetic technology, and no amount of instruction in molecular biology and genetics should allay its—our—legitimate human concerns. Rightly understood, these worries are, in fact, in touch with the deepest matters of our humanity and dignity, and we ignore them at our peril.

I aim to articulate some of those concerns, bearing in mind that genetic technology cannot be treated in isolation but must be seen in connection with other advances in reproductive and developmental biology, in neurobiology and in the genetics of behavior—indeed, with all the techniques now and soon being marshaled to intervene ever more directly and precisely into the bodies and minds of human beings. For the sake of this discussion, I will take the technical claims of the enthusiasts for genetic technology at face value, although I suspect that a fair number of their claims are exaggerated. Discovering the DNA sequences is far easier than learning how genes interact within the living body or what they mean, clinically speaking. Synthesizing a healthy gene to replace a defective one is much easier than delivering it safely to the right places in the body and having it work only as desired. Even the fine idea of perfected, individualized therapies based on genetic profiling is, I suspect, going to face great practical obstacles before it can be widely used, and even then, the *costs* of doing so may be prohibitive. Yet I will not dispute here about which of the prophesied technologies will in fact prove feasible or how soon.[1] To be sure, as a practical matter we must address the particular ethical issues raised by each new technical power as *it* comes into existence. But the moral meaning of the entire enterprise does not depend on the precise details regarding what and when. I shall proceed by raising a series of questions, the first of which is an attempt to say how genetic technology is different.

IS GENETIC TECHNOLOGY SPECIAL?

What is different about genetic technology? At first glance, not much. Isolating a disease-inducing aberrant gene looks fairly continuous with isolating a disease-inducing intracellular virus. Supplying diabetics with normal genes for producing insulin has the same medical goal as supplying them with insulin for injection.

Nevertheless, despite these obvious similarities, genetic technology is also decisively different. When fully developed, it will wield two powers not shared by ordinary medical practice. Medicine treats only existing individuals, and it treats them only remedially, seeking to correct deviations from a more or less stable norm of health. By contrast, genetic engineering will, first of all, deliberately make changes that are transmissible into succeeding generations and may even alter in advance specific *future* individuals through direct "germline" or embryo interventions. Second, genetic engineering may he able, through so-called genetic enhancement, to create new human capacities and, hence, new norms of health and fitness.[2]

For the present, it is true, genetic technology is hailed primarily for its ability to better diagnose and treat *disease* in *existing* individuals. Confined to such practices, it would raise few questions (beyond the usual ones of safety and efficacy). Even intrauterine gene therapy for existing fetuses with diagnosable genetic disease could be seen as an extension of the growing field of fetal medicine. But there is no reason to believe that the use of gene-altering powers can be so confined, either in logic or in practice. For one thing, "germ-line" gene therapy and manipulation, affecting not merely the unborn but also the unconceived,"[3] is surely in our future. The practice has numerous justifications, beginning with the desire to reverse the unintended dysgenic effects of modern medical success. Thanks to medicine, for example, individuals who would have died from diabetes now live long enough to transmit their disease producing genes. Why, it has been argued, should we not reverse these unfortunate changes by deliberate intervention? More generally, why should we not effect precise genetic alteration in disease carrying sperm or eggs or early embryos, in order to prevent in advance the emergence of disease that otherwise would later require expensive and burdensome treatment? And why should not parents eager to avoid either the birth of afflicted children or the trauma of eugenic abortion be able to avail themselves of germ-line alteration. In short, even before we have had more than trivial experience with gene therapy for existing individuals—none of it successful—sober people have called for overturning the current (self-imposed) taboo on germ-line modification.[4] The line between somatic and germ-line modification cannot hold.

Despite the naive hopes of many, neither will we be able to defend the boundary between therapy and genetic enhancement. Will we reject novel additions to the human genome that enable us to produce, internally, vitamins or amino acids we now must get in our diet? Will we oppose the insertion of engineered foreign (or even animal) genes fatal to bacteria and parasites or offering us increased resistance to cancer? Will we decline to make alterations in the immune system that will increase its efficacy or make it impervious to HIV? When genetic profiling becomes able to disclose the genetic contributions to height or memory or intelligence, will we deny prospective parents the right to enhance the potential of their children?[5] Finally, should we discover—as no doubt we will—the genetic switches that control our biological clock and that very likely influence also the maximum human life expectancy, will we opt to keep our hands off the rate of aging or our natural human lifespan? Not a chance.

We thus face a paradox. On the one hand, genetic technology really is different. It can and will go to work directly and deliberately on our basic, heritable, life-shaping capacities at their biological roots. It can take us beyond existing norms of health and healing—perhaps even alter fundamental features of human nature. On the other hand, precisely because the goals it will serve, at least to begin with, will be continuous with those of modern high interventionist medicine, we will find its promise familiar and irresistible.

This paradox itself contributes to public disquiet: rightly perceiving a powerful difference in genetic technology, we also sense that we are powerless to establish, on the basis of that difference, clear limits to its use. The genetic genie, first unbottled to treat disease, will go its own way, whether we like it or not.

HOW MUCH GENETIC SELF-KNOWLEDGE IS GOOD FOR US?

Quite apart from worries about genetic engineering, gaining genetic knowledge is itself a legitimate cause of anxiety, not least because of one of its most touted benefits—the genetic profiling of individuals. There has been much discussion about how knowledge of someone's genetic defects, if leaked to outsiders, could be damaging in terms of landing a job or gaining health or life insurance, and legislative measures have been enacted to guard against such hazards. Little attention has been paid, however, to the implications of genetic knowledge for the person himself. Yet the deepest problem connected with learning your own genetic sins and unhealthy predispositions is neither the threat to confidentiality nor the risk of "genetic discrimination" in employment or insurance, important though these practical problems may be.[6] It is, rather, the various hazards and deformations in living your life that will attach to knowing in advance your likely or possible medical future. To be sure, in some cases such foreknowledge will be welcome, if it can lead to easy measures to prevent or treat the impending disorder, and if the disorder in question does not powerfully affect self-image or self-command. But will and should we welcome knowledge that we carry a predisposition to Alzheimer's disease, schizophrenia, or some other personality or behavior disorder, or genes that will definitely produce, at an unknown future time, a serious but untreatable disease?

Still harder will it be for most people to live easily and wisely with less certain information—say, where multigenic traits are involved or where the predictions are purely statistical, with no clear implication for any particular "predisposed" individual. The recent case of a father who insisted that ovariectomy and mastectomy be performed on his ten-year-old daughter because she happened to carry the BRCA-1 gene for breast cancer dramatically shows the toxic effect of genetic knowledge.

Less dramatic but more profound is the threat to human freedom and spontaneity, a subject explored twenty-five years ago by the philosopher Hans Jonas, one of our wisest commentators on technology and the human prospect. In a discussion of human cloning, Jonas argued for a "right to ignorance":

> That there can be (and mostly is) too little knowledge has always been realized; that there can be too much of it stands suddenly before us in a blinding light. . . . The ethical command here entering the enlarged stage of our powers is: never to

violate the right to that ignorance which is a condition for the possibility of authentic action; or: *to respect the right of each human life to find its own way and be a surprise to itself.*[7]

To scientists convinced that their knowledge of predispositions can only lead to rational preventive medicine, Jonas's defense of ignorance will look like obscurantism. It is not. As Jonas observes, "knowledge of the future, especially one's own, has always been excepted [from the injunction to 'Know thyself'] and the attempt to gain it by whatever means (astrology is one) disparaged—as futile superstition by the enlightened, but as sin by theologians; and in the latter case with reasons that are also philosophically sound."[8] And although everyone remembers that Prometheus was the philanthropic god who gave fire and the arts to humans, it is often forgotten that he gave them also the greater gift of "blind hopes"—"to cease seeing doom before their eyes"[9]—precisely because he knew that ignorance of one's own future fate was indispensable to aspiration and achievement. I suspect that many people, taking their bearings from life lived open-endedly rather than from preventive medicine practiced rationally, would prefer ignorance of the future to the scientific astrology of knowing their genetic profile. In a free society, that would be their right.

Or would it? This leads us to the third question.

WHAT ABOUT FREEDOM?

Even people who might otherwise welcome the growth of genetic knowledge and technology are worried about the coming power of geneticists, genetic engineers and, in particular, governmental authorities armed with genetic technology.[10] Precisely because we have been taught by these very scientists that genes hold the secret of life, and that our genotype is our essence if not quite our destiny, we are made nervous by those whose expert knowledge and technique touch our very being. Even apart from any particular abuses and misuses of power, friends of human freedom have deep cause for concern.

C. S. Lewis, no friend of ignorance, put the matter sharply in *The Abolition of Man:*

> It is, of course, a commonplace to complain that men have hitherto used badly, and against their fellows, the powers that science has given them. But that is not the point I am trying to make. I am not speaking of particular corruptions and abuses which an increase of moral virtue would cure: I am considering what the thing called "Man's power over Nature" must always and essentially be. . . .
>
> In reality . . . if any one age really attains, by eugenics and scientific education, the power to make its descendants what *it* pleases, all men who live after

it are the patients of that power. They are weaker, not stronger: for though we may have put wonderful machines in their hands we have pre-ordained how they are to use them. . . . The real picture is that of one dominant age . . . which resists all previous ages most successfully and dominates all subsequent ages most irresistibly, and thus is the real master of the human species. But even within this master generation (itself an infinitesimal minority of the species) the power will be exercised by a minority smaller still. Man's conquest of Nature, if the dreams of some scientific planners are realized, means the rule of a few hundreds of men over billon upon billions of men. There neither is nor can be any simple increase of power on Man's side. Each new power won *by* man is a power *over* man as well. Each advance leaves him weaker as well as stronger. In every victory, besides being the general who triumphs, he is also the prisoner who follows the triumphal car.[11]

Most genetic technologists will hardly recognize themselves in this portrait. Though they concede that abuses or misuses of power may occur, especially in tyrannical regimes, they see themselves not as predestinators but as facilitators, merely providing increased knowledge and technique that people can freely choose to use in making decisions about their health or reproductive choices. Genetic power, they tell us, serves not to limit freedom, but to increase it. But as we can see from the already existing practices of genetic screening and prenatal diagnosis, this claim is at best self-deceptive, at worst disingenuous. The choice to develop and practice genetic screening and the choices of which genes to target for testing have been made not by the public but by scientists—and not on liberty-enhancing but on eugenic grounds. In many cases, practitioners *of* prenatal diagnosis refuse to do fetal genetic screening in the absence of a prior commitment from the pregnant woman to abort any afflicted fetus. In other situations, pregnant women who still wish not to know prenatal facts must withstand strong medical pressures for testing.

While a small portion of the population may be sufficiently educated to participate knowingly and freely in genetic decisions, most people are and will no doubt always be subject to the benevolent tyranny of expertise. Every expert knows how easy it is to get most people to choose one way rather than another simply by the way one raises the questions, describes the prognosis and presents the options. The preferences of counselors will always overtly or subtly shape the choices of the counseled.

In addition, economic pressures to contain health-care costs will almost certainly constrain free choice. Refusal to provide insurance coverage for this or that genetic disease may eventually work to compel genetic abortion or intervention. State-mandated screening already occurs for PKU (phenylketonuria) and other diseases, and full-blown genetic screening programs loom large on the horizon. Once these arrive, there will likely be an upsurge of economic pressure to limit reproductive freedom. All this will be done, of course, in the name of the well-being of children.

Already in 1971, geneticist Bentley Glass, in his presidential address to the American Association for the Advancement of Science, enunciated "the right of every child to be born with a sound physical and mental constitution, based on a sound genotype." Looking ahead to the reproductive and genetic technologies that are today rapidly arriving, Glass proclaimed: "No parents will in that future time have a right to burden society with a malformed or a mentally incompetent child."[12] It remains to be seen to what extent such prophecies will be realized. But they surely provide sufficient and reasonable grounds for being concerned about restrictions on human freedom, even in the absence of overt coercion, and even in liberal polities like our own.

WHAT ABOUT HUMAN DIGNITY?

Here, rather than in the more-discussed fears about freedom, lie our deepest concerns, and rightly so. For threats to human dignity can—and probably will—arise even with the free, humane and "enlightened" use of these technologies. Genetic technology, the practices it will engender, and above all the scientific teachings about human life on which it rests are not, as many would have it, morally and humanly neutral. Regardless of how they are practiced or taught, they are pregnant with their own moral meaning, and will necessarily bring with them changes in our practices, our institutions, our norms, our beliefs, and our self conception. It is, I submit, these challenges to our dignity and humanity that are at the bottom of our anxiety over genetic science and technology. Let me touch briefly on four aspects of this most serious matter.

"PLAYING GOD"

Paradoxically, worries about dehumanization are sometimes expressed in the fear of superhumanization, that is, that man will be "playing God." This complaint is too facilely dismissed by scientists and nonbelievers. The concern has meaning, God or no God. By it is meant one or more of the following: man, or some men, are becoming creators of life, and indeed, of individual living human beings (in vitro fertilization, cloning); they stand in judgment of each being's worthiness to live or die (genetic screening and abortion)—not on moral grounds, as is said of God's judgment, but on somatic and genetic ones; they also hold out the promise of salvation from our genetic sins and defects (gene therapy and genetic engineering).

Never mind the exaggeration that lurks in this conceit of man's playing God. (Even at his most powerful, after all, man is capable only of *playing*

God.) Never mind the implicit innuendo that nobody has given to others this creative and judgmental authority, or the implicit retort that there is theological warrant for acting as God's co-creator in overcoming the ills and suffering of the world. Consider only that if scientists are seen in this godlike role of creator, judge, and savior, the rest of us must stand before them as supplicating, tainted creatures. Despite the hyperbolic speech, that is worry enough.

Practitioners of prenatal diagnosis, working today with but a fraction of the information soon to be available from the Human Genome Project, already screen for a long list of genetic diseases and abnormalities, from Down syndrome to dwarfism. Possession of any one of these defects, they believe, renders a prospective child unworthy of life. Persons who happen still to be born with these conditions, having somehow escaped the spreading net of detection and eugenic abortion, are increasingly regarded as "mistakes," as inferior human beings who should not have been born.[13] Not long ago, at my own university, a physician making rounds with medical students stood over the bed of an intelligent, otherwise normal ten-year-old boy with spina bifida. "Were he to have been conceived today," the physician casually informed his entourage, "he would have been aborted." Determining who shall live and who shall die—on the basis of genetic merit—is a godlike power already wielded by genetic medicine. This power will only grow.

MANUFACTURE AND COMMODIFICATION

But, one might reply, genetic technology also holds out the promise of redemption, of a *cure* for these life-crippling and life-forfeiting disorders. Very well. But in order truly to practice their salvific power, genetic technologists will have to increase greatly their manipulations and interventions, well beyond merely screening and weeding out. True, in some cases genetic testing and risk management aimed at prevention may actually cut down on the need for high-tech interventions aimed at cure. But in many other cases, ever-greater genetic scrutiny will lead necessarily to ever more extensive manipulation. And, to produce Bentley Glass's healthy and well-endowed babies, let alone babies with the benefits of genetic enhancement, a new scientific obstetrics will be necessary, one that will come very close to turning human procreation into manufacture.

This process was already crudely begun with in vitro fertilization. It is now taking giant steps forward with the ability to screen in vitro embryos before implantation (so-called pre-implantation genetic diagnosis). And it will come to maturity with interventions such as cloning and, eventually, with precise genetic engineering. Just follow the logic and the aspirations of current practice: the road we are traveling leads all the way to the world of

designer babies reached not by dictatorial fiat, but by the march of benevolent humanitarianism, and cheered on by an ambivalent citizenry that also
dreads becoming merely the last of man's manmade things.

Make no mistake: the price to be paid for producing optimum or even
only genetically sound babies will be the transfer of procreation from the
home to the laboratory. Increasing control over the product can only be purchased by the increasing depersonalization of the entire process and its co-
incident transformation into manufacture. Such an arrangement will be profoundly dehumanizing, no matter how genetically good or healthy the
resultant children. And let us not forget the powerful economic interests that
will surely operate in this area; with their advent, the commodification of
nascent human life will be unstoppable.

STANDARDS, NORMS, AND GOALS

According to Genesis, God, in His creating, looked at His creatures and saw
that they were good—intact, complete, well-working wholes, true to the
spoken idea that guided their creation. What standards will guide the genetic
engineers?

For the time being, one might answer, the norm of health. But even before
the genetic enhancers join the party, the standard of health is being decon-
structed. Are you healthy if, although you show no symptoms, you carry
genes that will definitely produce Huntington's disease, or that predispose
you to diabetes, breast cancer, or coronary artery disease? What if you carry,
say, 40 percent of the genetic markers thought to be linked to the appearance of Alzheimer's disease? And what will "healthy" and "normal" mean
when we discover your genetic propensities for alcoholism, drug abuse,
pederasty, or violence?[14] The idea of health progressively becomes at once
both imperial and vague: medicalization of what have hitherto been mental
or moral matters paradoxically brings with it the disappearance of any clear
standard of health itself.

Once genetic *enhancement* comes on the scene, standards of health,
wholeness, or fitness will be needed more than ever, but just then is when all
pretense of standards will go out the window. "Enhancement" is, of course,
a euphemism for "improvement," and the idea of improvement necessarily
implies a good, a better, and perhaps even a best. If, however, we can no
longer look to our previously unalterable human nature for a standard or
norm of what is good or better, how will anyone know what constitutes an
improvement? It will not do to assert that we can extrapolate from what we
like about ourselves. Because memory is good, can we say how much more
memory would be better? If sexual desire is good, how much more would be
better? Life is good, but how much extension of the lifespan would be good

for us? Only simplistic thinkers believe they can easily answer such questions.[15]

More modest enhancers, like more modest genetic therapists and technologists, eschew grandiose goals. They are valetudinarians, not eugenicists. They pursue not some faraway positive good, but the positive elimination of evils: diseases, pain, suffering, the likelihood of death. But let us not be deceived. Hidden in all this avoidance of evil is nothing less than the quasi-messianic goal of a painless, suffering-free and, finally, immortal existence. Only the presence of such a goal justifies the sweeping aside of any opposition to the relentless march of medical science. Only such a goal gives trumping moral power to the principle "cure disease, relieve suffering."

"Cloning human beings is unethical and dehumanizing, you say? Never mind: it will help us treat infertility, avoid genetic disease, and provide perfect materials for organ replacement." Such, indeed, was the tenor of the June 1997 report of the National Bioethics Advisory Commission on *Cloning Human Beings*. Notwithstanding its call for a temporary ban on the practice, the only moral objection the commission could agree upon was that cloning "is not safe to use in humans at this time," because the technique has yet to be perfected.[16] Even this elite ethical body, in other words, was unable to muster any other moral argument sufficient to cause us to forgo the possible health benefits of cloning.[17]

The same argument will also justify creating and growing human embryos for experimentation, revising the definition of death to increase the supply of organs for transplantation, growing human body parts in the peritoneal cavities of animals, perfusing newly dead bodies as factories for useful biological substances, or reprogramming the human body and mind with genetic or neurobiological engineering. Who can sustain an objection if these practices will help us live longer and with less overt suffering?

It turns out that even the more modest biogenetic engineers. whether they know it or not, are in the immortality business, proceeding on the basis of a quasi-religious faith that all innovation is by definition progress, no matter what is sacrificed to attain it.

THE TRAGEDY OF SUCCESS

What the enthusiasts do not see is that their utopian project will not eliminate suffering but merely shift it around. Forgetting that contentment requires that our desires do not outpace our powers, they have not noticed that the enormous medical progress of the last half century has not left the present generation satisfied. Indeed, we are already witnessing a certain measure of public discontent as a paradoxical result of rising expectations in the health-care field: although their actual health has improved substantially in

recent decades, people's *satisfaction* with their current health status has remained the same or declined. But that is hardly the highest cost of success in
the medical/humanitarian project.

As Aldous Huxley made clear in his prophetic *Brave New World,* the road
chosen and driven by compassionate humaneness paved by biotechnology,
if traveled to the end, leads not to human fulfillment but to human debasement. Perfected bodies are achieved at the price of flattened souls. The joys
and sorrows of human attachment and achievement are replaced by facti-
tious ecstasies that come from pills. Procreation is replaced by manufacture,
family ties are absent, and people divide their time between meaningless
jobs and meaningless amusements. What Tolstoy called "real life"—life in its
immediacy, vividness, and rootedness—has been replaced by an utterly mediated, sterile, and disconnected existence. In one word: dehumanization,
the inevitable result of making the essence of human nature the final object
of the conquest of nature for the relief of man's estate. Like Midas, bioengi-
neered man will be cursed to acquire precisely what he wished for, only to
discover—painfully and too late—that what he wished for is not exactly
what he wanted. Or, worse than Midas, he may be so dehumanized he will
not even recognize that in aspiring to be perfect, he is no longer even truly
human. To paraphrase Bertrand Russell, technological humanitarianism is
like a warm bath that heats up so imperceptibly you don't know when to
scream.

The main point here is not the rightness or wrongness of this or that
imagined scenario; all this is, admittedly, highly speculative. I surely have
no way of knowing whether my worst fears will be realized, but you
surely have no way of knowing they will not. The point is rather the plau-
sibility, even the wisdom, of thinking about genetic technology, like the
entire technological venture, under the ancient and profound idea of
tragedy, in which success and failure are inseparably grown together like
the concave and the convex. What I am suggesting is that genetic technology's way of approaching human life, a way spurred on by the utopian
promises and perfectionist aims of modern thought and its scientific cru-
saders, may well turn out to be inevitable, heroic, and doomed. If this suggestion holds water, then the question regarding genetic technology is not
"triumph OR tragedy," because the answer is "both together"—necessarily
so.

To say that the technological approach to life, left to itself as *a way* of life,
is tragic does not yet mean *our* life must inevitably be tragic. To repeat,
everything depends on whether the technological disposition is allowed to
proceed to its self-augmenting limits, or whether it can be restricted and
brought under intellectual, spiritual, moral, and political rule. But here, I regret to say, the news so far is not encouraging. For the relevant intellectual,
spiritual, and moral resources of our society, the legacy of civilizing tradi-

tions painfully acquired and long preserved, are taking a beating—not least because they are being called into question by the findings of modern science itself. The technologies present troublesome ethical dilemmas, but the underlying scientific notions call into question the very foundations of our ethics.

In the nineteenth and early twentieth centuries, the challenge came in the form of Darwinism and its seeming opposition to biblical religion, a battle initiated not so much by the scientists as by the beleaguered defenders of orthodoxy. In our own time, the challenge comes from molecular biology, behavioral genetics, and evolutionary psychology, fueled by their practitioners' overconfident belief in the sufficiency of their reductionist explanations of all vital and human phenomena. Never mind "created in the image of God"; what elevated *humanistic* view of human life or human goodness is defensible against the belief, asserted by most public and prophetic voices of biology, that man is just a collection of molecules, an accident on the stage of evolution, a freakish speck of mind in a mindless universe, fundamentally no different from other living—or even nonliving—things? What chance have our treasured ideas of freedom and dignity against the reductive notion of "the selfish gene" (or, for that matter, of "genes for altruism"), the belief that DNA is the essence of life, or the teaching that all human behavior and our rich inner life are rendered intelligible only in terms of their contributions to species survival and reproductive success?

As sociologist Howard Kaye notes:

> For over forty years, we have been living in the midst of a biological and cultural revolution of which innovations such as artificial insemination with donor semen, in vitro fertilization, surrogacy, genetic manipulation, and cloning are merely technological offshoots. In both aim and impact, the end of this revolution is a fundamental transformation in how we conceive of ourselves as human beings and how we understand the nature and purpose of human life rightly lived. Encouraged by bio-prophets like Francis Crick, Jacques Monod, E. O. Wilson and Richard Dawkins, as well as by humanists and social scientists trumpeting the essential claims of race, gender, and ethnicity, we are in the process of redefining ourselves as biological, rather than cultural and moral beings. Bombarded with whitecoated claims that "Genes-R-Us," grateful for the absolution which such claims offer for our shortcomings and sins, and attracted to the promise of using efficient, technological means to fulfill our aspirations, rather than the notoriously unreliable moral or political ones, the idea that we are essentially selfreplicating machines, built by the evolutionary process, designed for survival and reproduction, and run by our genes continues to gain.[18]

These transformations are, in fact, welcomed by many of our leading scientists and intellectuals. In 1997, the luminaries of the International Academy of Humanism—including biologists Crick, Dawkins, and Wilson, and humanists Isaiah Berlin, W. V. Quine, and Kurt Vonnegut—issued a statement in defense of cloning research in higher mammals and human beings. Their reasons were revealing:

> What moral issues would human cloning raise? Some world religions teach that human beings are fundamentally different from other mammals—that humans have been imbued by a deity with immortal souls, giving them a value that cannot be compared to that of other living things. Human nature is held to be unique and sacred. Scientific advances which pose a perceived risk of altering this "nature" are angrily opposed. . . . As far as the scientific enterprise can determine, [however] . . . [h]uman capabilities appear to differ in degree, not in kind, from those found among the higher animals. Humanity's rich repertoire of thoughts, feelings, aspirations, and hopes seems to arise from electrochemical brain processes, not from an immaterial soul that operates in ways no instrument can discover. . . . Views of human nature rooted in humanity's tribal past ought not to be our primary criterion for making moral decisions about cloning. . . . The potential benefits of cloning may be so immense that it would be a tragedy if ancient theological scruples should lead to a Luddite rejection of cloning.[19]

In order to justify ongoing research, these intellectuals were willing to shed not only traditional religious views but *any* view of human distinctiveness and special dignity, their own included. They failed to see that the scientific view of man they celebrated does more than insult our vanity. It undermines our self-conception as free, thoughtful and responsible beings, worthy of respect because we alone among the animals have minds and hearts that aim far higher than the mere perpetuation of our genes. It undermines, as well, the beliefs that sustain our mores, practices, and institutions—including the practice of science itself. For why, on this radically reductive understanding of "the rich repertoire" of human thought, should anyone choose to accept as true the results of *these* men's "electrochemical brain processes" rather than his own? Thus do truth and error themselves, no less than freedom and dignity, become empty notions when the soul is reduced to chemicals.

The problem may lie not so much with the scientific findings themselves as with the shallow philosophy that recognizes no other truths but these and with the arrogant pronouncements of the bio-prophets. For example, in a letter to the editor complaining about a review of his book *How the Mind Works,* the well-known evolutionary psychologist and popularizer Stephen Pinker rails against any appeal to the human soul:

> Unfortunately for that theory, brain science has shown that the mind is what the brain does. The supposedly immaterial soul can be bisected with a knife, altered by chemicals, turned on or off by electricity, and extinguished by a sharp blow or a lack of oxygen. Centuries ago it was unwise to ground morality on the

dogma that the earth sat at the center of the universe. It is just as unwise today to ground it on dogmas about souls endowed by God.[20]

One hardly knows whether to be more impressed by the height of Pinker's arrogance or by the depth of his shallowness. But he speaks with the authority of science, and few are able and willing to dispute him on his own grounds.

There is, of course, nothing novel about reductionism, materialism and determinism of the kind displayed here; these are doctrines with which Socrates contended long ago. What is new is that, as philosophies, they seem (to many people) to be vindicated by scientific advance.[21] Here, in consequence, is perhaps the most pernicious result of our technological progress, more dehumanizing than any actual manipulation or technique, present or future: the erosion, perhaps the final erosion, of the idea of man as noble, dignified, precious, or godlike, and its replacement with a view of man, no less than of nature, as mere raw material for manipulation and homogenization.

Hence our peculiar moral crisis. We are in turbulent seas without a landmark precisely because we adhere more and more to a view of human life that both gives us enormous power and, *at the same time,* denies every possibility of nonarbitrary standards for guiding its use. Though well equipped, we know not who we are or where we are going. We triumph over nature's unpredictability only to subject ourselves, tragically, to the still greater unpredictability of our capricious wills and our fickle opinions. Engineering the engineer as well as the engine, we race our train to we know not where. That we do not recognize our predicament is itself a tribute to the depth of our infatuation with scientific progress and our naive faith in the sufficiency of our humanitarian impulses.

Does this mean that I am therefore in favor of ignorance, suffering, and death? Of killing the goose of genetic technology even before she lays her golden eggs? Surely not. But unless we mobilize the courage to look foursquare at the full human meaning of our new enterprise in biogenetic technology and engineering, we are doomed to become its creatures if not its slaves. Important though it is to set a moral boundary here, devise a regulation there, hoping to decrease the damage caused by this or that little rivulet, it is even more important to be sober about the true nature and meaning of the flood itself.

That our exuberant new biologists and their technological minions might be persuaded of this is, to say the least, highly unlikely. For all their ingenuity, they do not even seek the wisdom that just might yield the kind of knowledge that keeps human life human. But it is not too late for the rest of us to become aware of the dangers—not just to privacy or insurability, but to our very humanity. So aware, we might be better able to defend the increasingly beleaguered vestiges and principles of our human dignity, even as we continue to reap the considerable benefits that genetic technology will inevitably provide.

STUDY QUESTIONS

1. Why does Kass think that genetic technology is fundamentally different from other technologies we have employed in the past?
2. Why does Kass think we are better off not knowing many of our genetic predispositions? Do you agree with his reasoning? Explain.
3. How does the control of experts over genetic technology threaten autonomy and freedom, according to Kass?
4. What does Kass mean when he claims that genetic engineering will lead to the dehumanization of the reproductive process?
5. Kass implies that difficult questions such as how long humans should desire to live must be answered before allowing advances in genetic engineering to take place. Do you agree or disagree? Explain.
6. Kass argues that the scientific view of human nature undermines human dignity. Explain his reasoning. Do you agree or disagree?

NOTES

1. I will also not dispute here the scientists' reductive understanding of life and their treatment of rich vital activities solely in terms of the interactions of genes (and other lifeless molecules). I do, however, touch on the moral significance of such reductionism toward the end of this essay.

2. Some commentators, in disagreement with these arguments, insist that genetic technology differs only in degree from previous human practices that have existed for millennia. For example, they see no difference between the "social engineering" of education, which works on the next generation through speech or symbolic deed, and biological engineering, which inscribes its effects, directly and irreversibly, into the human constitution. Or they claim to see no difference between the indirect genetic effects of human mate selection and deliberate, direct genetic engineering to produce offspring with precise biological capacities. Such critics, I fear, have already bought into a reductionist view of human life and the relation between the generations. They speak about children not as gifts that we are duty-bound to humanize through speech and example in light of the good, but as products whose qualities we determine by manipulating their bodies, consulting only our own subjective prejudices. They fail to notice that education works through the soul, through *meanings* (necessarily immaterial) conveyed in speech and deed. And they ignore the fact that most people choose their mates for reasons different from stud farming. Though mindful of the heritable implications of choosing a spouse, people pay attention to character, tastes, and the things each partner esteems and aspires to in life, not merely

to some morally neutral, genetically determined capacity. The former are more important than the latter for rearing *human* offspring.

3. Correction of a genetically abnormal egg or sperm (that is, of the "germ cells"), however worthy an activity, stretches the meaning of "therapy" beyond all normal uses. Just who is the "patient" being "treated"? The potential person, the child-to-be that might be formed out of such egg or sperm is, at the time of the treatment, at best no more than a hope and a hypothesis. There is no medical analogue for treatment of nonexistent patients.

4. See, for example, LeRoy Walters, "Human Gene Therapy: Ethics and Public Policy," *Human Gene Therapy 2* (1991): 115–22.

5. To be sure, not all attempts at enhancement will require genetic alterations. We have already witnessed efforts to boost height with supplementary growth hormone, of athletic performance with steroids or "blood doping." Nevertheless, the largest possible changes in what is "normally" human are likely to come about only with the help of genetic alterations or the joining of machines (for example, computers) to human beings.

6. I find it odd that it is these issues that have been put forward as the special ethical problems associated with genetic technology and the Human Genome Project. Issues of privacy and risks of discrimination related to medical conditions are entirely independent of whether the medical condition is genetic in origin. Only if a special stigma were attached to having an *inherited* disease—for example, only if having thalassemia or sickle cell anemia were more shameful than having gonorrhea or lung cancer would the genetic character of a disease create special or additional reasons for protecting against breaches of confidentiality or discrimination in the workplace. It is, however, true that special questions of confidentiality and disclosure do arise for patients with genetic disease because, with heritable traits, a patient's relatives may be similarly afflicted; and they may arguably have a "need to know" that might put pressure on the right of privacy for the patient. Yet even here, the troubles such knowledge could produce within families go far beyond threats to privacy.

7. Hans Jonas, "Biological Engineering—A Preview," in his *Philosophical Essays: From Ancient Creed to Technological Man* (Englewood Cliffs, New Jersey: Prentice Hall, 1974), pp. 141–67, at p. 163. Italics in original.

8. "Biological Engineering—A Preview," p. 161.

9. Aeschylus, *Prometheus Bound,* lines 250ff.

10. Until the events of September 11 and the anthrax scare that followed, they did not worry enough. It is remarkable that most bioethical discussions of genetic technology had naively neglected its potential usefulness in creating biological weapons, such as, to begin with, antibiotic-resistant plague bacteria, or, later, aerosols containing cancer-inducing or mind-scrambling viral vectors. The most outstanding molecular geneticists were especially naive in this area. When American molecular biologists convened the 1975 Asilomar Conference on recombinant DNA research, which called for a voluntary moratorium on experiments until the biohazards could be evaluated, they invited to the meeting Soviet biologists who said virtually nothing but who photographed every slide that was shown.

11. C. S. Lewis, *The Abolition of Man* (New York: Macmillan, 1965), pp. 69–71. Italics in original.

12. Bentley Glass, "Science: Endless Horizons or Golden Age?" *Science* 171 (1971): 23–29, at p. 28.

13. In the early 1970s, I tried to grapple with this issue in an essay, "Perfect Babies: PreNatal Diagnosis and the Equal Right to Life," which appears as chapter 3 in my book *Toward a More Natural Science: Biology and Human Affairs* (New York: The Free Press, 1985). One of the most worrisome but least appreciated aspects of the godlike power of the new genetics is its tendency to "redefine" a human being in terms of his genes. Once a person is decisively characterized by his genotype, it is but a short step to justifying death solely for genetic sins.

14. Many scientists suspect that we have different inherited propensities for these and other behavioral troubles, though it is almost certain that there is no single "gene for x" that is responsible.

15. This strikes me as the deepest problem with positive eugenics: less the threat of coercion, more the presumption of thinking we are wise enough to engineer "improvements" in the human species.

16. National Bioethics Advisory Commission, *Cloning Human Beings, 1997,* p. iii. This is, of course, not an objection to cloning itself but only to hazards tied to the technique used to produce the replicated children.

17. I forbear mentioning what is rapidly becoming another trumping argument: increasing the profits of my biotech company and its shareholders, an argument often presented in more public-spirited dress: if we don't do it, other countries will, and we will lose our competitive edge in biotechnology.

18. Howard Kaye, "Anxiety and Genetic Manipulation: A Sociological View," *Perspectives in Biology and Medicine* 41, no. 4 (Summer 1998): 483–90, at p. 488. See also Kaye's book *The Social Meaning of Modern Biology,* 2nd ed. (New Brunswick, New Jersey: Transaction Publishers, 1997).

19. International Academy of Humanism, "Statement in Defense of Cloning and the Integrity of Scientific Research," 16 May 1997.

20. Steven Pinker, "A Matter of Soul," Correspondence Section, *Weekly Standard,* 2 February 1998, p. 6.

21. Needless to say, I do not share these views. To the contrary, I believe that one cannot give a true account even of animals without notions of form, wholeness, awareness, appetite, and goal-directed action—none of them reducible to matter-in-motion or even to DNA. But one cannot deny the growing cultural power of scientific materialism and reductionism. The materialism of science, useful as a heuristic hypothesis, is increasingly being peddled as the one true account of human life by a new breed of bio-prophets, citing as evidence the powers obtainable on the basis of just such reductive approaches to life. Many laymen, ignorant of any defensible scientific alternative to materialism, are swallowing and regurgitating these shallow soulless doctrines, because, as I say, "they *seem* to be vindicated by scientific advance." The result is likely to be serious damage to human self-understanding and the subversion of all high-minded views of the good life.

12

What's at the Bottom of the Slippery Slope: A Post-Human Future?

Jerry Weinberger

Jerry Weinberger is a professor of political science at Michigan State University. He is presently completing a new book entitled *The Technological Republican: The Political Thought of Benjamin Franklin*. Weinberger argues that, although the deployment of genetic engineering technology poses difficult moral and political issues, there is no reason to think that human beings will sacrifice essential human experiences in order to benefit from this technology. Genetic technology will not eliminate the experience of being rational, self-conscious, morally responsible, autonomous beings. Though the danger of dehumanization exists, future human beings will likely design moral norms and political institutions that resist dehumanization.

According to Leon Kass, the "darker truth about the present age" is that all contemporary societies are "wedded to the modern technological project; all march eagerly to the dreams of progress and fly proudly the banner of modern science; all sing loudly the Baconian anthem, conquer nature, relieve man's estate." Kass warns us that emerging bioscience and biotechnology, the cutting edges of the Baconian project, are propelling us to the brink of an unprecedented catastrophe: not to the end of ideology, not to the end of history, but, to use Frank Fukuyama's recent phrase, to "a post-human future." In our present Baconian circumstances, says Kass, "the future of our humanity hangs in the balance."[1]

Adam Wolfson glosses this theme as follows: The suicidal precipice at which we now teeter was inherent in the technological project from its beginning,

From *Perspectives in Political Science*, Spring 2003. Reprinted with permission of the Helen Dwight Reid Educational Foundation. Published by Heldref Publications, 1319 Eighteenth St., NW, Washington, DC 20036-1802. Copyright © 2003.

but it was not noticed as the project got under way and, with its enticing promises for the relief of man's estate, defined and propelled progress in the West.
At the outset, so the story goes, Bacon tied the power of science to benevo-
lence, to charity. But that Baconian attachment of science to charity was
"bound to fail," because charity is not grounded in modern science and springs
rather from "a transcendent source." Charity thus depends on religious faith
and absolute moral norms, and, contrary to Bacon's apparent expectations,
science has eroded both faith and absolute norms and now threatens to poison us with its most advanced and enticing candies.[2]

As I read these complaints about the Baconian project, I find two fundamental concerns. One is the fear that by using well-intentioned biotechnology we will so transform and degrade our human nature that we will become
incapable of essential human virtues, experiences, and happiness—perhaps
so much so that we will literally become something other than human. The
other fear is less that we will become deformed or morph ourselves into non-
or post-humans, than that, forsaking charity and humility, we will "play God"
and inevitably pay the price for such hubris. These two objections get to the
heart of things. The Baconian project of technology really is turning from
nonhuman nature to ourselves. When we ourselves are the objects of technology, as is the case in medicine and biotechnology, we now have to ask
what it means to degrade or endanger our humanity, or even to transform
ourselves into something new and radically different, as, for example, oil is
transformed into plastic.

So how do we inquire into the "nature" of humanity? Let me suggest two
different ways to pose this question. One I will call moral-teleological; the
other, ontological. Let us start with the moral-teleological. When we apply
our unbiased reason to the relevant evidence—to the array of human experiences and characteristics—we can discover, it is presumed, the one human
end or set of activities that is authoritative and trumps all others, makes us
genuinely happy, and without whose ordering the others will be in some
way defective. This is what is meant when we say, for instance, that heterosexuality is natural and homosexuality is unnatural, or when Aristotle (in his
Ethics) says that the gentleman is the peak of human virtue, or when Socrates
pronounces that the unexamined life is not worth living and that philosophers should rule, or when we say that human beings have natural rights that
confer on them an essential dignity that can be realized when these rights are
recognized and made the principles of our actions. In each case, the anchor
of the internal teleology—the ordering end or set of activities—is said to be
natural because its status as the anchor is given and does not depend on
mere, changeable agreement or convention or will, and because we must
bend our disparate inclinations to that anchor if we are to be at our best.

Now, the history of philosophy has not produced agreement on any one
answer as to what constitutes natural human perfection. The Aristotelian

gentleman, the Kantian moral person, the Hobbesian bourgeois man, and the Christian saint are really quite different and incompatible human types. Take your pick: Plato, Aristotle, Aquinas, Hobbes, Locke, Kant, Heidegger, Dewey. None is demonstrably refuted and all disagree. The problem, moreover, is that it can no longer be said that art is long but life is short. Life is getting somewhat longer but art is getting shorter by geometrical leaps and bounds. So, if we must wait for a compelling moral-teleological answer from philosophy, to cope with ever quickening biotechnological change, we are in a real pickle.

The ontological way of speaking about human nature is, I think, more promising. If we cannot determine the human *telos*—our natural perfection—with any reasoned consensus, perhaps we should focus on what a human must be simply to be open to the various and contending possibilities of human perfection and happiness. This approach requires thinking not about what is or is not the one, governing, genuine good for man—long life and commodious living, as Hobbes would say; or magnanimity or contemplation, as Aristotle would say; or a good will, as Kant would say. Rather, we consider whether a biotechnological advance or change would make us incapable of those experiences, or varying forms of those experiences, that the competing claims about perfection interpret and attempt to order. Although I might not think Christian saintliness or a Kantian good will particularly compelling, I can at least have those experiences (the experience of loving another as one loves oneself, or the immediate claim of honesty) that lead some to think of them as the telos of human life. Although I may think Aristotelian magnanimity to be foolishness or pride, I could have the experience (the awareness of not depending on the honor I deserve from others) that could lead some to think magnanimity the perfection of human life and happiness. And so forth.

We should think about the matter this way: If a being lacked one or more of the following characteristics or powers, it would be impossible for it to know of, or experience, those oft-contending possibilities that compete for our approbation and disapprobation—for our ordering. Such a creature would not be able to be fully human, and it would not answer to our hopes for a better future for ourselves, and it would be a misfortune for technology to create such a thing or to turn us into such a thing.

First and most obvious, the being must be rational. Of course rationality is multidimensional: it means the power to discover truth, to plan, to conjure alternative situations, to understand the finitude of human life (death) and hence the possibility and meaning of death, to engage in art and technology. Rationality would also include the capacity to imagine and hope for happiness, and thus to see and express the world, including the beautiful and the ugly, in aesthetic experience, and to be moved and even blinded by love and friendship (only a rational creature is capable of self-deception). In addition to rationality, the human being would have to be able to experience plea-sure and pain and to apply reason to that experience—I think mainly in the realms of sex, food, and bodily motion. The being would have to be able to experience the phenomena of inwardness and consciousness of self (indi-viduation), and to experience the sense of free will. These latter need not be fully explicable or even real—but even if we doubt them philosophically, it is, I think, impossible to imagine life without the feeling of them. The being would have to be capable of moral understanding and experience: it would have to be open to such things as benefits and harms; moral freedom and re-sponsibility; deserving and guilt; justice, nobility, and goodness; and per-sonal liberty. Again, even if these moral phenomena are, in truth, chimerical, it is hard to imagine human life (at least for a very long time) without at least the capacity for the subjective sense of them. That is my list.

I do not mean to claim or to imply that this list, and my approach, involves no moral judgment. It does imply some measure of what is good for us as human beings, and in this sense it is even teleological. I see no alternative to such a judgment if we wish to get a handle on the situation we now face. But this approach is minimally teleological in that it strives for the greatest gen-erality and especially strives not to rank-order the essential characteristics and powers or to claim that one particular form a power might take is itself essential to our happiness. For instance, that we are open to love does not mean that love must, for the sake of our fullest happiness, transpire only as romantic love within the bourgeois family as we know it—a phenomenon unknown to the Greeks of Plato and Aristotle's time. Likewise, that we are capable of moral experience does not mean that honesty must trump justice, or vice versa, or that courage trumps justice, or, more to the point, that some particular moral virtues might not become much less vivid under circum-stances of far less material necessity and far greater equality.

Now, if we imagine a being with all save one of the capacities on my list, we would think of it as no perfection or enhancement of ourselves and not as something we really want to be. And it might even be a danger to what we already are. For example, a real sociopath—a human being who, for rea-sons of deranged hard wiring, has never sensed or even overcome the calls of justice and responsibility—is a rare and frightening monster. If biotech-nology were to produce such a creature, it would surely have crossed over the ontological divide—as I will call the boundaries established by my list. The same would be true for rationality, sense of inwardness and individua-tion, free will, and so on.

With the ontological divide in mind, just what dangers do we face from biotechnology and genetic engineering, and how bad are they, really? The worst case of crossing the divide would be the deliberate manufacture of persons with one or more, but not all, of the characteristics radically di-minished or missing. Such persons would know of, and suffer from, their condition. This is unlikely to happen in any liberal, egalitarian society. And although it could happen in a place like China, we would simply be faced with a political task of stamping it out—as with slavery, genital mutilation, foot binding, the creation of eunuchs, the denial of education to girls, wife burning and disfiguration, and so forth. Although genetic engineering adds another tool by which illiberal societies might cause harm to people, I cannot see any reason why that engineering is, in itself, any more dangerous than gunpowder or worse than many long-established cultural stupidities.

The more serious worry is that we will, inadvertently, somehow enhance our way close to or over the divide. I think that biotechnological enhancement is the ultimate issue and that Kass is absolutely correct on this point. Genetic engineering will doubtless be used therapeutically to prevent or cure the myriad diseases for which there are genetic causes or contributions. This will be the immediate impetus to progress. And there is one disease that will stand out from all the rest in this regard. Bacon was perhaps the first to see the fact, but the point is made most vividly by an American icon and paragon: Benjamin Franklin.

In 1780, Franklin, then seventy-four years old, wrote the following in a letter to his friend Joseph Priestley:

> The rapid progress true science now makes, occasions my regretting sometimes that I was born so soon. It is impossible to imagine the height to which may be carded, in a thousand years, the power of man over matter. We may perhaps learn to deprive large masses of their gravity, and give them absolute levity, for the sake of easy transport. Agriculture may diminish in labor and double in its produce; all diseases may by sure means be prevented or cured, not excepting even that of old age, and our lives lengthened at pleasure even beyond the antediluvian standard.[3]

Important here is the phrase "even that of old age." It means that old age is simply another disease along with all the rest, and like all the rest, curable. When this position of Franklin's becomes widely accepted—as I think it soon will—there will be enormous, I would say unstoppable, pressure for advances in biotechnology and genetic engineering. By comparison with a malady that everyone has from birth, heart disease and stroke could well become orphan diseases. In our society in particular, but even in the world in general, it will be simply impossible to argue, with any effectiveness, in opposition to the war against the universal disease: old age and death. And as we learn how to push back Father Time, especially with genetic engineering, we will learn how to make our offspring and probably ourselves smarter, bigger, stronger, and so on. The overwhelming likelihood is that, in the not so distant future, each generation will be genetically better than the prior one.

Now the question is whether, and how, better could in fact wind up being worse. This brings us back to Leon Kass, who finds just such genetically engineered enhancement (eugenics) especially repugnant and dangerous. He objects to eugenics on two closely related grounds: eugenics will ultimately distort the best in our human nature, and eugenics will lead to the "commodification" of human life. In both cases, enhancement leads not to human improvement, but rather to human degradation and loss of dignity.

As regards the first ground, Kass maintains that our dignity and virtues consist, in part, in our proper comportment toward limits imposed on us by nature. The ultimate natural limitation is death, and death and its counterpoints, sex and procreation, provide occasion for depth and self-transcendence in human life. Since engineered eugenics sees natural limits, including aging and death, as mere obstacles to be overcome, they are the ultimate threat to human dignity. In pursuing the eugenic dream we run pell-mell toward the degrading belief that we can live well without ennobling sacrifice and without the strengths of character required to live with the reality of our finitude. Kass's position requires a positive connection between the human soul and the broader whole of nature to this extent: it requires the fact that our souls are embodied in organic stuff and that such embodiment, as the ultimate material source of death and progeny, is good—the lethal soul-nature nexus is, after all, the condition of our dignity and our possible virtues.[4]

But how nature, so understood, commands our respect is far from clear to me. At the very least, showing how our natural limits deserve respect requires a solution to the moral-teleological question discussed above: it requires a convincing argument that, for instance, the virtues of courage and noble sacrifice, as determined by our current life span, trump the goods and pleasures of long (even indefinitely long) life and commodious living—a convincing argument, say, for Aristotle's *Ethics* and against Hobbes or Bacon. But such an argument is not so easy either to come by or to reach consensus on. Moreover, I think this approach tends to close off our thinking about how what we really do admire about the virtues and experiences supposedly under threat—the accomplishments and strengths of will, mind, and character and the forms of happiness involved—might still be possible within different horizons or contexts, or might even take different forms in a world where science delivers physical comfort, expanded human powers, and three hundred years plus ten instead of our now meager three- or fourscore and change. And at any rate, I do not think an argument that death is good for us—as the condition of a particular ordering of the virtues and of a particular happiness, such as might occur within the bourgeois family—will have a ghost of a chance against the promise of the future predicted by Benjamin Franklin. (And that goes double for us in our capitalistic, pluralistic, and liberal society.) I think we can get a better handle on these issues, as a matter of effective public policy, by considering the ontological divide, rather than by trying to solve the moral-teleological problem once and for all, or by assuming that the virtues and excellences in question are fixed as regards context and form and not, perhaps, protean.

So what about engineered eugenics? Glasses and laser surgery restore us to visual health. Would genetically engineered visual enhancement, say x-ray vision that we could turn off and on like Superman, make us deformed or transhuman, and thus repugnant? Why would a person with genetically engineered x-ray vision be repugnant? I am not convinced that such a person would be, because I do not see how having such a power would propel her over the ontological divide. The obvious problem with x-ray vision has occurred to any adolescent fan of Superman: Why did Superman not use his powers to look into the girls' locker room or to check out what Lois Lane really had? Answer: Because Superman was a gentleman. That he had x-ray vision did not, perforce, make him a cad. Now, if we ever get to a point of genetically engineering x-ray vision, we will likewise be able, by some technological means, to have those who are gazed on know that they are under scrutiny and know just who does the scrutinizing. Modesty and politeness need not be eliminated by our new powers of sight: The human being with such x-ray vision is still a human being in this regard. The situation would be quite different—and more troubling—for a person or persons whose x-ray vision could not under any circumstance (including later genetic or other physical alteration) be turned off. Perhaps this would eventually make the world into a vast nudist camp, in which some crucial forms of privacy still existed (you can see, but you cannot touch). But we would approach this with much greater caution, for there would be a definite loss since human beings are, for the most part, more attractive with their clothes on than off.

And we would without doubt be crossing the divide if we provided not only x-ray eyes but also an x-ray mind so that we could read each other's thoughts. In this case, an array of human experiences associated with the consciousness of inwardness and self and sex and love would be radically altered, and we would not think of it as perfection of life as we know it. It is possible, in such a case, for us to discern between acceptable and unacceptable enhancement.

Now, assume that, by means of genetic engineering, a group or an entire generation were to be tall, physically adept and powerful, beautiful and extremely smart, very long-lived and healthy, and even endowed with Superman's x-ray vision. Would these people be degraded by their greater-than-normal capacities or become incapable of happiness and interest in life? In every ontological respect listed above, I think not. Life for them could well be more varied—given the heightened reason and creativity—not less, even though there would doubtless be fads as to hair and eye color, nose shape, and so forth. If we can design looks, we should expect marvelous variety side by side with bland standardization: just as with American food. And of course by the time we can engineer our offspring's looks or any other characteristic or personality trait, anyone who does not like what they got would probably be able to change it, either with easy surgery, later genetic intervention, or pharmacological adjustment. We cannot predict what will make such people happy, or how they will love, or what their aesthetic sensibilities and accomplishments may be. If they live youthfully to the age of three hundred years, childhood, death, family, and love will be experienced quite differently by them than they are by us. But then our experiences of childhood, death, family, and love are quite different from human beings whose life expectancy was forty years, or who lived in the polis, or in aristocratic Europe. Much about human experience will change—but so long as it is on the right side of the ontological divide it will be human, and there is no obvious reason to think that it must be degraded, flat-headed, and miserable.

The real problem, at least in the short run, would probably be political. As the result of private development and use of genetic engineering, it is possible to imagine much greater inequality than might be compatible with democracy as we know it today. At least at first, genetic enhancement would be more easily available to the well-off, who could with their money transform themselves into a real genetic superelite. And there is no guarantee that the supersmart people would not claim—with some logic on their side—that they and only they were fit to rule. This would be a very serious and difficult problem, but not one without at least a possible Baconian solution. If the poorer and less well endowed can be shown that the power—political and otherwise—of the superior human beings is in the inferior group's interest, because that power contributes to the technological cornucopia (which it will), then such inequality and even more limited democracy could be tolerated, and by both sides: The genetic inferiors would have no reason to revolt, and the genetic superiors would have no reason to be excessively repressive. There could well be a technologically advanced liberal society that is both more stable politically and less democratic than ours is today.

But even if this political outcome is avoided, there will be good reasons to keep a wary eye on the temptations of government to constrain individual liberty—especially reproductive liberty. The more likely long-term effects of genetic engineering will be toward intellectual and rough genetic equality, not rule by some small elite. First, it will proceed slowly enough so that wise political management and economic forces will prevent the quick development of a relatively small and insulated elite. As biotechnology becomes cheaper and easier, and feasible after development is complete, it will be more, not less, widely available. Smart pills will be available to the masses as well as the few. Why should we expect that our society, which is so concerned with improving education for all, would not also want more and more smart people, rather than a fixed number? In terms of social cohesion, will not widespread, engineered equality in intelligence be better than the rigid stratification that comes with natural meritocracy? Given these facts, one could well expect that those who, for whatever reasons, wish to reproduce without technology will be thought of much as we think of women who reproduce while consuming crack cocaine or excessive amounts of alcohol. Intervention by government could well be expected (so as to prevent social costs of the genetic inferiors), and along with that intervention would come bureaucratic control over private matters of reproduction and a significant diminution of personal liberty. We will have to be wary of this danger, which will accompany the new world to come. But each era in human life has its special problems, and the threat of government to individual liberty will not be particularly new.

Would increasing equality of brains be some kind of homogenized nightmare? I do not think so. That all have similar intellectual horsepower does not mean that all will be alike or that all will think and feel or do the same things. On the contrary. Along all of the ontological dimensions, we would not necessarily be faced by deformed, repulsive, or enervated human beings. In such conditions, political life, such as it is, could become very tame, because a basic cause of human conflict, inequality, would be much reduced. But that is surely not a bad thing. In many other areas of human life, however, the thrill and inventiveness of competition could proceed apace. In the contemporary worlds of auto racing and professional sports, for instance, all the cars and competitors are for all practical purposes equal. The competition consists of the subtlest of technical tweaks and strategic nuance, and winning and losing occur within mere seconds and fractions of seconds. But they are not for that reason boring.

It is possible that psychotropic drug therapies could result in some kind of slow and intentional self-lobotomizing. It does seem possible that, for the sake of avoiding anxiety, large numbers of people will so tranquilize themselves as to lose the edge that gives depth and interest to life and spurs creativity. (Like some kind of mass heroin epidemic.) Some degrees of unhappiness and angst are (probably) goads to artistic and imaginative originality, not to mention to intellectual and psychological seriousness. Thus stultifying chemical tranquillity is a threat to be avoided. But this threat is probably less serious than one might think at first glance. Human beings just do not like to be flat and bored; they crave excitement and novelty and some (daredevils and the like) even crave physical danger. The dopey happiness of a chemically tranquilized state is not one that people will long willingly endure if they are aware of what they give up. The threat is, of course, far greater if we are not aware of what we give up, if we are not able, once under the effect of the drugs, to judge and evaluate their effects. We will have to watch out for this problem, to be sure, because it would propel us over the ontological divide.

Still, the more likely possibility is as follows: The psychotropic drugs we know of today will seem exceedingly crude—like leeches and laudanum— by comparison to what the future will know. The drugs of the future will treat anxiety and depression, and even lesser forms of psychological dis- comfort, and arrange and affect our moods, but without interfering with— indeed, along with enhancing—our capacity for remembering other and prior moods, appreciating and feeling the strangeness of death and the un- happiness of disappointment, and the resulting depth, seriousness, and cre- ativity. Again, with such an array of drugs, there need be no diminution of the characteristics on the ontological list.

Another, related possibility is the genetic engineering of temperament and personality. One can well imagine an argument that could ensue over ge- netic manipulation of our sense of competitiveness or assertiveness: some would want their children—and would hope that most others would also want their children—to be shy, retiring, cooperative, and gentle, like Alan Alda and Mr. Rogers. These would be the kind of people who think testos- terone the root of human evil, who hate football, hunting, boxing, and Nascar, and who think discretion the better part of courage. Others would want children with much more competitive natures, like Rambo, Hulk Hogan, Margaret Thatcher, or hard-driving CEOs. Between these two camps something like a culture war might ensue. The hard driving could win out simply because parents might want their children not to have sand kicked in their faces. But then again, it is often hard to be a CEO, and many things that people want for themselves and for their children would call for more mod- erate temperaments: reflective thoughtfulness, scholarly rigor, philanthropy, any number of things.

But I would be reluctant to regulate this dispute at such a level of speci- ficity for three reasons: First, it would be very hard to reach consensus on which character and its virtues (cooperativeness versus hard-driving taking charge) should trump the other. Second, these types would still be on the hu- man side of the divide, and for the reason just mentioned, we should expect parents to choose a wide variety between them. And third, and most impor- tant, to regulate at this level would require a political and bureaucratic regime that would have to be extremely intrusive and powerful: such a regime would be subject to takeover by sets of partisans, each with some reason on their side, and once established, it could be used for other and ex- tremely dangerous and coercive policies that could shoot for some massive leap over the ontological divide.

Indeed, one way to produce human beings either for the wimpy side or for the macho side would be to take the extreme step of designing children with so little sense of self that they could see only the good of the collective, or with so little sense of engagement with, and deference to, others that they might think everyone merely of service to them and them alone. This would be to cross the ontological divide—to produce a human being for whom an array of human experiences associated with the tensions and connections among self and others would be massively distorted or impossible. The designing of such freaks should not be expected from free parents, but it could be expected from government. And so as regards the genetic (and pharmacological) manipulation of temperament, it will be extremely important to fear and watch out for and prevent a connection between political power and genetic and pharmacological choice. It will be better to let the individual choices of parents and individuals, and slowly emerging and unpredictable cultural trends, determine how things come out in fact.

But even if eugenics can be embraced along the lines that I have suggested, does it not, as Kass argues in his second point, threaten the commodification of human life, in which persons become mere extensions of others' designs, mere means to be used by their makers, or at least lacking, as the product of art, some fundamental independence? Kass argues: "As with any product of our making, no matter how excellent, the artificer stands above it, not as an equal, but as a superior, transcending it by his will and creative prowess."[5] But it is by no means obvious, to me, that the artist is necessarily superior (whatever that might mean) to the product of the art. The matter rather depends on the specific art and on the specific product. In the case of nuts and bolts, I would agree that the product is a mere means to be used by the producer. But with *Vermeer's Girl with a Pearl Earring* or with Shakespeare's dramatic corpus, could it not just as well be argued that the artist is the mere servant of the created thing? Do we not think of the artist at his peak as devoting his all to the service of his art? Is not the artist the mere vehicle for the masterpiece, which is "priceless"?

My point here is that there is no necessity that the work of art be subordinate to, or inferior to, the producer of that art. This point is even more relevant in the case of genetic engineering, in which the product and artisan are ontologically the same: when the product of the art is itself a human being. Surely we treat human beings as the objects of art in the sense of intellectual and moral cultivation—*Bildung*—and we hardly think of them as being dehumanized by the process. There is no reason why a genetically engineered and enhanced human person, who does not lack any of the ontological characteristics listed above, should necessarily be dehumanized by virtue simply of the artifice involved. To be determined by genetic engineering is, ontologically speaking, no more being determined than is being determined by a natural lottery.

Against this last point, someone might argue that the determination involved in engineered enhancement could be greater than reproduction by the natural lottery, because the intention governing the design of the hard wires can also apply to the subsequent nurture, with the effect of narrowing or unduly constraining the life choices of the product. An example—apparently a favorite—would be the cloning or reproducing by genetic engineering of, say, Michael Jordan.[6] In this extreme case, we could presume that the new Jordan would be constrained by expectations of basketball wizardry. A whole, already-lived life would stand as a model, and one could say that such expectations could be so confining as to be tyrannical. Even here, however, the new Jordan would still be free to tell Dad to buzz off—and would be under no harmful psychological compulsion to prove to anyone that he could be a basketball great. Should he decide to play, since so much of the game is mental and a matter of guts and effort, he could still have the opportunity to be better than the original Michael Jordan. And there is no basketball gene, after all; so the new Jordan—handsome, smart, tall, and athletically gifted— might decide to play soccer or to avoid sports and become a chef and restaurateur. As regards more likely possibilities, it is hard to see how genetic enhancement—on the right side of the ontological divide—would close off or overly determine life choices. The enhanced person could be better able, not less so, to resist the force of parental and social ambitions or intentions. The superior child would be more, not less, independent, with more, not fewer, life options available. And if a person should be engineered with traits of character so that they are simply unable to resist subordination to the parent, that would be a problem of crossing the ontological divide, which is quite different from the simple fact of having been subjected by art to parental hopes.

In general, it seems to me, genetic engineering for enhancement will not lead to the view that life is cheap. The engineered offspring will be better than their makers, not worse, and thus will be less likely to be objects of contempt, not more. Nor will such genetic engineering inadvertently and indirectly, but inevitably, make life seem cheap by dispelling the mystery of human life, which so much conditions our belief in human dignity.[7] As we manipulate the matter of life to enhance the experience of life, the connection between our matter and our experience—between our organic and electronic stuff, on the one hand, and the manifold aspects of consciousness, on the other—will likely become more intensely mysterious, not less. We will never know why electrical activity in the brain gives rise to self-consciousness—for example, to our awareness of death as we humans experience it or the smell of coffee as we experience it. And yet with genetic engineering we will more frequently and more immediately, and with greater complexity and specificity, confront and experience this inexplicable connection. To the extent that belief in human dignity is conditioned by the mystery of human life, we should not expect that belief to be endangered by our discovering ever new forms and elements of that very mystery.

I do not doubt that there will always be scientific misanthropes, who pronounce as humbug anything that cannot be touched or seen or measured. We will have to beware of them and also watch out for those who reason from control in some things to control in all. But by itself, science and ge-netic engineering will never convince human beings that they are nothing but matter in motion, nothing but complicated meat. The reason is very sim-ple: As soon as we hear and understand such claims, over cigarettes and cof-fee, we know that they are not true.

Although I do not agree with Leon Kass that our limit of fourscore years and ten is essentially good for us, it is not unreasonable for him to wonder if we will not, somehow, be made miserable and unhappy when we live to be three hundred and ten, with all of our enhanced powers. My guess is that in this future we will be as happy as or much happier in some respects than we are now, and also more, or at least no less, unhappy, in other respects—so long as we remain on the human side of the ontological divide. But it is very hard to predict such things, and to say it again, it will be futile to appeal to an unknown and unpredictable threat of such unhappiness—based on an account of what specific virtue or good trumps other virtues or goods—to ban or seriously impede what the vast mass of humanity will want and do most anything to get.

To return to a point made earlier, when we live to be three hundred and ten, much concerning love, sex, parenting, and the family will change. Will a couple married for fifty years be likely to go for another fifty or a hundred? Probably not. But nothing will prevent those who believe their marriage made in heaven from sticking it out for the duration. Will there be different relations among generations and between particular parents and children? Probably so. Will procreation be mediated by technology? Almost undoubt-edly. All this will change specific forms of sex and love, friendship and par-enting—but this will not mean that we will not have and enjoy sex, experi-ence love, be friends, and be parents, so long as we remain on the human side of the ontological divide.

As the threat of natural death recedes, there is no doubt that our sensibil-ities in this regard—what and how we fear, how we comport toward risk, and how we are aware of our finitude—will change. And if we were ever to reach some kind of immortality (beyond entropy) or near-immortality (to the point of entropy) we may well have reached a world where some of what we think of as our fundamental experiences might be drastically altered be-cause our circumstances will have been so drastically altered. In such a case, we will not be dogs or cats or robots, but still rational beings who will be able to live fully in the world as it then is. (And even death will not be gone as a possibility—after 2,000 years one could still commit suicide.) We may then even bid farewell to some items on the ontological list, not, however, as self-deprivation, but rather as an adjustment to a world where some pos-sibilities on the list will be so heightened as to make others fade to insignif-icance by comparison. But that world is much too far away to take seriously as a matter of public policy.

My temporary conclusion is this. I do not worry too much that biotechno-logical and pharmacological enhancement (smarter, bigger, stronger, health-ier, and so on) will perforce make us miserable or transform us into flat-headed last men or even into monsters. All things considered, the good things promised us by Bacon's project for conquering nature outweigh the bad ones and the dangers. One could object that I simply look too much on the bright side of life. But I see no alternative to doing so, since the biotech-nological revolution is coming and there is nothing we can do to stop it. Moreover, looking on the bright side does not preclude taking seriously the serious objections to genetic enhancement, such as those of Leon Kass, nor does it preclude, as I hope I have shown, awareness of other dangers that the future portends. We will have to keep the ontological divide in mind, for it will be possible for us to cross it, especially if genetic choice falls under ill-managed political power. And despite all that I have said, mankind could suffer some farfetched genetically engineered accident, or even endure some science-fiction-like development by which humanity becomes, say, one single, giant, disembodied brain. Is the mere existence of these possi-bilities altogether bad and enough to stop us in our tracks? I think not. One frequent complaint about technological modernity is that it just makes life too boring and drab. And it has often been argued that modern technology replaces real thinking by mere technical calculation. I would say that the new dangers we face, and the complicated moral and political task of avoid-ing them, will make life really interesting. And does not technology now compel us to one of the most interesting and enlivening questions for thought: What is humanity?

So much for the threat to our human nature. Not to worry too much, I would say. The hubris issue is another matter altogether. In my abstract on-tological list, I purposely left out one very important characteristic: made-in-the-image-of-God. One could argue that this characteristic is not essential to an ontological understanding of human nature. Certainly Aristotle did not think it worth including in the *Nicomachean Ethics*, nor did Heidegger in *Sein und Zeit*. But I think there is a real problem here, and I think that most biotechnology enthusiasts deceive themselves about the possible conflict be-tween religion and the project for conquering nature. Bacon had a lot to say about this matter, and it will be helpful to turn to him again for some clarifi-cation.

According to Bacon, "natural philosophy proposes to itself, as its noblest work of all, nothing less than the restitution and renovation (restitutio et in-stauratio) of things corruptible."[8] Bacon could not be clearer about this: The only impediments to overcoming death and resurrecting the dead are the de-ficiencies of natural science. These deficiencies are remediable, and it was Bacon's object to show us how to fix them. For Bacon—and I would say for Franklin and for modern biotechnology as it is moving—death is a curable genetic disease, not the wages of sin. Bacon was not interested in playing God; he wanted simply to put God out of business. Bacon sometimes argues that God actually intends to retire: the project of technology is God's will, and Providence works through our God-given reason. But Bacon knew the obvious, more orthodox objection to this progressive argument: Science is another Tower of Babel, watched by a jealous and righteous God who wants salvation to be entirely his work or gift of grace. If we fall for the temptation to play God he will punish us, and if we do not fall for that temptation he will reward us. The hubris consists not in what we get, but in how we try to get it. We know this to be true because it has been disclosed to us by a divine miracle: revelation and Scripture. Thus might an orthodox believer respond to the wild ambitions of Baconian biotechnology.

Bacon's utopian fable *New Atlantis* describes a future society in which everything is geared to accommodate the project of conquering nature. The heart of the society is a huge institution for conducting all varieties of scientific research and technological development. But the fable is also an account of the relationship between modern science and miracles. There are some remarkable facts about the story told in *New Atlantis*: The founding, in the island of Bensalem, of the scientific academy for the project of technology, is followed by an original miracle of revelation, which establishes the society's religion and whose veracity is attested by the scientists of the academy. These scientists have, by the grace of God, been vouchsafed with the power to understand the secrets of creation and to discern between "divine miracles, works of nature, works of art, and impostures and illusions of all sorts." Then, later in the story, we learn that the scientists have the power to create all manner of deceits of the senses (false apparitions, impostures, illusions) and to make natural phenomena seem, to the ignorant, miraculous.[9] And Bensalem, the society dedicated to the technological conquest of nature, is suffused with religion, but one that is a bland mishmash that includes Jews believing in the divinity of Jesus and that bows completely to the authority of science.

Bacon presents us with the following extraordinary picture. On the one hand, he gives a scoffer or skeptic plenty of evidence to conclude that the scientists faked the miracle in Bensalem and that the religion of Bensalem was created and tailored by the scientific establishment merely to suit its purposes. But on the other hand, Bacon pulls the rug out from under the scoffer by his very presentation and verification of the miracle. How so? The only way for the scientists to certify the miracle is for them to have penetrated and mastered every single corner of material nature. Such a science—conceivable, in Bacon's eyes—could indeed prove a given phenomenon to be a miracle outside the realm of all natural causes. Far from ruling out the possibility of miracles, perfect science is the ground for proving, according to reason, that a miracle has occurred. Although an imperfect science—one that is not yet complete or can never be complete—cannot in this way prove a miracle to have occurred, neither can it prove that miracles are impossible. And this is not to mention that every course of nature as we know it scientifically could, in fact, be the product of an extraworldly, divine, miraculous cause. It is thus not impossible that miracles as people experience them are a modulation in the continuing miracle that causes every event, natural or otherwise, in the universe.

This leads us back to the hubris problem. If Baconian natural science cannot know that miracles are impossible, then is Bacon not bolder than bold—indeed foolhardy in the extreme—to urge mankind toward the "noblest work" of natural philosophy? Why on earth would he—or we—do such a thing and risk the revealed wrath of God? In Bacon's case, it was not because he thought this project consistent with charity and hence with God's true and ultimate will. Bacon was one of the nastiest characters in the history of philosophy, did not have a charitable bone in his body, and thought charity to be nonsense—a product of the mind's deeply embedded conceit that things that are in fact discrete are connected, as is implied in the claim that some noble end obliges one man to sacrifice himself to, or for, another. Bacon expected payoffs from his project for himself, in the form of an extended life. He did not die from experimenting with refrigeration (which he himself did not need), as Hobbes later claimed. He died by accident, as the result of inhaling impure potassium nitrate, with which he intended the "induration and conservation" of his body.[10]

Bacon's death was an accident, not an act of self-sacrifice. He was a coldly prudent, selfish, and calculating man. And so, as regards the risk of divine revenge, Bacon proceeded as he did because he was convinced that such revenge was impossible. After all, no sane person—not to mention a person with such a powerful intellect and sense of self-interest as Bacon—would simply gamble that for a few extra years of life on this earth (bought by a science aimed at conquering death altogether) the cost would not be eternal damnation. But Bacon was convinced of his safety not by his technological natural science. That science was, he knew, just getting under way and could not—even when complete—prove the nonexistence of God and miracles. Bacon was convinced of his safety rather by philosophy more traditionally and generally understood—by his observations and reasoning about the human mind and moral and political opinions.

I cannot here discuss Bacon's observations and reasoning about man, God, and miracles. But there is an important point I want to make on this score. Bacon was much tougher than we are on the issue of science and religion. Whereas we commonly and blithely think that religion is one thing and science another, and that only fundamentalist lunatics believe that science is the work of the devil (the Great Satan), Bacon knew from the get-go that, ultimately, science and God are very possibly on a collision course: If there is a God, then the noblest work of science is, potentially, in direct competition with his greatness and powers of salvation. From Bacon's point of view, the technological project required a prior settling, for himself, of the issue of *quid sit deus*.

Bacon's personal certainty about this matter could become widespread or universal. Perhaps universal atheism will follow from really long life and really commodious living—not to mention from virtual immortality. But we cannot be sure of this dream of the Enlightenment. Bacon himself thought it would take a long, long time; and if we follow his suggestion, we should not count on it any time soon (and this merely presumes, it does not know, that there is no God). It could well happen, then, that the emerging and accelerating project for conquering that "mere disease," death, a hitherto-unheard-of challenge to divine power, will at some point provoke tensions that strain our liberal procedures for managing political and religious matters. We may fool ourselves, for instance, when we think of militant religious fundamentalism as merely the product of envy or frustrated ambitions and ignore completely the fundamentalist view that modern technology and science are in themselves arrogant to the point of impiety. And it is far from impossible that such extremism could arise, not just at the periphery of the technological world, but right at its heart. We could well be faced again with solving the tension between the powers who rule on this earth and those who fear powers invisible.

I will repeat a point made earlier. Many recent opponents of the Baconian project—those who worry about a looming "post-human" future—are in fact the heirs of an antimodernist argument that springs from Nietzsche. Convinced that pain, suffering and struggle, and religion provide human depth and character and make us interesting, they fear that the technological conquest of nature will make us contented cows, capable only of shallow, instrumental reasoning and for whom the word "awesome" can be used to describe a pair of shoes. If Bacon is correct, this is not likely to happen for a very long time. Rather, the technological project may sooner or later propel us to the other most interesting and enlivening question for thought and especially for politics: the one concerning God and the tension between reason and revelation. This may prove a real challenge to reason and to politics, and the task of solving or managing it will not be a bore.

STUDY QUESTIONS

1. What are the two fears that Weinberger attributes to critics of modern techno-science?
2. Describe the differences between the moral-teleological and ontological approaches to describing human nature.

3. According to Weinberger, what is the problem with the moral-teleological approach?
4. What experiences are defining characteristics of human beings, according to Weinberger?
5. What does Weinberger mean by the ontological divide?
6. Why do critics such as Kass think that genetic engineering is dangerous?
7. Why does Weinberger think that genetic enhancement is probably not dangerous? Do you agree with his reasoning? Explain.
8. According to Weinberger, what is the most serious and difficult issue raised by techno-science?

NOTES

1. Leon Kass, "Preventing a Brave New World," TNR.com (21 May 2001): 1; and Leon Kass and James Q. Wilson, "The Wisdom of Repugnance," in *The Ethics of Human Cloning* (Washington D.C.: AEI Press, 1998), 13.

2. Adam Wolfson, "Biodemocracy in America," www.ThePublicInterest.com (winter 2002): 4.

3. Benjamin Franklin, *Writings*, ed. J. A. Leo Lemay (New York: Library of America, 1987), 1017. Franklin made the same point in other letters in which he expected this new life span to be possible in about three hundred years, that is, about now.

4. "The Wisdom of Repugnance," 24–31, 45–46. In the follow-up essay ("Family Needs Its Natural Roots") in the same volume, Kass speaks of "the moral pointings of nature" (80–83).

5. "The Wisdom of Repugnance," 39.

6. "The Wisdom of Repugnance," 35–36, 46.

7. For this objection, I thank my colleague Arthur Melzer.

8. Francis Bacon, "Of The Wisdom of the Ancients: Orpheus," in *The Works of Francis Bacon*, vol. 6 (London: Longman and Co., 1861), 720–2.

9. Jerry Weinberger, ed., *New Atlantis and the Great Instauration* (Arlington Heights: Harlan Davidson, 1989), 48, 80.

10. See Lisa Jardine and Alan Stewart, *Hostage to Fortune* (London: Victor Gollancz, 1998), 502–11.

INTERVENTIONS: CAN WE CONTROL TECHNOLOGY?

Technology seems to give us greater individual control over our activities and projects. Yet, technology subtly influences the people who produce and consume it, and we are not entirely aware of these effects. For instance, communications technology (cell phones, e-mail, etc.) gives us the ability to reach anyone, anytime, but also enables others to reach us. These innovations fundamentally change our concepts of private space and private time and muddle the distinction between work and home. Yet, these substantial changes in how we live are not necessarily part of the deliberative processes of cell phone producers and consumers. Transportation technologies allow us to live in suburbs far away from places of work, food sources, etc. This has fundamentally transformed everything from the structure of families to the kinds of careers we choose, though early producers and consumers of automobiles never envisioned these changes. Kass worries that, as a society, we may lack control over the effects of technology, thus raising questions about whether humanity is in control of its destiny.

Unfortunately, the models of autonomy we have been working with thus far do not help us think about the appropriate response to technological advance. In the face of rapid technological advance, some people focus primarily on the promise of new technologies, professing the end of poverty and disease, and welcoming the opportunities made available by disrupting traditional ways of thinking, while opposing calls for restraint. Others call for either a return to earlier, less technologically dependent forms of life or advocate that we place very strict constraints on technological development, refusing any new developments until we can be certain of the consequences.

Both of these responses express their own version of self-sufficiency. The most enthusiastic champions of new technologies wish to be independent of the limitations placed on us by physical obstacles of space, time, and biology—an extreme form of self-sufficiency. On the opposing side, technophobes seek greater self-reliance by becoming less dependent on technological devices and the social systems required to maintain them. Neither response seems reasonable because both require that we give up too much. Champions of technology threaten to impose a form of life on us the outlines of which we can only dimly grasp, sacrificing security and stability. Technology's detractors threaten human creativity and innovation, not to mention the reduction in suffering new technologies provide.

Self-direction requires only that we assess whether new technologies conform to our basic values. However, despite Weinberger's thoughtful attempt to provide such an assessment, our deliberations on this question are bound to be tentative and not well grounded, given our well-documented inability to predict the effects of technology. Furthermore, as Kass points out, the need to rely excessively on experts in genetic technology may place the autonomy of individuals at risk. The relatively weak conditions that characterize self-direction may not explain why such reliance on experts is a threat to autonomy.

Perhaps we can begin to resolve these dilemmas by recognizing that whether technology is destructive or not depends on the social relations within which it is designed and deployed. When technology is designed and developed in a context in which only profit, production efficiency, and marketing matter, we are likely to get technologies that are incompatible with other values, because there is no incentive to let humanistic and environmental values into the design and production process. Thus, humanistic and environmental values are not captured in the price of the product and are not represented in the market.

As individual consumers, we have limited influence over techno-capitalism. We are free to choose, but only among the choices made available to us by producers who may have no incentive to incorporate the full range of human value into their products. Thus, finding ways of collectively influencing techno-capitalism through the introduction of democratic decision-making processes is crucial to developing technology that remains sensitive to human value.

Weinberger makes the sensible suggestion that future generations will be concerned with their humanity. However, that will matter only if a large swath of humanity has significant input into how technologies are developed. This entails that we reject individualistic interpretations of autonomy. Paradoxically, we can gain autonomy only by recognizing that our individual deliberative processes are dependent on the actions and deliberations of others. Personal autonomy can function as a dominant value only if it is elaborated in a way that avoids the excessive individualism of self-sufficiency and the tendency of self-direction to avoid addressing issues of the social conditions in which autonomy is exercised.

V

IN GOD WE TRUST—OR DO WE?

Public discussion of society's moral failings often involves the claim that moral decline is the product of advancing secularism, a decline that can be reversed if more people conscientiously embrace a religious point of view. However, the connection between religion and ethics is not obvious. Religion cannot be necessary for moral conduct, given that there are many nonreligious people who are morally respectable. Neither can religion be sufficient for ethics since there are many religious scoundrels.

In light of these facts, defenders of religion as the foundation of ethics tend to argue that although there may be many nonreligious reasons to be good, these reasons will not suffice in all contexts at all times. When ethics is based on personal conscience, cultural norms, or practical reason, ethical principles reflect particular interests or perspectives. Only an absolute authority—God—can explain the existence of absolute moral principles that apply to all people at all times. Thus, religion provides a stable foundation for ethics because only such an absolute authority can encourage us to suspend our narrow interests and act for the common good.

Secularists, however, deny that ethics must rest on religion, arguing that there are many nonreligious reasons to promote the interests of others even when the needs of others conflict with our self-interest. Feelings of empathy, compassion, and revulsion are powerful motives that when accompanied by informed, logically consistent reasoning provide a sufficient basis for morality.

13

Can We Be Good without Hell?

Jerry L. Walls

Jerry L. Walls teaches theology at Asbury Theological Seminary and is the author of *Hell: The Logic of Damnation* (1993) and *Heaven: The Logic of Eternal Joy* (2001). Walls argues that self-interest coincides with morality much of the time, explaining why many people can lead moral lives without God. But when self-interest conflicts with morality, people have no reason to be moral. This is especially the case when the sacrifice is extreme. Thus, he argues that only belief in heaven and hell explains extraordinary self-sacrifice.

Crime is rising because the fear of hell is declining—or so said Britain's Secretary of State for Education and Science John Patten in 1992. The British newspapers deemed the argument so preposterous that Britain needed a renewed fear of damnation and hope of redemption in order to return to civility.

The secretary's essay not only drew sharp reaction in the press, it also sparked a considerable debate over the moral foundations of modern society. One critical editorial gives the flavor of the prevailing opinion. Entitled "Hell: who needs it?" it concluded with this parting shot: "We may well need to renew our sense of the bad and the good, but the renewal will not be prompted by thoughts of a dreadful eternity elsewhere, even if we imagine Mr. Patten to be there with us, sharing it!"

On our side of the Atlantic, the popular press has likewise regularly fed us stories about the need to "renew our sense of the bad and the good" and about how we need to rediscover America's moral foundations. *Time* and *Newsweek* have splashed former drug czar William Bennett and his "Virtuecrats" on their covers and sympathetically described their "crusade against

America's moral decline." These now regular articles seem to take for granted that there is a moral void at the heart of our society.

While Christians should applaud this reopening of the debate about morality, we do not have to be satisfied with how it is being conducted. There is a tension, an ambivalence, that pervades this discussion. Oxford philosopher Basil Mitchell calls this tension the "dilemma of the traditional conscience." It is the quandary faced by those who affirm traditional moral convictions but who deny the theological framework that historically provided those convictions with meaning and motivation. Without the framework, it is not clear whether or why those convictions of right and wrong are true or why they should be followed.

Our cultural debate over morals and virtues does not meet this dilemma head-on. One *Time* article came the closest by offering the opinion that "interestingly, and perhaps reassuringly, some of the most thoughtful ethicists feel that the elements for an enduring moral consensus are right at hand—in the Constitution and the Declaration of Independence, with their combination of Locke's natural rights and Calvin's ultimate right." But this merely evades the issue. What remains unacknowledged is the obvious fact that for Locke and Calvin these rights are ultimately grounded in the will of a living God. Perhaps it is time to admit that Mr. Patten was onto something.

I do not believe there is any adequate account of moral authority or of moral motivation on secular principles. More specifically, I believe we need God, heaven, and yes, even hell, to make sense of morality. Indeed, we need to define our very selves in light of these eternal realities. If there is no God, no heaven, no hell, there simply is no persuasive reason to be moral.

I do not mean to claim there is no reason at all to behave morally without these beliefs. A person might decide to adhere to traditional morality if he thought it a good thing that most people should behave that way. But there is a profound difference between being moral and believing it is a good thing to behave morally most of the time. This is a key point in the virtue tradition, and one of the main reasons for its appeal.

But there is a deeper reason why it ultimately makes no sense to be moral without God, heaven, and hell. Being moral is often at odds with self-interest. There are times when virtue may exact a large price and occasions when commitment to moral integrity can even cost moral agents their own lives.

An obvious example here is the young soldier who chooses to die for his country rather than to flee in battle. It is noteworthy that C. S. Lewis used this case in *The Abolition of Man* to illustrate the difference between those who stand within what he calls the Tao in their approach to moral education, and those who do not. By the Tao Lewis simply meant the consensus of traditional morality that he believed was held in common by all cultures. Here is his illustration: "When a Roman father told his son that it was a sweet and seemly thing to die for his country, he believed what he said. He was communicating to the son an emotion which he himself shared and which he believed to be in accord with the value which his Judgement discerned in noble death."

Those who reject the absolute authority of the Tao and attempt to reconstruct morality on some other basis Lewis gives the label "moral innovators." Such innovators are faced with a dilemma at this point: "Either they must go the whole way and debunk this sentiment like any other, or must set themselves to work to produce, from outside, a sentiment which they believe to be of no value to the pupil and which may cost him his life, because it is useful to us (the survivors) that our young men should feel it." The latter course assumes—indeed, creates—a conflict between what is good for individuals and what is good for society as a whole. Another way to state it is to see the conflict as being between what is arguably moral (defending your country) and what is merely in one's self-interest (staying alive).

How can it be a sweet and seemly thing for the soldier to die for his country? Those who survive and remember him may view his death in this fashion, but of what value is that to him? How then can this mode of behavior be thought rational? If it is not rational, how can it be right? For self-sacrifice to be rational, one must discover some clear justification for acting decisively against one's immediate self-interest.

Here is where God, heaven, and hell come in. These are the resources that enable us to give a satisfying account to our young soldier (and everybody else, for that matter) of why we should not only behave morally but also be moral, and not only generally but always. For these are the best, if not the only, resources to make sense of how it is always in our best interest to be moral.

The doctrines of heaven and hell are the supreme articulation of the claim that we can evade neither responsibility for our actions nor the motives behind them. They represent the epitome of the notion that we never serve our ultimate self-interest by doing what is immoral, just as we always serve our ultimate self-interest by our steadfast commitment to do what is right in all situations, including those that are the most costly to us. In fact, the logic of heaven dictates that only by losing your life will you find it. We are eternal beings, being groomed for an existence that transcends our this-worldly goods. In heaven all forfeited good is restored in a better mode than before.

The recent papal encyclical (*The Splendor of Truth*) argues along these lines in its emphasis on martyrdom as a witness to Christian moral commitments. What so surprises and challenges current sensibilities is the fact that the whole discussion of morality is set in the context of eternity. Martyrs are described as those who "obediently trusted and handed over their lives to the Father, the one who could free them from death" (cf. Heb. 5:7). Morality has an altogether different basis if a sacrificial death is a life handed over to a loving Father who cares for his children than it has if such a life is given over to oblivion.

In our post-Enlightenment setting, this appeal to heaven is, ironically, likely to strike many as immoral. Any concern with self-interest may seem incompatible with genuine morality. The unfortunate result of this supposed conflict is that our society continues to fluctuate between moral self-restraint and immoral self-indulgence. Happily, this tension, with its disastrous consequences, is not inevitable.

To be sure, Christianity is opposed to self-indulgence, but this should not be equated with legitimate self-interest. Basil Mitchell makes this point in showing the positive moral significance of heaven and hell.

> If a man longs for a heaven that is genuine communion with God and with other men, what he hopes for is not self-interested in any objectionable sense, for he desires this for others as well as for himself; and, if he does not, then he has not yet made the required metanoia—he has not repented. He has to be born again, but what he then receives is what he most deeply wants, a bliss that cannot be enjoyed without selfless devotion to God and to others. When understood in this way—a profoundly traditional way—the emphasis in the Gospels upon heaven and hell can be seen to fulfill morality, not to distort it.

Only with the help of heaven and hell can "the dilemma of the traditional conscience" be resolved. Because only an appeal to a reality that transcends biological survival will allow morality and self-interest to merge.

In one of *Time*'s recurring articles on this subject, the essayist wrote: "If Americans wish to strike a truer ethical balance, they may need to reexamine the values that society so seductively parades before them: a top job, political power, sexual allure, a penthouse or lakefront spread, a killing on the market." The "ethical balance" he has in mind is between service to self and service to society. So conceived, the balance represents a sort of compromise between a thorough-going self-interest and a selfless service to others.

Here is how heaven and hell change the picture. They bring God in! And at once everything looks different. No compromise is necessary. If we are eternal persons whose lives have an eternal context, then self-interest dictates that we follow the laws of heaven. Heaven is the true fulfillment of all human desire. And so without seeing ourselves as heaven's citizens, we cannot order our desires the right way. We will desire lesser goods (the goodness of sexual acts) over higher ones (the goodness of fidelity). In other words, we cannot redefine our wants without challenging the secular definition of who we are.

So the moral significance of hell is not to serve as a threat to deter uncivil behavior. Hell in its adjudication is the judgment of God, but in its nature it is the intrinsic consequence of pursuing the wrong means to happiness. It is the natural outcome of not considering carefully who we are and profoundly pursuing what will truly satisfy us. So understood, hell cannot be used in a simplistic way as a club to keep in line people who never seriously reflect on these basic questions about the meaning of life.

Or to put the point another way, if the ideas of heaven and hell are in fact lost on us, it is because we have lost our grasp on the larger matrix of convictions that give them life; for the concepts of heaven and hell cannot survive in any meaningful sense outside their natural habitat. Outside the context of God, eternity, goodness, evil, salvation, and ultimate human fulfillment, these notions will inevitably appear to be relics from the past that are all but unintelligible to us today.

In his 1984 Ingersoll Lecture on immortality entitled "Hell Disappeared. No One Noticed. A Civic Argument," Martin Marty maintained that the doctrine of hell is no longer "culturally available" in our society. Marty advanced this argument against those who press for the return of "God-talk in public education." These persons contend that if God is not restored to our schools, there is no proper basis for teaching values and civic virtue.

As Marty points out, however, this is not as simple a matter as it may seem. For the God who figured prominently in America's educational past, whether theistic or deistic, was a morally active God who held people accountable for moral wrongdoing, both in this life and in the life to come. In short, God played an important role in moral education because of the attendant doctrine of judgment. So we cannot bring God back into our schools in any morally significant sense unless we also bring back the doctrines of heaven and hell. And, Marty further argued, if we did unilaterally bring God-talk back into the classroom, the practical effect would be to reduce God to a mere "syllable." Since the idea of hell is culturally unavailable to us, Marty concludes that civil institutions should learn to develop moral systems that do not need to "invoke the syllable 'God' as an instrument for promoting 'traditional values.'"

Now Marty is correct in pointing out that the idea of hell has been linked with the idea of God in traditional Western moral education. I would argue, however, that there is more involved here than a historical link. There is also a logical link. More specifically, any idea of God worth believing entails the doctrine of heaven and also some version of the doctrine of hell—or at least judgment. I do not claim it entails the doctrine of eternal hell, although that is the account of hell that I believe is true. But some version of the doctrine follows from the idea of God.

Here is the essential argument: If God is supremely powerful as well as good, then he has both the ability and the desire to preserve and perfect his relationship with his rational creatures. A good God would not create us with the kind of aspirations we have and then leave those aspirations unsatisfied. The doctrine of heaven is the claim that our deepest aspirations can be satisfied in a perfected relationship with God and other persons. However, a loving God would not force this relationship upon us; indeed, he cannot do so if we are truly free. So we can, if we prefer, destroy our own happiness by rejecting the only true means to that happiness. This is the heart of the traditional doctrine of hell.

As a matter of logic, then, any idea of God that does not entail reward and punishment is neither morally relevant nor worthy of our worship. He is certainly not a god Christians would recognize.

Now this has interesting implications for Marty's argument. If the idea of hell is culturally unavailable, this is because the idea of God is culturally unavailable. And when we reflect on the current state of our society, it is not too far-fetched to suggest that in terms of his actual cultural impact, God has been reduced to a syllable. If this is so, we are far worse off than Marty suggests.

I have my doubts, however, whether hell is really as culturally unavailable as Marty claims. There are signs that hell is being taken more seriously today than it was even a decade ago when he delivered his lecture. In 1991, *U.S. News & World Report* published a story entitled "Hell's Sober Comeback" in which it reported that belief in hell is on the rise among Americans. According to a Gallup poll, 60 percent of Americans professed to believe in hell in 1990, compared to 53 percent in 1981. Belief in heaven rose from 71 percent to 78 percent during the same period. It is also noteworthy that several serious books and articles have been published about hell in the past few years, whereas a decade ago Marty reported that a survey of religious literature turned up almost nothing.

Recently, a controversy erupted in response to a Church of England document that affirmed the possibility of damnation—albeit, on two pages in a two-hundred-page document. The very suggestion, from a credible source, that hell might be a reality to be faced is still enough to elicit passionate reaction. This surely indicates that the issue of hell is far from dead in the public consciousness, even in deeply secularized Britain.

Cultural trends are, of course, mercurial and not easily read without benefit of several years of hindsight. So perhaps we should not make too much of this alleged change in the public mind. But it is also possible that the statistics cited above reflect a substantive change at a deeper level of our culture. For there has been taking place in the past several years a change in the intellectual climate with respect to belief in God and other religious matters. This too has been noticed by the popular media. In 1980, *Time* magazine observed the following: "In a quiet revolution in thought and argument that hardly anyone could have foreseen only two decades ago, God is making a comeback. Most intriguingly, this is happening . . . in the crisp, intellectual circles of academic philosophers, where the consensus had long banished the Almighty from fruitful discourse."

What is worth reflecting on here is the possibility that "hell's sober comeback" is at least partly a result of God's "comeback" in circles of sober reflection. A recovery of intellectually serious belief in God is a culturally significant development whose effects would likely, in time, include a renewed consideration of the implications of theistic belief. And if this is true, it is not too much to hope that it may enable us to recover some hard reasons to be moral, not the least of which would flow from a renewed vision of heaven and hell.

We cannot be moral without God, and we cannot have God without hell. Hell needs to make a comeback.

STUDY QUESTIONS

1. According to Walls, why does adherence to traditional values require belief in God?
2. According to Walls, aside from the rewards and punishments of religion, what reasons do we have for sacrificing our self-interest? Do you agree with Walls on this point? Explain.
3. Can you think of examples of moral conduct that are not explained by a motive of self-interest or a religious motive?
4. Does Christian morality require extreme self-sacrifice on Walls's view?
5. What reasons does Walls give for thinking that acting out of a concern for eternal reward and punishment is not self-interested?
6. Why, according to Walls, does the concept of God logically entail the concept of hell? Do you agree?

14

Everything I Like about Religion I Learned from an Atheist

Barbara Ehrenreich

Barbara Ehrenreich is an essayist, columnist, and social critic. Her books include *Global Woman: Nannies, Maids, and Sex Workers in the New Economy* (with Arlie Hochschild and Arlie Russell Hochschild, 2003) and *Nickel and Dimed* (2002). The following article is adapted from her acceptance speech for the 1998 Humanist of the Year Award, presented by the American Humanist Association. Ehrenreich uses her personal experience to raise counter examples to the claim that religion is necessary for ethics. Ehrenreich suggests that the recognition of human suffering and a strong sense of self-reliance are the essential ingredients for a moral point of view.

One of the most alarming developments in my lifetime has been the increasing identification of patriotism and other so-called traditional values, like family, with religion. Religion is such a tricky thing. We try to teach our kids to avoid cults and sects but then, sooner or later, they get old enough to ask you to explain the difference between a cult and a genuine religion.

Is it that cults have irrational belief systems and engage in peculiar, lurid practices? No. Some religions do that, too. Is it because cults are always trying to take your money? Well, no. Religions have a tendency to do that, as well. So eventually you have to admit to your kids that it's really just a matter of size.

A couple of dozen people committing suicide in preparation for boarding the mother ship somewhere is a cult, while a hundred million people bowing down before a flesh-hating, elderly celibate is considered a world-class

Barbara Ehrenreich, "Everything I Like about Religion I Learned from an Atheist," *The Humanist*, November 1999. Reprinted by permission.

religion. A half-dozen Trotskyists meeting over coffee is considered a sect, while a few million gun-toting, Armageddon-ready Baptists is referred to as the Republican Party.

This fusion of patriotism and religion all started when I was a child. When they put the words "under God" in the Pledge of Allegiance, for a long time I couldn't accept it. When they were saying "one nation under God," I thought they were saying "one Asian under dog." There was also the whole question of why we had to recite the Pledge of Allegiance every morning in school in the first place. Did they actually think that second-graders would defect to the Soviet Union overnight if we didn't renew that pledge every day?

And then there are all the travesties involving the founding fathers, who are usually portrayed by the Christian right as a bunch of born-again members of the Christian Coalition, even though they were mostly deists. They were exactly what many people today would call "godless atheists"—like John Adams, who described the Judeo-Christian tradition as "the bloodiest religion that ever existed" or Ethan Allen (the revolutionary hero, not the furniture store), who wrote the first anti-Christian text published in America.

It's not just a matter of religion infiltrating patriotism, however. There's also the ongoing attempt in the United States to turn patriotism into a religion.

Every year Congress takes up the issue of whether to amend the Constitution to prevent the "desecration" of the American flag. This gets members into all kinds of trouble when they realize that today you can find the American flag on almost anything: T-shirts, bathing suits, even men's underwear. So they seriously discussed, in the august halls of Congress, whether underwear could be a flag and if it were ruled to be a flag in one state, would it then be a flag in all states—and whether it would then, I suppose, have to be saluted. The way it was going, I almost expected them to eventually get to the vexing issue of whether small lapses in personal hygiene committed by guys wearing the flag underwear would qualify as acts of desecration.

Not only have religion and patriotism been merging, but religion has been seeping into public policy in the form of "family values." James Dobson, a leading member of the Christian right (now there's an oxymoron for you, like conservative Marxist or airline schedule), publishes a pro-family newsletter in which I was described a couple of years ago as someone who had "devoted her life to the destruction of the American family." This despite the fact that I raised two perfect children and remain in close contact with dozens of relatives around the country—some of whom are kind of annoying, I admit, but I have never tried to destroy any of them.

I think the reason Dobson believes I must be trying to destroy the family is that I'm a feminist—which shows a typical Christian-right understanding of feminism. For example, a couple of years ago, Christian leader Pat Robertson sent out a mailing to the Iowa members of the Christian Coalition in which he explained feminism for them. He explained that the goals of feminism are to get women to (1) leave their husbands, (2) kill their children, (3) overthrow capitalism, (4) become lesbians, and (5) practice witchcraft. This is a very exhausting agenda. My question then is, if we're so good at witchcraft, why hasn't Pat Robertson turned into a little green frog yet? We'll have to work on our spells.

For the record, feminists have not tried to "destroy the family." We just thought the family was such a good idea that men might want to get involved in it, too. And these are not partisan issues anymore. The Democrats today have been as big on family values and religion as have the Republicans. For example, President Bill Clinton signed the welfare reform bill in 1996, which effectively ended this nation's obligation to the poorest of the poor. At the time he signed it, Monica Lewinsky was working in the White House and Dick Morris, the presidential aide who pushed hardest for welfare reform, was embroiled in a relationship with a Washington prostitute. But the interesting thing is that the welfare reform bill, among many ingeniously sadistic measures, provides money to bring abstinence education to unmarried poor women. Why waste that abstinence education on the poor? There are so many sites in Washington where it could be very effectively applied.

The reason why the constant linkage of God, family, and flag is particularly upsetting to me has to do with the history of my own family. I am a fourth-generation atheist. My ancestors were not members of the so-called liberal elite—so hated by our current conservative elite. They were miners and railroad workers and farmers and farm workers. Once they had been religious people, many of them Catholics.

The story of how my family became irreligious begins with my great-grandmother, a Montana farmer named Mamie O'Laughlin. When her father was dying, she sent for a priest. The priest didn't want to be bothered and sent back a message saying he would come only if he were paid a fee of $25, a huge sum in those days and way beyond the means of my great-grandmother. So her father died without the consolation of the sacrament and that was the end of religion for Mamie O'Laughlin.

A couple of years after her father died, she herself lay dying in childbirth at the age of thirty-one. This time a priest showed up, without being called, to administer last rites to her. But Mamie had never forgiven the church. So when the priest placed the cross on her chest, she sat up and, with her last burst of strength, threw it across the room. Then she lay back and died.

This is what I was told as a child to explain why my family had been atheists going way back, and had become atheists without the benefit of any higher education. But as I learned later, my family members were hardly the only blue-collar atheists in the United States, and certainly not the only ones in Butte, Montana, where my grandparents lived and I was born.

What I learned through my own reading later was that there is a vast and largely forgotten tradition of working-class American atheism, usually called freethought in the nineteenth century. At one time there were dozens of freethought newspapers published throughout the United States. In the Northeast, the freethought newspaper movement was linked to the working men's movement of the early 1800s, which was a progenitor of the trade union movement. In the West it flourished among miners and other low-paid working people who were drawn to the Wobblies and other unions at the early part of this century.

These were poor people whose distrust of priests and ministers was part and parcel of their hatred of bosses and bankers. Their ethos was, put briefly: think for yourself, because those who offer to do your thinking for you are usually planning to get hold of your wallet. This is the family tradition I came out of and which I'm proud to claim as my own.

When I mention this I sometimes get funny looks—like I must be some kind of morally depraved degenerate. This is because the common religionist view is that religion is the only possible source of morality, that there is no point in doing good unless you're going to be rewarded for it in the afterlife.

But that's not how it worked in my family. One bizarre but still meaningful-to-me example is my great-grandfather John Howes. His earliest rebellion against religion—I'm not totally proud to admit—was that he urinated in the holy water before Easter service when he was a boy in Canada and was thus involuntarily ejected from the church. Later he moved to Butte, and the story is told that, after working in the copper mines for many years and saving his money, he finally had enough to achieve his dream of getting out of the mines and buying a small farm. So he hitched up his wagon and started driving out of town. And there he came across—hitchhiking, I guess—an Indian woman, who had no money at all, and her child. So John Howes gave her all his money and turned around and went back to Butte to the mines.

I can't attribute any fancy existential philosophy to my great-granddad, but I think the idea was, if there is no God or no evidence of God and certainly no evidence of a very morally engaged God, then whatever has to be done has to be done by us. This is how I was raised and how my children were raised. I felt very deeply affirmed a few years ago when somebody sent me a story about a certain wise old rabbi who advised that, if you ever really need help, go to an atheist—because an atheist isn't going to wait around for God to get the job done.

And that is the philosophical basis of my own social activism. God, if there is one, has never shown a great interest in stopping wars, ending patriarchy, feeding the hungry, curing the sick, or so many other urgent tasks, which is why we have to do those things ourselves. If there isn't a God to care for us, then we have to care for each other.

As a social activist I have come to know and respect many religious traditions and many religious people. I like the fierce old prophets of the Old Testament, railing against the rich and the mighty. I admire the transcendent philosophy of Buddhism, which, I should point out, is completely nontheistic. And I'm a great fan of that inveterate troublemaker, permanent vagrant, and socialist revolutionary, Jesus Christ.

In fact, sometimes I think it would be great if the United States were a "Christian nation," assuming anyone could remember what Christianity originally meant. Originally, it was not a program for persecuting gays, poor people, abortionists, and teachers of evolution. It was a program for the abolition of militarism and for the radical redistribution of wealth.

It seems to me I've spent a lot of time in the past few years speaking to bona fide Christians about what their religion was originally about. I talked to them about Jesus' encounter with the wealthy young fellow who said, "I've obeyed all the laws; am I going to get into heaven?" and Jesus said, "No, you have to give away everything you have to the poor; then you might have a chance." And so on and so forth.

It's a sad day, I think, for Christianity—or maybe a great day for secular humanism—when a fourth-generation atheist has to remind Christians what their religion really says. As one of my favorite T-shirts pleads, "Jesus Christ, protect me from your followers."

In many ways I've often thought atheists would probably fit in better in this very religious society if we adopted some sort of organized religion—even if it were just that innocuous way of getting through Sunday mornings, like Unitarianism. After all, you can't really hope to get elected to public office if you're openly atheist. Even the Boy Scouts don't want us; that's been made clear. George Bush said he didn't believe an atheist could be a real American. So I know plenty of closet atheists and agnostics who go to church and go along with it and mouth the words just so they can be "part of the community, too," as they put it.

Well I'm happy to be part of the atheist community. Despite all my respect for the liberation theologists and the Buddhist monks and the Christian peace activists and so forth, there's no way I could sign on to one of those religions. And not just because of my own irrepressible skepticism. In my case there's another reason why I have to remain a practicing atheist, and that's family values.

STUDY QUESTIONS

1. Ehrenreich uses humor to make many of her points, but there is a serious question lurking in her question regarding the difference between cults and religion. What point is she making?

2. Ehrenreich pokes fun at the alleged connection between religion, patriotism, and family values. Are there non-religious reasons to make sacrifices for one's country or family?

3. Ehrenreich writes that the way of thinking that encouraged atheism in the 19th and early 20th centuries was "think for yourself, because those who offer to do your thinking for you are usually planning to get hold of your wallet." What assumptions about social reality support this way of thinking?

4. What do the actions of John Howes, Ehrenreich's great-grandfather, illustrate about morality?

5. What, does Ehrenreich imply, is the basis of morality? On this view, why would people sacrifice their own interests to support a larger purpose?

INTERVENTIONS: IS OBEDIENCE TO GOD COMPATIBLE WITH MAKING MY OWN DECISIONS?

Moral autonomy (or moral freedom) refers to our capacity to choose the moral beliefs we live by. The claim that we are not genuine moral agents unless we choose our moral beliefs and principles has been a central tenet of our philosophical tradition. The intuitive idea supporting this view is that if I were to follow a moral command regardless of what that command requires me to do and regardless of what my conscience requires me to do, I would not be functioning as an independent human being.

Many people find moral clarity and stability in a religiously based ethic. The problem is that moral actions grounded in God's commands seem in conflict with moral autonomy. According to many religious doctrines, to properly worship God is to obey God's commands. But in what sense can an action be autonomous if it is merely a matter of obedience? Doing what God wants because God wants it is not the same as thinking for yourself or acting on your own.

Much of the conflict in society between secular and religious concerns is a product of this tension between our desire for moral freedom and our desire for moral stability. However, whether there is genuine conflict between moral autonomy and religious ethics depends on how we understand the idea of moral autonomy.

If we interpret autonomy to mean self-sufficiency then autonomy is clearly incompatible with the authority of religious commandments. To be self-sufficient means that I must not look outside myself for ultimate authority on moral questions. Thus God, tradition, society, moral exemplars, or other authorities cannot provide the ultimate warrant for moral judgment if autonomy is to be achieved.

Many philosophical arguments have been offered for such a position. The most influential, introduced by the eighteenth-century philosopher Immanuel Kant and articulated by contemporary philosophers such as John Rawls, is the view that such external authorities corrupt our moral reasoning by introducing into our deliberations biases and prejudices based on emotion and desire. Instead, each person is to rely on her inherent human ability to reason impartially when making moral judgments. This is incompatible with arguments based on religion, which represent only particular, sectarian, religious viewpoints rather than an objective point of view.

However, this version of moral autonomy may not be coherent. In what sense am I "living life from the inside" if I must reason from a standpoint that ignores my inclination to care about certain things and not others? Responding to the needs of others around us, especially loved ones, simply because it is what they want is an essential component of a meaningful life. Yet, moral autonomy as self-sufficient independence precludes such a motive for one's actions. Furthermore, in many areas of life, it is necessary to accept the authority of the judgments of others. We routinely accept the authority of doctors, scientists, and teachers because we are often not in a position to independently assess their claims. Yet, such reliance on authority does not necessarily undermine our autonomy. Why should reliance on religious authorities regarding ethical matters be different?

Autonomy understood as self-direction is friendlier toward the role of religious authorities if beliefs are the product of sufficient critical reflection. In order to satisfy the conditions for self-direction we need only critically reflect on our actions to make sure they can be endorsed from the point of view of our deepest values, with some endorsement of the process through which those values were acquired. (See p. 130, "Interventions," for a more detailed account of self-direction.) If someone's deepest values are religious, autonomy understood as self-direction appears to be compatible with religious ethics.

The important point here is that, when the conditions for self-direction are satisfied, the agent's active, informed deliberation in part explains the actions that follow from her deliberation. Religious influences must not fully determine one's beliefs and judgments. Thus, much will depend on the nature of the religious influences. If proper worship requires unquestioning obedience to God's commands, then deliberation is not playing a substantive role and autonomy is undermined.

It is important to note that autonomy would be undermined even if a person had chosen freely to submit, unreflectively, to God's commands. To see this, an analogy may be helpful. Suppose an able-bodied mother with time on her hands were to demand of her adult daughter that she perform all the mother's household chores without compensation. If the daughter were to claim she is autonomous because she freely decided to submit to her mother's demands with unquestioning obedience, we would question whether the daughter understands her situation or the meaning of the word "autonomy." Similarly, only religious perspectives that permit some degree of independent evaluation of moral claims are compatible with self-direction.

Yet, the problems with self-direction discussed in "Interventions," p. 130, arise in this context as well. In social contexts where alternative religious perspectives are not permitted or are treated with contempt, are the resources for deliberation sufficient to guarantee self-directedness? At what point does religious education become religious indoctrination, thus undermining the capacity for independent thought? As I noted in "Interventions," p. 130, the ability to imagine otherwise, as well as the presence of social conditions that provide us with genuine alternatives, are crucial to our capacity for autonomy. Thus, the compatibility of religion and moral autonomy depends on particular approaches to religious education and worship.

VI

GLOBAL CONFLICT

The events of September 11, 2001, pose a variety of moral challenges, but perhaps the most far-reaching implication of the terrorist attacks is that they clarified the degree to which we must place questions about moral values in a global context.

Warnings about a moral crisis are essentially about the prospects of preserving a way of life, elements of which include material prosperity, democracy, personal liberty, and religious and cultural pluralism. In a world where cultural, economic, and political institutions have a global reach, our ability to preserve the values of Western culture depends upon how others perceive these values and the degree to which they constitute shared goals and aspirations. When liberal societies committed to pluralism confront nonliberal societies, these issues are acute. To what degree must liberal societies tolerate the illiberal, and what actions do toleration require? Immigration patterns make this an issue within borders as well as between them.

These issues are too complex to be treated adequately here, but the essays below pose one fundamental question—do Islamic and Western cultures have similar aspirations or are there fundamental, irreconcilable differences between them?

In his 1992 book *The End of History and the Last Man,* political commentator Francis Fukuyama argued that at bottom all human beings aspire to the goods that Western culture offers. Thus, we can expect, in the future, the end of sharp ideological conflicts. The forces of modernization—capitalism, democracy, and science—will continue to expand, mitigating cultural differences between civilizations. In 1993, historian Samuel Huntington wrote an influential article, later expanded to a book, in which he argues that the requirements of identity formation prevent a convergence of worldviews and aspirations. Writing specifically about Muslim conflicts with Western culture, Huntington argued that Muslim identity is, in part, constructed in opposition to Western influence. Thus, we can expect a clash of civilizations that will persist for the foreseeable future. Part of what is at stake in this debate is whether traditional cultures can coexist with the commitment to personal autonomy which is so central to Western culture.

Assumptions regarding shared values drive debates about the morality and effectiveness of military responses to terrorism, foreign policy initiatives, and immigration policy. The prospects for the expansion of democracy and human rights, in this country and abroad, depend upon whether these values are widely shared.

15

The Future of "History": Francis Fukuyama vs. Samuel P. Huntington

Stanley Kurtz

Stanley Kurtz is a research fellow at the Hoover Institution, the author of many articles on contemporary social issues, and a contributing editor at *National Review Online*. Stanley Kurtz summarizes and assesses the arguments in the widely discussed debate between Francis Fukuyama and Samuel Huntington regarding the potential for conflict between Islam and Western culture. Writing from a perspective after the terrorist attacks of September 11, Kurtz argues that understanding the impact of modernization on traditional cultures is essential in assessing the potential for continued conflict.

This is Samuel P. Huntington's moment. The world of cultural and religious strife anticipated by Huntington in his much-discussed (and widely excoriated) book, *The Clash of Civilizations*, has unquestionably arrived. Yet whether we might also someday see an alternative world—the global triumph of democracy envisioned in Francis Fukuyama's brilliant work, *The End of History and the Last Man*—is also a question that seems very much before us as we contemplate what it would mean to "win" the war in which we are engaged. The question of our time may now be whether Huntington's culture clash or Fukuyama's *pax democratica* is the world's most plausible future.

This is a question with policy implications, of course, and both *The Clash of Civilizations* and *The End of History* are, in part, books about policy— what the United States government should do. Ultimately, however, to choose between Fukuyama and Huntington is to articulate a vision of human

From Stanley Kurtz, "The Future of History: Francis Fukuyama vs. Samuel P. Huntington," *Policy Review*, June–July 2002. Reprinted by permission.

social life. What are the mainsprings of human action? How salient is religion as a cultural force? Is democracy the most civilized and natural way of life? Questions like these are at the heart of the contest between Huntington and Fukuyama, and we can take the measure of the concomitant policy disputes only by moving through these larger problems, not around them.

Philosophically and spiritually, *The End of History* and *The Clash of Civilizations* could hardly be more different (although each book can fairly be called "conservative"). Read closely, unexpected areas of convergence emerge. Nonetheless, ultimately, neither Huntington nor Fukuyama tells us what we need to know in order to synthesize their perspectives—or to finally decide between them. The books are at once complementary and irreconcilable. Taken together, they frame our current perplexity. So let us explore the dilemma that is the state of the world at the moment by considering each book in turn.[1]

TEMPLATES OF CONFLICT

Anyone who has followed the war and the debates surrounding it will find something familiar and thought-provoking on nearly every page of *The Clash of Civilizations*. The book often reads as though it had been written this year. It's easy to forget how controversial it was when it appeared. For all the respectful (if often skeptical) attention Huntington's views have garnered from the policy community, his reception within the academy, among liberal opinion makers, and in many overseas capitals has been, and remains, overwhelmingly hostile.

The reason why is that *The Clash of Civilizations* sticks a thumb in the eye of liberalism and multiculturalism alike. For Fukuyama, the mainspring of history is the liberal yearning for equal recognition. Huntington gruffly retorts, "It is human to hate." Humans require identity, and they acquire it, says Huntington, through the enemies they choose. With the collapse of Cold War enmities, new forms of identity will inevitably be constructed upon new patterns of hostility. Differences of religion and culture, says Huntington, will provide the needed template for the clashes to come.

This vision of a civilizational state of nature in which hatred is rife and trust and friendship rare was bound to get a rocky reception in a nation where every other ad or song is about harmony. But Huntington pushes his argument further. Not content to affirm the inevitability of human hatred, or to predict the rise of cultural antagonisms in general, Huntington singles out "the Muslim propensity toward violent conflict" as the most important coming challenge to world peace and American power. "Muslim bellicosity and violence," says Huntington, "are late-twentieth-century facts which neither Muslims nor non-Muslims can deny." Yet until last September, deny they did.

For the post—September 11 reader, watching Huntington demolish President Clinton's contention (SO like the current president's) that the West has no problem with Islam, but only with violent Islamic extremists, is a fascinating bit of reverse *deja vu*: The underlying problem for the West is not Islamic fundamentalism. It is Islam, a different civilization whose people are convinced of the superiority of their culture and are obsessed with the inferiority of their power. The problem for Islam is not the CIA or the U.S. Department of Defense. It is the West, a different civilization whose people are convinced of the universality of their culture.

The litany of Huntington's insults to liberalism does not end there. Whereas Fukuyama is at pains to point out how seldom established democracies take up arms against one another, Huntington insists that promoting democracy and modernization abroad means more war, not less. Electoral competition in non-Western countries, says Huntington, heightens appeals to nationalism and brings belligerent fundamentalists to power, thus increasing international conflict. Social and economic modernization, he adds, uproots societies and thereby spurs traditionalist reaction. But Huntington's deepest assault on liberalism may be his insistence on treating our belief in democracy's global appeal as a characteristic (and characteristically naive) trait of Western culture rather than as a universal truth.

Multiculturalist ideas fare no better at the point of Huntington's sword than do liberal ones. Picking up on Max Weber's classic (but now taboo) thesis, for example, Huntington maintains that cultural factors are responsible for the differential rates at which various societies have modernized. More than that, Huntington launches a frontal assault on the carriers of both democratic and postmodern culture worldwide.

Huntington pokes fun at the educated international elite that favors the spread of democracy and capitalism, needling them by showing just how small a minority they are—culturally marginalized within their own societies, even where they rule. The neo-Marxist carriers of "post-colonial" theory within the academy are a sub-group of this class—highly educated, multicultural migrants, fully at home neither in the West nor in their countries of origin.

The term of art among aficionados of post-colonial theory these days is "hybridity." Over and above its reference to the mixing of cultures, "hybridity" doesn't mean much. Instead of using it to build a systematic theory of cultural interaction, post-colonial critics simply employ the term to undermine claims that coherent and bounded cultures can be usefully defined or analyzed. Pouncing on any indications of cultural mixing, the post-colonialists label these "hybridity" and satisfy themselves thereby that the demon of unbridgeable cultural difference has been slain.

From this perspective, then, Huntington's greatest sin is his cultural "essentialism"—his insistence on dealing with cultures as bounded wholes with defining "essences" instead of as indefinite, interpenetrating hybrids. When Huntington singles out "the Muslim propensity for violent conflict," scholars rarely reproach him openly for cultural bigotry. Instead they deride him for his naive "essentialism"—his "propensity for violent generalization," so to speak. But the post-colonial theorists are only selectively critical of generalization. In fact, their own work depends upon the highly generalized concept of "Orientalism" to discount, at a blow, several hundred years of Western scholarship on the Middle East.

Read in the wake of September 11, it is more than clear that Huntington's book is filled, not with impermissible "essentialism," but with useful generalizations. Again and again, and in so many words, Huntington successfully predicts the future. Repeatedly, Huntington tells us that we're in for a long-term struggle (including periods of intense violence) with the Muslim world. But these generalized predictions are the least of it. Not only is Huntington right, he is right for all the right reasons—and correct in depth and detail as well. The *Clash of Civilizations*, for example, features an extended and still quite useful analysis of the social roots of Islamic fundamentalism.

How did Huntington manage to predict the future so uncannily? He recognized that the future already existed in the present. He acknowledged and explored what others failed to recognize—that America was already engaged in a war of sorts with the Islamic world, even before September 11. And in yet another uncanny moment, Huntington casts his eye eastward and effectively predicts the advent of an "axis of evil"—an alliance of Middle Eastern and East Asian states in opposition to America and the West. He also points to a future in which weapons of mass destruction will act as military equalizers between civilizations in confrontation.

But even this summary does not do justice to the level of detail at which Huntington reflects upon our current dilemma. Here are some developments anticipated and discussed in *The Clash of Civilizations*: the advent of terrorist attacks on core cultural symbols; the emerging importance of the "floating army" originally created by volunteers from many Muslim lands to fight against the Soviets in Afghanistan; the tendency of Muslim fundamentalism to push Russia and the United States more closely together; the key military dynamic of terror versus air power.

Huntington has done remarkably little crowing about all this since September 11. Wisely, he has adopted the most conservative possible interpretation of his own work by maintaining publicly that we have not yet arrived at a full-fledged civilizational clash between the Muslim and Western worlds. That is true, in a sense. Only the coming attack on Iraq will reveal just how completely and forcefully the Arab and Muslim world will line up in opposition to America and the West.

But in large measure, the world is already living out the truth of Huntington's thesis. The very possibility of a definitive, radical, and large-scale mobilization of the Muslim world is already at the center of Western policy calculations. And of course, the threat of such a mobilization explains the entirely sensible decisions of Presidents Clinton and Bush to publicly proclaim that our problem is only with the extremists and has nothing to do with Islam or Islamic society itself.

So Huntington's triumph must be acknowledged. This is not to say, however, that his thesis is free of problems. On the contrary, there are a slew of them. Nor does Huntington's prescience gainsay the possibility that Fukuyama might ultimately be proven right about the global spread of democracy. Before turning to Huntington's troubles, however, let us take stock of Fukuyama's optimistic vision in the light so harshly cast upon it by the present crisis.

FUKUYAMA'S TRADITION PROBLEM—AND OURS

Since September 11, and despite the apparent vindication of Samuel Huntington's prophecies in *The Clash of Civilizations*, Francis Fukuyama has steadfastly maintained that the end of history is nigh. For Fukuyama, the war itself is a tribute to the forces driving fundamentalist reaction in the Islamic world—the forces of modernization. And Fukuyama points out that Islamism is an inherently parochial phenomenon, not a universal ideology that can serve as an authentic rival to democracy. So Fukuyama maintains that, while the revolt against modernity in parts of the Muslim world may briefly slow the spread of democracy and capitalism, it cannot ultimately halt or replace it.

These are important points. We cannot assess them, however, without confronting certain problems in Fukuyama's thought. *The End of History and the Last Man* is constructed around a Hegelian framework that is at once the source of Fukuyama's extraordinary insights and the reason why he seems to have missed or slighted the phenomena at the center of Huntington's work. So it is to the intellectual framework of *The End of History and the Last Man* that we must turn.

Fukuyama's great accomplishment in *The End of History* is to establish that democratic rights and participation are fundamental ends in themselves, not mere epiphenomena of capitalism. Communist dictatorships and capitalist autocracies alike rob human beings of their dignity, and Fukuyama successfully shows how the growing turn toward democracy in both types of society is not simply a demand for wealth but, at the deepest level, an insistence upon equal personal dignity and recognition.

To establish these points, Fukuyama makes use of the philosopher G. W. F. Hegel to revive and reformulate the Anglo-American tradition of liberalism.[2] The liberalism of Hobbes and Locke is founded upon the relatively "low" human goals of self-preservation and the desire for wealth. Hobbes, for example, singles out "vainglory" as the greatest threat to peace. Only by abandoning the wish to be acknowledged as superior to others, says Hobbes, can we escape the war of all against all, thereby attaining both security and prosperity. So in its classic form, liberalism eschews the drive for recognition in favor of the safer, if humbler, pleasures of prosperity and peace.

Yet Fukuyama notices that liberal theory, in grounding itself on security and prosperity, overlooks something fundamental about democracy— namely, the desire for recognition by others of one's freedom and equality as a human being. This desire for recognition has actually been driving the worldwide democratic revolution. So rather than simply reject the quest for superiority as dangerous and alien, Fukuyama makes use of Hegel to show how democracy actually tames the human craving for superiority by transforming it into a thirst for equal recognition.

This is what Hegel's famous account of the master and slave is all about. In Hegel's reconstruction of the prototypical human situation, a master subdues a slave through his willingness to risk his life in a battle for pure prestige. The slave, valuing life above prestige, submits to the master and acknowledges his conqueror's superiority. Yet the master's seeming triumph turns out to be hollow since the recognition obtained from a slave is necessarily inferior in quality. Through a series of transformations, both the master and the slave eventually discover that only formal and mutual recognition of their equal dignity achieves authentic self-respect for each.

Fukuyama's extraordinary accomplishment is to give life to Hegel's abstract account by using it to illuminate the dynamics of the global democratic revolution. Unfortunately, however, while Hegel's story brilliantly illuminates the dynamics of decrepit communist dictatorships, the parable nonetheless falls flat as an account of life in other large areas of the world: those known as "traditional" societies. Fukuyama treats traditional societies as simple variants of slave-states or dictatorships, where recognition is granted to a supreme leader or a small ruling class, and the humanity of the masses is denied. Yet that is far too simple an account of the actual distribution of recognition in traditional societies. Nor can the problem be solved, as Fukuyama sometimes tries to do, by classifying traditional societies as stuck in some transitional stage of "irrational" recognition on the pathway toward the rational endpoint of modern democracy.

Fukuyama's impressive reworking of liberal "state of nature" teachings by way of Hegel suffers from a problem common to such theories. It assumes what is to be proven, in his case by constructing an imaginary history that, unlike actual history, takes the individual as the fundamental unit of society. In the actual history of human societies, it is far too simple to say either that the individual is denied recognition by his masters or that he gains recognition at the expense of his rulers. On the contrary, in most traditional societies, the interests of individuals are inextricably intermingled in the groups with which they identify. Individual recognition is a function of the honor both of the larger group and of leaders of that group. By devising an imaginary state of nature in which the subjects are a single master and a single slave, and by treating more complex social structures of recognition as mere elaborations of this fictitious individualist construction, Hegel elides the fundamental question— the extent to which human beings are individual subjects in the first place.

Throughout the bulk of *The End of History*, Fukuyama writes as though recognition in traditional societies was effectively denied to the great mass of people. Yet late in the book, when he is probing the vulnerabilities of democracy, Fukuyama abruptly reverses ground and for the first time acknowledges that mutual recognition in traditional societies may actually be more widely distributed than in modernity. Recognition in such societies, says Fukuyama, may not be equal in the modern sense, but in small, pre-industrial agricultural communities, life is built upon small and stable social groups knit together by ties of kinship, work, and religion. In that sense, mutual recognition in such societies may actually be more pervasive and satisfying than in our own.

That isolated passage notwithstanding, Fukuyama never grasps the principle of hierarchy that structures the distribution of recognition in traditional societies. Traditional hierarchies are not so much master-slave relationships as they are by-products of group solidarity. Real solidarity is impossible without a leader who embodies the honor and interests of the group. The patriarchs who rule families, tribes, and states in traditional societies are bound by webs of responsibility and customary obligation to their subjects, just as those subjects gain much from the reputation and success of the groups (and thus the leaders) with which they identify.

Most traditional religious and kinship systems are mechanisms for distributing recognition within hierarchy—again, meaning "hierarchy" not in the simple sense of a master's domination of a slave, but in the sense of a leader as the embodiment of a larger and mutually dependent group. Not coincidentally, as with Fukuyama's Hegelianism, Marx's own adaptation of Hegel also stumbles on the problem of religion and traditional societies. Precisely because it is grounded on an underlying master-slave dynamic rather than on solidarity-based hierarchies, Marx's class analysis has never managed to unravel the secrets of religion or family life in traditional societies. And of course, it is upon the recrudescence of religion in kin-based societies that Huntington rests his analysis in *The Clash of Civilizations*.

True, Marx and Fukuyama alike are seemingly able to handle these problems by classifying traditional solidarities as "transitional" forms and by dismissing them as false consciousness. Yet, in the end, neither Fukuyama nor Marx is able to turn Hegelian categories to the task of producing a truly nuanced analysis of traditional solidarities.

To put it another way, Fukuyama portrays the structure of the desire for recognition as the willingness to risk one's life in a battle for pure prestige—the battle of a master to conquer and rule a slave. Yet this is only a single version of the human desire for recognition, and not the most fundamental. Historically, the desire for recognition has been structured not simply by the quest for individual mastery, but by the willingness to sacrifice one's life in a battle for the prestige of one's group. Following Hegel, Fukuyama brilliantly traces the path from dictator to democrat—from the quest for individual mastery to the solution of equal mutual recognition. What's left out is the way of the suicide bomber and of the solidarities that the suicide bomber embodies and defends. In actual—rather than fanciful—human history, self-sacrifice on behalf of group prestige is at least as fundamental as personal risk for the sake of individual domination.

Fukuyama also presents yet another fascinating account of democratic evolution. In contrast to the foregoing, more "spiritual," story, the other one is an economic argument, grounded on the mechanism of modern natural science. Simply put, scientific progress yields economic, technological, and especially military power. In order to harness that power and thereby avoid subjugation by other states, traditional societies have no choice, Fukuyama says, but to modernize economically. Yet economic modernization invariably disrupts traditional social forms and, in time, creates a society of individuals—independent subjects who are bound at some point to demand the equal forms of recognition embodied in democracy. So for Fukuyama, the economic effects of modern natural science dovetail with Hegel's dialectic of recognition to produce an inevitable triumph for democracy.

But what if the mechanism of modern natural science does in fact push us toward a world of democratic individualism, even though (contra Fukuyama) democratic individualism may not necessarily be the only fulfilling, or even the most fulfilling, way of life? In that case, we might expect a certain persistent dissatisfaction to trouble the spirit of democracy. In a sense, Fukuyama takes that dissatisfaction as his subject, as in his extraordinarily insightful application of Nietzsche's "last man" problematic to the malaise of modernity. Indeed, Fukuyama's use of Hegel to dignify and elevate an otherwise "low" and excessively "bourgeoisified" democratic theory is in many ways a response to the dissatisfactions inherent in modern democracy. More than Fukuyama concedes, however, these chronic problems of modernity are tributes to the ongoing power and appeal of traditional solidarities, and explain why history's end has so lately been delayed.

CLASH OF PARADIGMS—AND POLICIES

This is not at all to say that Fukuyama is mostly wrong while Huntington is mostly right. The truth, both trickier and messier, is something that Hunting-

ton and Fukuyama are equally reluctant to allow. Read closely, these two extraordinary books overlap far more than one might think.

Huntington, like Fukuyama, is too wise to entirely ignore the phenomena
that preoccupy his counterpart. For example, Huntington acknowledges the
global power of technological and economic modernization; he simply
stresses the fact that modernization is actually driving the worldwide rise of
fundamentalist reaction. Fukuyama, on the other hand, acknowledges the
importance of reactionary antimodernism; he simply notes that the cultural
reaction is testimony to the power and reach of the modernizing process.

Both are right, of course, and each is wise enough to touch lightly upon
the truth in his counterpart's assertion. Yet each is also reluctant to alter his
theory according to the other's insights. This is because both Huntington and
Fukuyama have some very specific policy goals in mind. Fukuyama wants to
see America actively promote democracy abroad. Huntington, on the other
hand, ever the realist, warns about the potentially disastrous effects of an arrogant and naive democratic imperialism. Were Huntington to treat the modernization process as something other than the mere occasion for cultural reaction, or were Fukuyama to explore the deeper social and spiritual roots of
Third World fundamentalism, these clashing but relatively clear and consistent policy prescriptions would each be called into question.

At one point in *The End of History*, Fukuyama at least acknowledges that
the global advent of capitalism and democracy might well leave room for the
persistence of cultural differences on the "sub-political" level (for example,
family life, kinship structure, religion). Yet Fukuyama never really integrates
that insight into his Hegelian account—never develops a convincing way of
looking at cultural difference in his own theoretical terms. Nor does
Fukuyama grant that the persistence of certain traditional social forms in,
say, capitalist East Asia could be a significant spur to conflict within a future
international system dominated by capitalist democracies. And of course,
Fukuyama doesn't consider that the partial retention of traditional social
forms in East Asia might suggest that a still more tenacious cultural resistance
to capitalism and modernity might be conceivable in a region like the Middle East (a region about which Fukuyama has relatively little to say in *The
End of History*).

By the same token, while Huntington stresses the disruptive effects of
modernity on traditional social forms, he never considers that a nativist or
fundamentalist response might ultimately fail to reverse that disruption. Nor
does Huntington consider that the very fact of his being right about the clash
of civilizations might actually help to push the international system in
Fukuyama's direction. Arguably, in fact, that is what we are witnessing right
now.

For all of his eerily prescient statements in *The Clash of Civilizations*, there
are a number of discordant declarations. In accordance with his cultural-
regional realism, for example, Huntington is at pains to stress that "no country,

including the United States, has global security interests." In the wake of September 11, with American security interests and power rapidly expanding across the globe, that statement is almost embarrassingly false. A major theme of Huntington's book, in fact, is the coming decline of American power, which will inevitably be reined in by the demographic growth of the Muslim world and the economic development of East Asia. Huntington will not likely prove entirely wrong on that score in the long run, yet certainly one plausible effect of the war on terror is a significant extension of American power across the globe in the short and medium term.

Huntington notes that the Islamic resurgence in the Middle East has given the Muslim world renewed confidence in itself, confidence spurred on by the defeat of a world power like the Soviets in Afghanistan. Of course, he was right about renewed Islamic confidence—so right that he might now be proven wrong by the American response to Islamic overreach. With the Taliban defeated, Osama bin Laden taken down a notch or two, and perhaps the ousting of Saddam Hussein and the installation of a pro-Western regime in Iraq, can the forces of Islamic reaction remain as confident and ascendant as Huntington once suggested?

Ultimately, therefore, the resolution between Fukuyama and Huntington is still in doubt. Huntington was right about a conflict in the offing between the Middle East and the West. But we still don't know whether that clash is just the beginning of a long-term civilizational stand-off or a stimulus to democracy's and capitalism's final and successful push to establish themselves around the world.

Consider Pakistan, which plays a central role in Huntington's treatment of the Islamic world. Huntington sees Pakistan, because of its role in supplying the Afghan resistance to the Soviets, as a leading power in the Muslim world and a key potential partner in any anti-American alliance between Islam and East Asia. Of course, that all changed after September 11, when President Bush forced Pakistan to fall in with America or be deemed an enemy, after which Pakistan switched sides.

Will the change hold? That is an open question. Certainly President Pervez Musharraf has enjoyed considerable success to date, with relatively few domestic protests erupting against his tilt toward America. Yet the murder of journalist Daniel Pearl and other terrorist incidents make it clear that Musharraf's government will face continued internal pressure from Islamists.

Huntington's model would explain Pakistan's tilt toward America as an attempt by a "secondary" civilizational power to stifle a cultural "fault-line" war that could cut against its own interests. Yet that only begs the question. What is the source of Pakistan's interest in moving toward closer cooperation with the West in the first place? I think Fukuyama explains this better than Huntington. The military and economic advantages of being part of the Western camp are the carrots held out by President Bush to President Musharraf. Ultimately, therefore, it is Fukuyama's scientific-economic mechanism of modernization that has enabled the United States to pry Pakistan loose from its erstwhile Islamist allies.

Yet the new pattern of alliance is clearly unstable. Musharraf, as noted, is still under internal pressure from Islamists, and an American attack on Iraq may yet produce a change of mood within Pakistan, just as fighting between Israelis and Palestinians has put pressure on moderate Arab leaders to cut their ties with Israel. And even if Pakistan's American alliance holds, the nation may turn into what Huntington calls a "torn country"—a society unable to resolve the contradiction between its global economic and security interests and its cultural center of gravity. Nor is a future American tilt toward India inconceivable. A civilizational alliance between victims of Islamic terror could put further pressure on Pakistan's pro-Western stance. In short, both Huntington and Fukuyama are right, although we cannot yet know in what measure. In the real world, the policy prescriptions that flow so neatly from their crisply consistent theoretical frameworks are profoundly muddled.

Realist restraint or democratic missionizing? Which shall it be? We have to be prepared for both, I believe. The coming years will be a time of reluctant imperialism for the United States. Inevitably, our victories in the war against terror will give us greater and greater power within the Muslim world. We exercise that power now in Afghanistan; soon we are likely to hold it in Iraq. Should our policy be to spread the gospel of democracy to these newly conquered Muslim lands, or should we eschew cultural arrogance and thereby escape the danger of a traditionalist reaction? That is a question that will be answered only in the doing. We have to be ready to experiment, to learn from our failures, and to quickly shift gears if need be. When it comes to the question of exporting democracy to the non-Western world, a foolish consistency will be the hobgoblin of small policy.

Even in their own terms, we can see certain paradoxes and contradictions built into both Fukuyama's and Huntington's policy recommendations. Maybe more than he knows, Fukuyama really does succeed in casting Hobbes aside—and not just on the question of liberalism's internal rationale. Fukuyama's commitment to the global spread of democracy may well dignify liberalism by restoring to it a certain nobility of spirit. Yet at a cost, for all we need do is recall Hobbes's warning that nothing is more disruptive to peace within a state of nature than vainglory. In effect, Huntington's complaint about Fukuyama's foreign policy is borrowed from Hobbes. If the world is a state of nature on a grand scale, then surely a foreign policy governed by a "vainglorious" missionizing spirit rather than a careful calculation of national (and civilizational) interest promises dangerous war and strife.

Yet Huntington's policy prescriptions are also rent by paradox. Huntington wants the West to defend its democratic traditions as a specifically Western cultural heritage, not as magical solutions to the problems of the world.

The trouble, one might say, is that it's not in our culture to see our culture as simply a culture. Huntington's anti-universalist realism, even insofar as it may be correct, will always be "counter-cultural" policy in an inherently missionizing Western democracy.

MODERNIZATION: THE MISSING LINK?

In the end, the most fundamental issue separating Fukuyama and Huntington receives only very passing treatment from either thinker. Ultimately, it is impossible to adjudicate the Fukuyama–Huntington debate without a well-grounded theory of modernization. In the absence of a clear conception of how, why, and when modernization blends, or fails to blend, with particular social forms, there is simply no basis for making decisions about the relative long-term prescience of either man. And while both Huntington and Fukuyama touch on these underlying social-structural questions, neither explores them in anything like systematic fashion.

As noted, Huntington does put forward a very nice account of the social roots of Islamic fundamentalism. Yet that account only begs the question of the long-term effects of modernization. Huntington rightly notes that the tendency of modernization to break traditional social bonds has actually stimulated an identity-preserving return to Islam. Yet if the forces of modernization continue to disrupt the older social solidarities, a long-term cultural shift toward individualism is entirely conceivable, and that is a possibility Huntington does not entertain. In an effort to distinguish between modernization and Westernization, Huntington rightly points out that the West's cultural individualism predates modernity and cannot be treated as entirely synonymous with it. Yet that does not preclude the possibility that the long-term effect of technological and economic modernization might be to dissolve traditional social forms and thereby generate exactly the sort of cultural individualism long familiar to us in the West.

This is precisely Fukuyama's claim, yet he does not substantiate it so much as assume it. Fukuyama does show how urbanization and bureaucratization served to undercut traditional social ties in the West, thereby leading to an individualist world of capitalism and democracy. Unfortunately, he simply presumes that this pattern will hold for the non-Western world. That is too simple. Western feudalism, for example, was structured around localized patron-client relationships and tied to agricultural production. Feudalism was therefore effectively broken when an uprooted peasantry flooded the towns. Dense systems of kinship, however, were never critical to the Western social system. In most of the non-Western world, on the other hand, kinship is at the core of traditional social structure, and kinship ties have proven highly portable and adaptable to urban environments. The urban shanty towns of

Cairo and Istanbul (filled with migrant peasants soon to become the foot soldiers of Islamism) are still very much structured by traditional kinship bonds.

In Cairo, for example, the resources, time, and energy that Westerners channel into developing a business, a unique career, or a civic association are instead devoted to complex marriage negotiations. The family alliances built through such marriages stand as the surest security against poverty and the helplessness of aging, even as those same connections feed the endemic corruption that hampers the development of capitalism and bureaucratic competence in Muslim lands.

Likewise, the shanty towns of Istanbul have in many respects recreated village life, except for the fact that in the more Islamic sectors, women's observance of proper Islamic dress is more strict than in the countryside.

Even regional ties remain strong among peasant immigrants in Istanbul, who often travel to other sectors of the city just to arrange marriages for their children with immigrants from their old localities—people with whom they already have ties of kinship.

When it comes to modernization, these traditional social forms can cut in different directions. On the one hand, the persistence of arranged marriage and other kinship practices has clearly helped to fuel the rise of Islamism, which is in many respects an attempt to protect traditional family forms from the "acid of modernity." On the other hand, kinship connections have sometimes proven adaptable to capitalism. Many women in the poorer quarters of Istanbul, for example, do piecework for businesses that export clothing to Europe. The piecework ateliers are organized around kinship connections, real or fictive. Yet, as in Egypt, that very same kinship ethos impedes the efficiency of Turkish bureaucracy. Without a link, real or fictive, through your kinship network, it can take up to six years in many sections of Istanbul just to get a phone connected. Much of the piecework activity, moreover, is hidden from the state, and so represents a serious tax loss to the government.

So while Fukuyama is correct to say that the power that emerges from economic and technological development exerts a constant pressure on non-Western states to modernize, the actual nature and extent of the social changes that flow from, say, urbanization are not predictable from that fact. Some Third World countries have barely begun to modernize. Others, like Turkey and Japan, nicely bear out Fukuyama's model of non-Western states drawn into the web of modernization by the need to maintain military-economic parity with the West. Yet Japan retains much of its traditional social structure, while Turkey is still very much what Huntington calls a "torn country."

The future, therefore, is anyone's guess. In contrast to Fukuyama's expectations of a quick and easy link between economic and technological modernization, urbanization, and cultural individualism, a traditional kinship structure has reconstituted itself at the center of the great urban migration that is driving the spread of Islamism. Yet that same traditional structure is under siege from the forces of modernity—a siege that at once provokes the fundamentalist reaction and threatens, over the long term, to undercut that reaction. Will we ultimately see a slow but complete dissolution of traditional Muslim social forms and the emergence of something recognizably modern and even "Western" in the Islamic world, or will we see instead some complex social blend—and with what political-cultural consequences? No one knows the answers to these questions, and neither Fukuyama nor Huntington comes close to giving us the tools we need to puzzle out the long-term problem.

Maybe with time, for example, the "acid of modernity" will dissolve Turkey's traditional social structure and the modernizers will win out. Or maybe the piecework ateliers of Turkey will develop into a working blend of capitalism and the traditional social structure. Or will the kinship structure's formidable interference with bureaucratic and capitalist efficacy tell the tale in the end? To begin to answer the question, we need detailed case studies and hard analyses of the social and economic riddles at the heart of the urbanizing Islamic world (and the Third World more generally). At the moment, however, we have too little in the way of either data or theory to make an informed decision. That, in the end, is why neither Huntington, nor Fukuyama, nor anyone else at the moment can plausibly resolve the issue.

The question of time, moreover, is a central, though hidden, difficulty in the Huntington-Fukuyama debate. There is a tension in Fukuyama's account between his long-term prediction of the triumph of capitalism and democracy and his near-term critique of foreign-policy "realism." When democracy swiftly spreads, Fukuyama can take credit for having predicted the change. On the other hand, when Huntingtonian civilizational clashes emerge to complicate the picture, Fukuyama can fall back on his confidence in the eventual triumph of democracy and remind us that he never said that universal democratization would come swiftly or easily, only that democracy is the sole remaining political ideology with universal potential. Between the short- and long-term prediction, there is a fair amount of wiggle room.

In response to Huntington's apparent vindication by the events of September 11 and their aftermath, Fukuyama has written, "Modernity is a very powerful freight train that will not be derailed by recent events." One wants to know the precise speed at which this powerful train is traveling. It hardly seems a stretch to say that the current dynamic of civilizational strife could last for decades, even if a worldwide triumph of democracy and capitalism is eventually in the cards. Huntington explicitly notes that his proposed foreign policy paradigm will likely be every bit as time-limited as was the Cold War paradigm that preceded it. So conceivably, Fukuyama could be correct about the long term, while Huntington could nonetheless be correct about the next several decades. Yet that would leave Fukuyama's policy proposals in tatters.

In fact, however, our present global dilemma borrows liberally from both *The Clash of Civilizations* and *The End of History*. Policy prescriptions will therefore have to be cribbed unsystematically, and on the fly, from Huntington and Fukuyama alike. Ultimately, this is because both thinkers are on to something fundamental about human social life. There is no doubt that, worldwide, we continue to live out the process of social and cultural democratization and individualization described most brilliantly by Tocqueville more than a century and a half ago.

Yet it is nonetheless the case that the war between modern democracy and traditional society may never quite come to an end—even if, at a given moment, democracy appears triumphant. This is because (notwithstanding assorted "state of nature" fantasies), until relatively recent times, human societies have always assigned more weight to the collective than to the individual. The mechanism of modern natural science may lately have uprooted those traditional social forms and created a novel human ideal, but the chronic disenchantment at the heart of modernity bespeaks a yearning for the firm direction, shared identity, and common purpose that the old hierarchical collectivities used to provide.

In a sense, Fukuyama's charge to spread democracy around the globe is a very modern attempt to restore that feeling of collective purpose. Yet nothing entirely modern can fully replace the satisfactions of traditional religious and family life. That is why, even within triumphant capitalism and democracy, our domestic culture war lurches on inconclusively. That culture war is simply an internal manifestation of the incomplete and unnatural character of modernity. And even if modernity's external enemies are someday vanquished, its internal upheavals and doubts will remain, forever unresolved and irresolvable.

Of course traditional societies have more than their fair share of social and psychological costs, and especially in a modernizing environment those costs can be profound indeed. Nonetheless, we are, all of us, perpetually suspended between tradition and modernity, neither of which will quite do, yet one of which now has the weight of science and technology (and therefore of "history") on its side. The only good solution to this dilemma is a blend, in the best Tocquevillian sense, of the old and the new. Different societies will find (or fail to find) that blend in different ways and at different rates. Perhaps someday, the peoples of the world will all be seeking to strike the balance of modernity and tradition within a broadly liberal democratic framework. Until that day, however, the end of history and the clash of civilizations will remain perplexing and simultaneous truths, the measure of which we shall be compelled to take without benefit of overarching formula or guide.

STUDY QUESTIONS

1. What is Huntington's main thesis about identity formation? What are the implications of this thesis on the prospects for peaceful co-existence?
2. What is cultural essentialism and why is Huntington often accused of it?
3. What evidence does Kurtz present supporting Huntington's claims?
4. What is Fukuyama's main thesis regarding identity formation when influenced by democracy?
5. According to Kurtz, why do traditional societies pose a problem for Fukuyama's thesis? Explain.
6. How would you answer the question that Kurtz in his commentary on Fukuyama poses? Is your deepest desire a desire for recognition as a free and equal human being, or is it recognition as a member of a family or religious tradition? Or is there some other desire even more fundamental?
7. According to Fukuyama what happens to traditional societies when they are exposed to science and capitalism? How do traditional societies react to these changes?
8. If Fukuyama is right, what policy implications follow? If Huntington is right, what policy implications follow?
9. Briefly characterize Kurtz's objections to both Huntington and Fukuyama.
10. Kurtz claims that the main issue dividing Huntington and Fukuyama is the issue of modernization. What does he mean by this?
11. What does Kurtz mean when he says that modernity is incomplete and unnatural? If this is the case, what implication does it have for the Huntington/Fukuyama debate?

NOTES

1. Huntington first put forward his thesis in an essay, "The Clash of Civilizations," in *Foreign Affairs* (Summer 1993). He published his book-length elaboration, *The Clash of Civilizations and the Remaking of World Order*, in 1996. A paperback edition is available from Touchstone Books. Fukuyama likewise first advanced his argument as an essay, "The End of History?" in the *National Interest* (Summer 1989). His book appeared in 1992 as *The End of History and the Last Man*. It is available in paperback from Avon Books.

2. It is important to note that rather than directly adapting Hegel, Fukuyama is actually drawing on the interpretation of Hegel articulated by the Marxist philosopher Alexandre Kojeve. In fact, Fukuyama makes a point of instructing the reader that,

when he says "Hegel," he is actually making reference to a sort of composite philosopher who might be called "Hegel-Kojeve." Here, too, I will speak of Hegel when "Hegel-Kojeve" is actually at issue. It will emerge, in fact, that some of the difficulties I point to in "Hegel" below may more appropriately be laid at the door of Kojeve or at Fukuyama's reading of Hegel-Kojeve—perhaps a third philosopher, Hegel-Kojeve-Fukuyama.

16

The Clash of Ignorance

Edward W. Said

Edward W. Said was University Professor of English and Comparative Literature at Columbia University. The author of many books of literary criticism,
his writing on a variety of contemporary issues also appeared regularly in *The
Nation*, London's *Guardian, Le Monde Diplomatique,* and the Arab-language
daily *al-Hayat*. Professor Said died in September 2003. Said argues that both
Huntington and Fukuyama are mistaken. Islamic culture is pluralistic, characterized by many competing ideologies like most other modern cultures,
and already deeply involved in Western culture. Thus, predictions of further
conflict depend upon how we approach the current crisis.

Samuel Huntington's article "The Clash of Civilizations?" appeared in the
Summer 1993 issue of *Foreign Affairs*, where it immediately attracted a surprising amount of attention and reaction. Because the article was intended to
supply Americans with an original thesis about "a new phase" in world politics after the end of the Cold War, Huntington's terms of argument seemed
compellingly large, bold, even visionary. He very clearly had his eye on rivals in the policy-making ranks, theorists such as Francis Fukuyama and his
"end of history" ideas, as well as the legions who had celebrated the onset of
globalism, tribalism, and the dissipation of the state. But they, he allowed,
had understood only some aspects of this new period. He was about to announce the "crucial, indeed a central, aspect" of what "global politics is likely
to be in the coming years." Unhesitatingly he pressed on:

> It is my hypothesis that the fundamental source of conflict in this new world will
> not be primarily ideological or primarily economic. The great divisions among

Reprinted with permission from the October 22, 2001, issue of *The Nation*.

humankind and the dominating source of conflict will be cultural. Nation states will remain the most powerful actors in world affairs, but the principal conflicts of global politics will occur between nations and groups of different civilizations. The clash of civilizations will dominate global politics. The fault lines between civilizations will be the battle lines of the future.

Most of the argument in the pages that followed relied on a vague notion of something Huntington called "civilization identity" and "the interactions among seven or eight [*sic*] major civilizations," of which the conflict between two of them, Islam and the West, gets the lion's share of his attention. In this belligerent kind of thought, he relies heavily on a 1990 article by the veteran Orientalist Bernard Lewis, whose ideological colors are manifest in its title, "The Roots of Muslim Rage." In both articles, the personification of enormous entities called "the West" and "Islam" is recklessly affirmed, as if hugely complicated matters like identity and culture existed in a cartoonlike world where Popeye and Bluto bash each other mercilessly, with one always more virtuous pugilist getting the upper hand over his adversary. Certainly neither Huntington nor Lewis has much time to spare for the internal dynamics and plurality of every civilization, or for the fact that the major contest in most modern cultures concerns the definition or interpretation of each culture, or for the unattractive possibility that a great deal of demagogy and downright ignorance is involved in presuming to speak for a whole religion or civilization. No, the West is the West, and Islam Islam.

The challenge for Western policy-makers, says Huntington, is to make sure that the West gets stronger and fends off all the others, Islam in particular. More troubling is Huntington's assumption that his perspective, which is to survey the entire world from a perch outside all ordinary attachments and hidden loyalties, is the correct one, as if everyone else were scurrying around looking for the answers that he has already found. In fact, Huntington is an ideologist, someone who wants to make "civilizations" and "identities" into what they are not: shut-down, sealed-off entities that have been purged of the myriad currents and countercurrents that animate human history, and that over centuries have made it possible for that history not only to contain wars of religion and imperial conquest but also to be one of exchange, cross-fertilization, and sharing. This far less visible history is ignored in the rush to highlight the ludicrously compressed and constricted warfare that "the clash of civilizations" argues is the reality. When he published his book by the same title in 1996, Huntington tried to give his argument a little more subtlety and many, many more footnotes; all he did, however, was confuse himself and demonstrate what a clumsy writer and inelegant thinker he was.

The basic paradigm of West versus the rest (the Cold War opposition reformulated) remained untouched, and this is what has persisted, often insidiously and implicitly, in discussion since the terrible events of September 11. The carefully planned and horrendous, pathologically motivated suicide attack and mass slaughter by a small group of deranged militants has been turned into proof of Huntington's thesis. Instead of seeing it for what it is— the capture of big ideas (I use the word loosely) by a tiny band of crazed fanatics for criminal purposes—international luminaries from former Pakistani Prime Minister Benazir Bhutto to Italian Prime Minister Silvio Berlusconi have pontificated about Islam's troubles, and in the latter's case have used Huntington's ideas to rant on about the West's superiority, how "we" have Mozart and Michelangelo and they don't. (Berlusconi has since made a half-hearted apology for his insult to "Islam.")

But why not instead see parallels, admittedly less spectacular in their destructiveness, for Osama bin Laden and his followers in cults like the Branch Davidians or the disciples of the Rev. Jim Jones at Guyana or the Japanese Aum Shinrikyo? Even the normally sober British weekly *The Economist*, in its issue of September 22-28, can't resist reaching for the vast generalization, praising Huntington extravagantly for his "cruel and sweeping, but nonetheless acute" observations about Islam. "Today," the journal says with unseemly solemnity, Huntington writes that "the world's billion or so Muslims are 'convinced of the superiority of their culture, and obsessed with the inferiority of their power.'" Did he canvas one hundred Indonesians, two hundred Moroccans, five hundred Egyptians and fifty Bosnians? Even if he did, what sort of sample is that?

Uncountable are the editorials in every American and European newspaper and magazine of note adding to this vocabulary of gigantism and apocalypse, each use of which is plainly designed not to edify but to inflame the reader's indignant passion as a member of the "West," and what we need to do. Churchillian rhetoric is used inappropriately by self-appointed combatants in the West's, and especially America's, war against its haters, despoilers, destroyers, with scant attention to complex histories that defy such reductiveness and have seeped from one territory into another, in the process overriding the boundaries that are supposed to separate us all into divided armed camps.

This is the problem with unedifying labels like Islam and the West: They mislead and confuse the mind, which is trying to make sense of a disorderly reality that won't be pigeonholed or strapped down as easily as all that. I remember interrupting a man who, after a lecture I had given at a West Bank university in 1994, rose from the audience and started to attack my ideas as "Western," as opposed to the strict Islamic ones he espoused. "Why are you wearing a suit and tie?" was the first retort that came to mind. "They're Western too." He sat down with an embarrassed smile on his face, but I recalled the incident when information on the September 11 terrorists started to come in: how they had mastered all the technical details required to inflict their homicidal evil on the World Trade Center, the Pentagon, and the aircraft they had commandeered. Where does one draw the line between "Western" technology and, as Berlusconi declared, "Islam's" inability to be a part of "modernity"?

One cannot easily do so, of course. How finally inadequate are the labels, generalizations and cultural assertions. At some level, for instance, primitive passions and sophisticated know-how converge in ways that give the lie to a fortified boundary not only between "West" and "Islam" but also between past and present, us and them, to say nothing of the very concepts of identity and nationality about which there is unending disagreement and debate. A unilateral decision made to draw lines in the sand, to undertake crusades, to oppose their evil with our good, to extirpate terrorism and, in Paul Wolfowitz's nihilistic vocabulary, to end nations entirely, doesn't make the supposed entities any easier to see; rather, it speaks to how much simpler it is to make bellicose statements for the purpose of mobilizing collective passions than to reflect, examine, sort out what it is we are dealing with in reality, the interconnectedness of innumerable lives, "ours" as well as "theirs."

In a remarkable series of three articles published between January and March 1999 in *Dawn*, Pakistan's most respected weekly, the late Eqbal Ahmad, writing for a Muslim audience, analyzed what he called the roots of the religious right, coming down very harshly on the mutilations of Islam by absolutists and fanatical tyrants whose obsession with regulating personal behavior promotes "an Islamic order reduced to a penal code, stripped of its humanism, aesthetics, intellectual quests, and spiritual devotion." And this "entails an absolute assertion of one, generally de-contextualized, aspect of religion and a total disregard of another. The phenomenon distorts religion, debases tradition, and twists the political process wherever it unfolds." As a timely instance of this debasement, Ahmad proceeds first to present the rich, complex, pluralist meaning of the word *jihad* and then goes on to show that in the word's current confinement to indiscriminate war against presumed enemies, it is impossible "to recognize the Islamic—religion, society, culture, history or politics—as lived and experienced by Muslims through the ages." The modern Islamists, Ahmad concludes, are "concerned with power, not with the soul; with the mobilization of people for political purposes rather than with sharing and alleviating their sufferings and aspirations. Theirs is a very limited and time-bound political agenda." What has made matters worse is that similar distortions and zealotry occur in the "Jewish" and "Christian" universes of discourse.

It was Joseph Conrad, more powerfully than any of his readers at the end of the nineteenth century could have imagined, who understood that the distinctions between civilized London and "the heart of darkness" quickly collapsed in extreme situations, and that the heights of European civilization could instantaneously fall into the most barbarous practices without preparation or transition. And it was Conrad also, in *The Secret Agent* (1907), who described terrorism's affinity for abstractions like "pure science" (and by extension for "Islam" or "the West"), as well as the terrorist's ultimate moral degradation.

For there are closer ties between apparently warring civilizations than most of us would like to believe; both Freud and Nietzsche showed how the traffic across carefully maintained, even policed boundaries moves with often terrifying ease. But then such fluid ideas, full of ambiguity and skepticism about notions that we hold on to, scarcely furnish us with suitable, practical guidelines for situations such as the one we face now. Hence the altogether more reassuring battle orders (a crusade, good versus evil, freedom against fear, etc.) drawn out of Huntington's alleged opposition between Islam and the West, from which official discourse drew its vocabulary in the first days after the September 11 attacks. There's since been a noticeable de-escalation in that discourse, but to judge from the steady amount of hate speech and actions, plus reports of law enforcement efforts directed against Arabs, Muslims, and Indians all over the country, the paradigm stays on.

One further reason for its persistence is the increased presence of Muslims all over Europe and the United States. Think of the populations today of France, Italy, Germany, Spain, Britain, America, even Sweden, and you must concede that Islam is no longer on the fringes of the West but at its center. But what is so threatening about that presence? Buried in the collective culture are memories of the first great Arab-Islamic conquests, which began in the seventh century and which, as the celebrated Belgian historian Henri Pirenne wrote in his landmark book *Mohammed and Charlemagne* (1939), shattered once and for all the ancient unity of the Mediterranean, destroyed the Christian-Roman synthesis and gave rise to a new civilization dominated by northern powers (Germany and Carolingian France) whose mission, he seemed to be saying, is to resume defense of the "West" against its historical-cultural enemies. What Pirenne left out, alas, is that in the creation of this new line of defense the West drew on the humanism, science, philosophy, sociology, and historiography of Islam, which had already interposed itself between Charlemagne's world and classical antiquity. Islam is inside from the start, as even Dante, great enemy of Mohammed, had to concede when he placed the Prophet at the very heart of his *Inferno*.

Then there is the persisting legacy of monotheism itself, the Abrahamic religions, as Louis Massignon aptly called them. Beginning with Judaism and Christianity, each is a successor haunted by what came before; for Muslims, Islam fulfills and ends the line of prophecy. There is still no decent history or demystification of the many-sided contest among these three followers—not one of them by any means a monolithic, unified camp—of the most jealous of all gods, even though the bloody modern convergence on Palestine furnishes a rich secular instance of what has been so tragically irreconcilable about them. Not surprisingly, then, Muslims and Christians speak readily of crusades and *jihads*, both of them eliding the Judaic presence with often sublime insouciance. Such an agenda, says Eqbal Ahmad, is "very reassuring to the men and women who are stranded in the middle of the ford, between the deep waters of tradition and modernity."

But we are all swimming in those waters, Westerners and Muslims and others alike. And since the waters are part of the ocean of history, trying to plow or divide them with barriers is futile. These are tense times, but it is better to think in terms of powerful and powerless communities, the secular politics of reason and ignorance, and universal principles of justice and injustice, than to wander off in search of vast abstractions that may give momentary satisfaction but little self-knowledge or informed analysis. "The Clash of Civilizations" thesis is a gimmick like "The War of the Worlds," better for reinforcing defensive self-pride than for critical understanding of the bewildering interdependence of our time.

STUDY QUESTIONS

1. What is Said's main objection to Huntington's "clash of civilization" thesis?
2. What examples does Said use to defend his claim that the boundaries between the West and Islam are not as sharply defined as Huntington suggests?
3. Said's discussion of the novelist Joseph Conrad suggests an alternative explanation for violence and hatred. What is that alternative explanation?
4. Said suggests that we are all swimming in the deep waters between modernity and tradition. What does he mean by this? Is he right? Explain.

INTERVENTIONS: HYBRID IDENTITIES AND AUTONOMY

Identity formation, the capacity to see oneself as a stable, distinct, and reasonably coherent individual, is a central component in autonomy, and involves a process of coming to know what one most deeply cares about. This self-knowledge is a necessary condition for leading a self-directed life, because it is essential in avoiding the conflicts that arise when our desires are not integrated with more basic values and commitments.

However, we don't achieve coherent identities on our own. How others see us is very much a part of how we view ourselves—identity formation requires recognition by others. Thus, there is tension within the concept of autonomy. Autonomy, at least as traditionally construed, requires that we establish our independence from others; but a central component of autonomy, the process of identity formation, is dependent on our connections to others. Are identity formation and autonomy really in conflict? The answer to this question depends on the content of identity formation, which brings us to the essays in this section.

Attachments to cultural or ethnic traditions contribute to seeing oneself as a stable, coherent individual. After all, much about each of us would be quite different if we grew up in a different culture. If it is the case that identity formation is dependent on recognition by others, it is likely that among the kinds of recognition that a person would find meaningful is recognition of his or her cultural or ethnic identity. But how deep down does cultural identity reach? Is cultural identity a necessary component of identity or is it something we can acknowledge or not, depending on our particular interests?

Disagreement on this issue is fundamental to the debate between Huntington and Fukuyama. Fukuyama argues that the deepest desire of all human beings is recognition as a free and equal citizen. Although as private individuals we might be deeply involved in sustaining a particular cultural identity, as a public citizen what matters most is that we be treated as free and equal citizens. For example, I may be a member of a particular religion or ethnic group and my membership in that group may be terribly important to my family and me. But when I go to work, attend meetings of the PTA, or vote, my religion or ethnicity should be a matter of public indifference. I should receive no special benefits or burdens vis-à-vis public institutions as the result of my religion or ethnicity. It is a private matter, not part of my public identity. Thus, for Fukuyama cultural identity and autonomy are not at odds because my deepest desire is to be recognized as autonomous.

However, Huntington makes very different assumptions regarding identity formation. Although in Western culture, we may be satisfied with public recognition as a free and equal citizen, that is not true universally, and certainly not within Islam, according to Huntington. Many people want to be recognized primarily as a member of a religion, or as a participant in a tradition or ethnic group, etc. Public recognition of membership in these traditions is an essential component of who one is. Importantly, according to Huntington, part of that recognition is a sense of superiority that feeds the sense of identity and helps to sustain it. Identity is based on conflict. Thus, in Huntington's view, personal autonomy is primarily a Western value. Many people throughout the world more deeply desire recognition as a member of a group; their sense of themselves as coherent individuals is derived from group identification.

Fukuyama and Huntington disagree about whether autonomy is a universal value. However, Said argues that this contrast between the West and Islam is too starkly posed. As Said points out, the populations of Western societies include substantial Muslim populations, and even within countries that are primarily Muslim, there is sharp disagreement over Islam's approach to democracy, liberalism, and autonomy. If Said is right, the conflict between Islam and the West, and between cultural identity and autonomy, takes place within societies and indeed within individuals who, because they live within multicultural societies, must negotiate social norms that may conflict with particular identities. The question of how modernization processes affect traditional belief systems has a personal dimension.

Does entry into modernity demand of individuals a stark choice between recognition as free and equal citizens and recognition as members of social groups? If the ideal of autonomy requires self-sufficiency, then we should see ourselves as individuals distinct from the encumbrances of cultural or ethnic traditions. We may participate in these traditions, but only as a product of conscious, thoughtful, and persistently renewed decisions that treat the commitment as optional. This is because, according to the model of self-sufficiency, no cultural practice can have authority over the free choices of individuals. We must, to be genuinely autonomous, have the capacity to choose our own ends, and that means we must be able to assess and revise, in the light of that assessment, all commitments and entanglements.

But many argue that if we see ourselves as self-sufficient, much of what is meaningful and important to us cannot find public expression—it is a recipe for alienation and contributes to the decline in moral values. This is especially true of cultural and ethnic identifications. If we question or distance ourselves from deep attachments that confer meaning and provide stability, we will have no point of view from which to understand our lives and thus no standards by which to evaluate our goals. The very idea of assessing goals and life plans presupposes a background of unquestioned, inalterable commitments, which for many people involves attachments to cultural and ethnic traditions. To restrict these commitments to a private sphere is oppressive, since it precludes public expression of precisely those identities that require recognition for their stability.

This difficult choice between freedom and meaning has encouraged many people to adopt hybrid identities as a way of sustaining autonomy while participating in essential groups. They view themselves as free and equal for some purposes, but maintain solidarity with ethnic and religious traditions for other purposes. The self-direction model of autonomy best explains hybrid identities, because it permits cultural, religious, and ethnic traditions to powerfully guide individuals as long as they engage their critical faculties. But given that self-direction requires integration between an agent's various desires and values, this will not be a promising approach if, as Huntington argues, the meaning of identity requires contempt for ways of life that fall outside the definitions of one's core identity. For hybrid identities, competing ways of life must somehow be wholeheartedly incorporated into the self if integration is to be achieved, and if the components of hybrid identities involve values that are in fundamental conflict, then integration and thus autonomy would appear to be out of the question. The recent case of a Muslim woman who was required to remove her traditional headdress and reveal her face to the DMV camera in order to acquire a driver's license is just one of many such conflicts that individuals confront.

Yet, it seems implausible to suggest that all people of hybrid identities, Muslim-Americans, Italian-Americans, etc., who achieve autonomy have done so at the expense of their traditional beliefs. Perhaps the way out of these dilemmas is to think differently about the integration condition that is central to self-direction. Philosopher Diane Meyers has argued that an integrated person is not only one who has a clear idea of her values and is able to make her desires conform to them. An autonomous person is one who has the capacity to imagine ways of living that reconcile competing values. Autonomous people know what they want, but they also need the ability to revise their values and attachments without sacrificing them when new information or unforeseen conflicts arise.

In this view, autonomy is not a condition of coherence between all our values and desires, which in a complex world most of us cannot achieve. Rather, autonomy is a set of cognitive, volitional, and interpersonal skills that individuals employ to resolve conflicts as the self evolves. Such resolutions involve more than self-reflection and imagination. They also involve analytical and communication skills that enable persons to engage the groups of which they are a part, encouraging those groups to redefine the elements of traditions in order to sustain their meaning in ways that are compatible with autonomy. Establishing one's identity as a member of a group need not involve passive acquiescence to group norms, but rather an active process of mutual evolution. Notice, however, that achievement of autonomy requires the active involvement and support of others. Mutual evolution cannot be a solitary pursuit. As I will argue in more detail in part 8, autonomy is an achievable goal only if dependence on others is acknowledged.

However, if persons with hybrid identities are to achieve autonomy it must be the case that traditions are not static, monolithic entities, and the benefits achieved through adherence to tradition are not thoroughly dependent on resistance to influence and change. Furthermore, the capacity to achieve autonomy in the context of adherence to group identities requires that aspects of the self—personal characteristics, long-standing emotional attachments, cultural, racial, religious, and ethnic identifications—are subject to revision. The difficulty is that it is implausible to think that we can revise everything about ourselves. Thus, inevitably, autonomous hybrid identities will be difficult to achieve and subject to periodic failure, and may sometimes be impossible.

VII

IT'S ALL GOOD:
LIFE AMONG THE RELATIVISTS

Discussions of our moral condition inevitably raise the specter of moral relativism. It is often claimed that contemporary Americans lack guiding principles because we no longer believe that there is a set of objective moral prescriptions that all human beings are obligated to follow regardless of their circumstances. Instead, according to this critique, we have come to believe that morality is relative to particular cultures or subcultures. Thus, what is wrong in one group may not be wrong in another, and there are no independent standards by which to evaluate competing moral claims. Judging what people of different times and places do is therefore a sign of intolerance.

Criticisms of relativism often include criticisms of moral subjectivism and moral freedom as well. Moral subjectivism is the view that ultimate moral authority rests with an individual's private preferences. Because there may be considerable differences between an individual's private preferences and group norms, moral relativism and moral subjectivism are not identical positions. Moral freedom, as I have been developing it in this text, is the view that moral authority is based on an individual's competent, socially informed decisions. Because our competent, socially informed decisions are not necessarily identical to our preferences, moral freedom is not reducible to moral subjectivism; and because our competent, informed decisions often differ from group norms, moral freedom differs from relativism as well.

This part focuses especially on the claim that there are no objective moral truths. Thus, it addresses one of the underlying assumptions of moral relativism, subjectivism, and moral freedom.

17

Are We Living in a Moral Stone Age?

Christina Hoff Sommers

Christina Hoff Sommers is a resident fellow at the American Enterprise Institute, Washington, D.C. She is the author of *The War Against Boys: How
Misguided Feminism is Harming Our Young Men* (2001) and *Who Stole
Feminism: How Women Have Betrayed Women* (1994). Sommers argues
that moral relativism and/or subjectivism afflicts many students today. As a
remedy, educational institutions must place greater emphasis on the moral
truths expressed in the great literary, philosophical, and political works of
the Western cultural tradition. By embracing traditions, we learn the moral
truths that all human beings must recognize. Traditions are the means
through which basic moral truths such as the importance of honesty, integrity, and the dangers of selfishness are taught to succeeding generations.

A lot is heard today about how Johnny can't read, can't write, and the trouble he has finding France on a map. It also is true that Johnny is having difficulty distinguishing right from wrong. Along with illiteracy and innumer-
acy, deep moral confusion must be added to the list of educational
problems. Increasingly, today's young people know little or nothing about
the Western moral tradition.

This was demonstrated by "Tonight Show" host Jay Leno, who frequently
does "man-on-the-street" interviews. One night, he collared some young
people to ask them questions about the Bible. "Can you name one of the Ten
Commandments?" he asked two college-age women. One replied, "Freedom
of speech?" Leno said to the other, "Complete this sentence: Let he who is
without sin. . . ." Her response was "Have a good time?" Leno then turned to

Reprinted from the *USA Today* magazine, March 1999, by the Society for the Advancement of
Education.

a young man and asked, "Who, according to the Bible, was eaten by a whale?" The confident answer was "Pinocchio."

As with many humorous anecdotes, the underlying reality is not funny at all. These young people are morally confused. They are the students I and other teachers of ethics see every day. Like most professors, I am acutely aware of the "hole in the moral ozone." One of the best things schools can do for America is to set about repairing it—by confronting the moral nihilism that is the norm for so many students. Schools at all levels can do a lot to improve the moral climate of our society. They can help restore civility and community if they commit themselves and have the courage to act.

When you have as many conversations with young people as I do, you come away both exhilarated and depressed. Still, there is a great deal of simple good-heartedness, instinctive fair-mindedness, and spontaneous generosity of spirit in them. Most of the students I meet are basically decent individuals. They form wonderful friendships and seem to be considerate of and grateful to their parents—more so than the baby boomers were.

In many ways, they are more likeable than the baby boomers, being less fascinated with themselves and more able to laugh at their faults. A large number are doing volunteer work (70 percent of college students, according to one annual survey of freshmen). They donate blood to the Red Cross in record numbers and deliver food to housebound elderly people. They spend summer vacations working with deaf children or doing volunteer work in Mexico. This is a generation of youths that, despite relatively little moral guidance or religious training, are putting compassion into practice.

Conceptually and culturally, though, today's young people live in a moral haze. Ask one of them if there are such things as "right" and "wrong," and suddenly you are confronted with a confused, tongue-tied, nervous, and insecure individual. The same person who works weekends for Meals on Wheels, who volunteers for a suicide prevention hotline or a domestic violence shelter, might tell you, "Well, there really is no such thing as right or wrong. It's kind of like whatever works best for the individual. Each person has to work it out for himself." The trouble is that this kind of answer, which is so common as to be typical, is no better than the moral philosophy of a sociopath.

I often meet students incapable of making even one single confident moral judgment, and the situation is getting worse. The things students say are more and more unhinged. Recently, several of my students objected to philosopher Immanuel Kant's principle of humanity—the doctrine that asserts the unique dignity and worth of every human life. They told me that, if they were faced with the choice between saving their pet or a human being, they would choose the former.

We have been thrown back into a moral Stone Age, wherein many young people are totally unaffected by thousands of years of moral experience and moral progress. The notion of objective moral truths is in disrepute, and this mistrust of objectivity has begun to spill over into other areas of knowledge. The concept of objective truth in science and history is being impugned as well. For example, an undergraduate at Williams College reported that her classmates, who had been taught that "all knowledge is a social construct," were doubtful that the Holocaust ever occurred. One of her classmates said, "Although the Holocaust may not have happened, it's a perfectly reasonable conceptual hallucination."

A creative writing teacher at Pasadena City College wrote an article in the *Chronicle of Higher Education* about what it is like to teach Shirley Jackson's famous short story "The Lottery" to today's college students. It is a tale of a small farming community that seems normal in every way, with people who are hardworking and friendly. As the plot progresses, however, the reader learns this village carries out an annual lottery in which the loser is stoned to death.

It is a shocking lesson about primitive rituals in a modern American setting. In the past, most students had understood "The Lottery" to be a warning about the dangers of mindless conformity, but now they merely think it is "Neat!" or "Cool!" They will not go out on a limb and take a stand against human sacrifice.

It was not always thus. When Thomas Jefferson wrote that all men have the right to life, liberty, and the pursuit of happiness, he did not say, "At least that is my opinion." He declared it as an objective truth. When suffragette Elizabeth Cady Stanton "amended" the Declaration of Independence by changing the phrase "all men" to "all men and women," she was not merely giving an opinion; she was insisting that females are endowed with the same rights and entitlements as males.

The assertions of Jefferson and Stanton were made in the same spirit—as self-evident truths, not personal judgments. Today's young people enjoy the fruits of the battles fought by such leaders, but they are not being given the intellectual and moral training to argue for and justify truth. In fact, the kind of education they are getting is systematically undermining their common sense about what is true and right.

Let me be concrete and specific: Men and women died courageously fighting the Nazis. They included American and Allied soldiers, as well as resistance fighters. Because brave people took risks to do what was right and necessary, Germany eventually was defeated. Today, with the assault on objective truth, many college students find themselves unable to say why the U.S. was on the right side in that war. Some even doubt that America was in the right. They are not even sure the salient events of World War II ever took place. They simply lack confidence in the objectivity of history.

Too many young people are morally confused, ill-informed, and adrift. This confusion gets worse, rather than better, once they go to college. If they are attending an elite school, they actually can lose their common sense and become clever and adroit intellectuals in the worst sense. Author George Orwell reputedly said, "Some ideas are so absurd that only an intellectual could believe them." The students of such intellectuals are in the same boat. Orwell did not know about the tenured radicals of the 1990s, but he was presciently aware that they were on the way.

The problem is not that young people are ignorant, distrustful, cruel, or treacherous. It is not that they are moral skeptics. They just talk that way. To put it bluntly, they are conceptually clueless. Students are suffering from "cognitive moral confusion."

What is to be done? How can their knowledge and understanding of moral history be improved? How can their confidence in the great moral ideals be restored? How can they be helped to become morally articulate, morally literate, and morally self-confident?

In the late 1960s, a group of hippies living in the Haight-Ashbury District of San Francisco decided that hygiene was a middle-class hang-up they could do without. So, they decided to live without it. Baths and showers, while not actually banned, were frowned upon. Essayist and novelist Tom Wolfe was intrigued by these hippies, who, he said, "sought nothing less than to sweep aside all codes and restraints of the past and start out from zero."

Before long, the hippies' aversion to modern hygiene had consequences that were as unpleasant as they were unforeseen. Wolfe describes them: "At the Haight-Ashbury Free Clinic there were doctors who were treating diseases no living doctor had ever encountered before, diseases that had disappeared so long ago they had never even picked up Latin names, such as the mange, the grunge, the itch, the twitch, the thrush, the scroff, the rot." The itching and the manginess eventually began to vex the hippies, leading them to seek help from the local free clinics. Step by step, they had to rediscover for themselves the rudiments of modern hygiene. Wolfe refers to this as the "Great Relearning."

The Great Relearning is what has to happen whenever earnest reformers extirpate too much. When, "starting from zero," they jettison basic social practices and institutions, abandon common routines, and defy common sense, reason, conventional wisdom—and, sometimes, sanity itself.

This was seen with the most politically extreme experiments of the 20th century—Marxism, Maoism, and fascism. Each movement had its share of zealots and social engineers who believed in starting from zero. They had faith in a new order and ruthlessly cast aside traditional arrangements. Among the unforeseen consequences were mass suffering and genocide. Russians and Eastern Europeans are beginning their own Great Relearning. They now realize, to their dismay, that starting from zero is a calamity and that the structural damage wrought by the political zealots has handicapped their societies for decades to come. They are learning that it is far easier to tear apart a social fabric than to piece one together again.

America, too, has had its share of revolutionary developments—not so much political as moral. We are living through a great experiment in "moral deregulation," an experiment whose first principle seems to be: "Conventional morality is oppressive." What is right is what works for us. We question everything. We casually, even gleefully, throw out old-fashioned customs and practices. Writer Oscar Wilde once said, "I can resist everything except temptation." Many in the 1960s generation made succumbing to temptation and license their philosophy of life.

We jokingly call looters "non-traditional shoppers." Killers are described as "morally challenged"—again jokingly, but the truth behind the jests is that moral deregulation is the order of the day. We poke fun at our own society for its lack of moral clarity. In our own way, we are as down and out as those hippies knocking at the door of the free clinic.

MORAL CONSERVATIONISM

We need our own Great Relearning. Let me propose a few ideas on how we might carry out this relearning. The first, which could be called "moral conservationism," is based on this premise: We are born into a moral environment just as we are born into a natural environment. Just as there are basic environmental necessities—clean air, safe food, and fresh water—there are basic moral necessities. What is a society without civility, honesty, consideration, and self-discipline? Without a population educated to be civil, considerate, and respectful of one another, what will we end up with? The answer is, not much. For as long as philosophers and theologians have written about ethics, they have stressed the moral basics. We live in a moral environment. We must respect and protect it. We must acquaint our children with it. We must make them aware it is precious and fragile.

My suggestions for specific reforms are far from revolutionary and, indeed, some are pretty obvious. They are commonsense ideas, but we live in an age when common sense is increasingly hard to come by.

We must encourage and honor colleges that accept the responsibility of providing a classical moral education for their students. The last few decades of the 20th century have seen a steady erosion of knowledge and a steady increase in moral relativism. This is partly due to the diffidence of many teachers confused by all the talk about pluralism. Such teachers actually believe that it is wrong to "indoctrinate" our children into our own culture and moral tradition.

Of course, there are pressing moral issues around which there is no consensus. In a modern pluralistic society, there are arguments about all sorts of things. This is understandable. Moral dilemmas arise in every generation. Nevertheless, humanity long ago achieved consensus on many basic moral questions. Cheating, cowardice, and cruelty are wrong. As one pundit put it, "The Ten Commandments are not the Ten Highly Tentative Suggestions."

While it is true that we must debate controversial issues, we must not forget there exists a core of noncontroversial ethical issues that were settled a long time ago. Teachers must make students aware there is a standard of ethical ideals that all civilizations worthy of the name have discovered. They must be encouraged to read the Bible, Aristotle's *Ethics*, William Shakespeare's *King Lear*, the *Koran*, and the *Analects* of Confucius. When they read almost any great work, they will encounter these basic moral values: integrity, respect for human life, self-control, honesty, courage, and self-sacrifice. All the world's major religions proffer some version of the Golden Rule, if only in its negative form: Do not do unto others as you would not have them do unto you.

The literary classics must be taught. The great books and great ideas must be brought back into the core of the curriculum. The best of political and cultural heritage must be transmitted. Author Franz Kafka once said that a great work of literature melts the "frozen sea within us." There are any number of works of art and philosophy that have the same effect.

American children have a right to their moral heritage. They should know the Bible. They should be familiar with the moral truths in the tragedies of Shakespeare and the political ideas of Jefferson, James Madison, and Abraham Lincoln. They should be exposed to the exquisite moral sensibility in the novels of Jane Austen, George Eliot, and Mark Twain, to mention some of my favorites. These great works are their birthright.

This is not to say that a good literary, artistic, and philosophical education suffices to create ethical human beings, nor to suggest that teaching the classics is all that is needed to repair the moral ozone. What is known is that we can not, in good conscience, allow America's children to remain morally illiterate. All healthy societies pass along their moral and cultural traditions to their children.

This suggests another basic reform. Teachers, professors, and other social critics should be encouraged to moderate their attacks on our culture and its institutions. They should be encouraged to treat great literary works as literature and not as reactionary political tracts. In many classrooms today, students are encouraged to "uncover" the allegedly racist, sexist, and elitist elements in the great books.

Meanwhile, pundits, social critics, radical feminists, and other intellectuals on the cultural left never seem to tire of running down our society and its institutions and traditions. We are overrun by determined advocacy groups that overstate the weaknesses of our society and show very little appreciation for its merits and strengths. I urge those professors and teachers who use their classrooms to disparage America to consider the possibility that they are doing more harm than good. Their goal may be to create sensitive, critical citizens, but what they actually are doing is producing confusion and cynicism. Their goal may be to improve students' awareness of the plight of exploited peoples, but they are producing individuals capable of doubting that the Holocaust actually took place and incapable of articulating moral objections to human sacrifice.

In my opinion, we are not unlike those confused, scrofulous hippies of the late 1960s who finally showed up at the doors of the free clinics in Haight-Ashbury to get their doses of traditional medicine. I hope we have the good sense to follow their example. We need to take an active stand against the divisive unlearning that is corrupting the integrity of our society.

Writer Williams Butler Yeats talked of the "center" and warned that it is not holding. Others talk of the threats to our social fabric and tradition. Nevertheless, we remain a sound society. We know how to dispel the moral confusion and get back our bearings and confidence. We have traditions and institutions of proven strength and efficacy, and we still are strong.

We need to bring back the great books and the great ideas. We need to transmit the best of our political and cultural heritage. We need to refrain from cynical attacks against our traditions and institutions. We need to expose the folly of all the schemes for starting from zero. We need to teach our young people to understand, respect, and protect the institutions that protect us and preserve our free and democratic society.

If we do, when we engage in the Great Relearning that so badly is needed today, we will find that the lives of our morally enlightened children will be saner, safer, more dignified, and more humane.

STUDY QUESTIONS

1. Is Sommers primarily concerned with the inability of young people to act well, or to make proper judgments? Is the ability to act well related to the ability to make proper judgments? Explain.
2. If you were faced with the decision to save a pet or save an unrelated human being, which would you choose? Why?
3. According to Sommers, we are morally confused because we lack an understanding of what concept? What does she mean by this?
4. Sommers discusses a variety of cases in which students failed to make rational judgments. Some denied the reality of the Holocaust and Nazi aggression; others refused to condemn arbitrary murder. Why do you think students would make such judgments?
5. What does Sommers advocate as a solution to moral confusion? Do you agree?

6. Why, according to Sommers does the study of moral traditions lead to the recognition of objective moral truths?
7. Are great works from our literary tradition effective ways of transmitting moral knowledge? Explain.
8. Is it possible to endorse and honor a tradition while criticizing it? Discuss.

18

Of Cave Dwellers and Spirits: The Trouble with Moral Absolutes

Dwight Furrow

Dwight Furrow teaches philosophy at San Diego Mesa College, and is the author of *Against Theory: Continental and Analytic Challenges in Moral Philosophy* (1995).

In this essay, I argue that both moral relativism and moral absolutism are indefensible positions. Furthermore, moral absolutism is a more significant source of moral uncertainty than is relativism because moral absolutism promises more than it can deliver and distracts us from acknowledging genuine sources of moral responsibility.

Distress over the murky morals of contemporaries is not unique to our age of terrorists and technoscience. Some 2,500 years ago, Plato had similar concerns, likening the human condition to that of prisoners shackled to the walls of a cave, credulous, and unwittingly seduced by mere shadows of transcendent, divine reality. Plato's allegory of the cave represents our human intellect trapped inside a desiring body bound to a particular place and time, too distracted by worldly concerns to comprehend timeless and universal truths.

Our intellectual tradition has taken this image of the human condition seriously, agreeing with Plato that if our intellects are confined to the fleshly here and now our judgments are likely to be provincial and transient, tied so closely to narrow self-interest and impulsive, evanescent motives that humans would careen like novice roller-bladers from one catastrophe to the next. Without enduring, universal truths, all judgments are provisional and contingent, lacking both the authority to vanquish bullies and cranks and the steadfastness to stiffen the spineless. So on the coattails of Plato, we have plumbed heaven and earth for these objective, universal truths while treating relativist dissent as a scourge, akin to attacks by locusts or the smallpox virus.

However, the worry that our fragile hunches and vagrant apprehensions might lead us to ruin has apparently not trickled down to the culture at large. For 2,500 years after Plato's lament, a steady parade of moralist scribes have documented the inability of contemporary Americans to make clear and consistent moral judgments.

The culprit in this scandal, according to these social critics, is skepticism regarding the existence of objective moral truths. This skepticism apparently infects our moral judgments with fatal hesitation induced by the worry that in raining on someone else's parade we are simply making room for our own prancing horses. Reporting on attitudes typical of today's undergraduates, the historian Gertrude Himmelfarb laments in her book *One Nation, Two Cultures*: "To pass judgment, they fear, is to be a moral 'absolutist,' and having been taught that there are no absolutes, they now see any judgment as arbitrary, intolerant, and authoritarian." Himmelfarb's observations are correct, I can report without hesitation, for my students, at least on first thought, tend to concur. The persistence of moral relativism is even deemed newsworthy on occasion, as in a *Newsweek* commentary by Yale student Alison Hornstein who reported shortly after September 11 that campus discussions of the terrorist attacks focused on how the life circumstances of the terrorists explained their actions, largely ignoring the moral wrongness of the acts, and seeming to excuse them.

Should one mistakenly think this reluctance to judge, like belief in one's indestructibility, is an affliction of the young, Alan Wolfe's sociological reports on the moral beliefs of contemporary Americans in *Moral Freedom: The Search for Virtue in a World of Choice* demonstrates the persistence of moral relativism among those old enough to remember Woodstock.

Moralists variously explain the popularity of relativism by pointing to widespread ignorance of our intellectual and religious traditions and their time-honored truths, an excessively critical stance toward that tradition by intellectuals with a political agenda, or intellectual laziness encouraged by a distracted, hedonistic culture that finds stringent moral judgments to be uncomfortable like cold showers and bitter medicine. In striving to exit the cave, we seem to have merely decorated its walls with an empire of irresistible temptations, which dazzle and distract the intellectual weaklings in our midst, according to these critics.

Plato's solution to such intellectual infirmity was to prepare the mind for a noble death that would free the properly nurtured soul from its dependence on the located, temporal, desiring body, enabling the unencumbered spirit to grasp mega-concepts so precise and powerful that ambiguity and uncertainty could be thrust aside like discarded demons from a benighted past.

Plato's solution has an obvious downside though; even philosophers enjoy life enough to want its perpetuation. So philosophers have spent the intervening millennia devising clever ways to separate truth from morality.

Each generation of thinkers has loudly trumpeted success in this enterprise, much to everyone's relief. Until recently, the idea that we are progressively accumulating moral truths that will ultimately and finally speak Sweet Reason's commandments (if not reality's very own moral language) represented the consensus among intellectuals. Today, though debates over postmodernism and multiculturalism challenge that consensus, there remains substantial agreement that our basic judgments regarding the true and the good rest on stable, objective standards immune to reasonable doubt. Reports in the media to the contrary notwithstanding, relativism is a minority position in the academy.

Of course, we defend the objectivity of moral judgment with more modesty than Plato's heaven-storming. Our pragmatic age is inclined to think that because our bridges stay up and the stock market flourishes we must know something about the good life's innermost secrets. Social scientists armed with superior accounting methods and billions of megahertz dream of the day their computer models spit out the rules of human cohabitation artfully arranged to instantly stanch the flow of unruly desire. Even in the area of morals, the idea that all human beings have intrinsic worth has generated widespread theoretical agreement regarding a baseline for treatment that all of us are obligated to uphold. That this idea has proved recalcitrant in practice seems not to have diminished the enthusiasm with which it is promoted.

But what to do about the "still discordant wavering multitude" who resist the blandishments of absolutists? Far from being a mere academic concern, the fate of Civilizations is alleged to rest on our ability to defend the authority of moral absolutes, for such truths are the ordnance with which we fight the barbarians at the gate who appear no longer in loincloths but in the seductive costumes of homosexuals, divorcees, multiculturalists, and most recently terrorists.

The erstwhile emperor is once again making an appearance in nature's garb. This debate between absolutists and relativists is both irrelevant and pernicious. It is irrelevant because relativism in its virulent, harmful form is rare while something akin to relativism is benign and intellectually honest. The debate is pernicious because for purposes of stanching moral decline, foot stomping about moral truths is largely ineffective and distracts us from the real moral challenges that confront modern societies.

The form of moral relativism that gets everyone's knickers in a twist is the view that all claims about what is right or good are equally valid, because individual preference is the only authority on moral questions. As the aforementioned commentators suggest, students in a thoughtless moment often endorse this sort of "anything goes" relativism, especially when discussing the moral implications of historical events. If my students really believed this, it would be cause for alarm, but it is an easy task to show them that in fact they don't believe such a thing at all.

We philosophers love to browbeat the brave undergraduate, who timorously asserts that no belief is more or less valid than any other, with the arch wisdom that the generalization applies to her own claim as well; thus the speaker denies what she intends to assert. But many find logical hygiene less appealing than gripping narratives, so a more convincing approach is to point out that if their mother were raped they would quickly overcome their reluctance to pass judgment. In a world where beliefs have consequences, we could not manage even minimally competent social interactions without making judgments that are non-arbitrary and reasonably consistent. The brute resistance of the world will not allow us the fantasy of utterly collapsing the distinction between thinking one is right and being so. I doubt that anyone can live as if "anything goes," nor could anyone consistently endorse it when forced by circumstances to judge. The silliest forms of relativism are just straw men invented to beat the momentarily unreflective into submission.

What my students and many other inhabitants of contemporary culture are unable to explain is why an action is right or wrong outside the context of their immediate concerns and interests. Confronted by differences too substantial to fully comprehend, and compelled from all sides to view their own lives as both insular and singular, today most people implicitly recognize that there are a variety of ways of seeing the world and what looks right or wrong from one point of view may not appear that way from another. Modestly assuming they cannot presume a God's eye view of how things stand, when pressed about why they are reluctant to pass judgment, the most common response is "what gives me the right to judge?" Such reticence, of course, can be a sign of intellectual laziness or self-absorption. But the tendency afflicts the bright and industrious as well as the dim and inert; and people with the most genuinely altruistic motives can twist logic into knots to avoid judging. Students who devote their precious spare time to community service are as likely as their less caring classmates to claim that Hitler was not evil, just different. "You know, like really wacked—totally." Such apparent moral catatonia is best explained not by indifference, but by the recognition that our capacity for understanding is limited by time and distance and, when the luxury of skepticism can be afforded, we should withhold judgment until forced by circumstances to get off the fence.

This cagey, tentative attitude toward moral judgment, though sometimes obtuse and puerile, harbors an important insight. Moral judgment has its strongest purchase within a form of life, and unless you walk in the shoes of those about whom you pass judgment, your judgment will likely lack nuance and credibility. Skepticism about the usefulness of the idea of objective, universal moral truths is obvious and natural in a world that so often shoves the unfamiliar under our noses.

The insight that moral judgments are deeply personal and complicated by the vicissitudes of circumstance suggests to the theoretically inclined with their penchant for generalizing, that all moral judgments are therefore relative to a person's social context or cultural background. Encouraged by anthropological discoveries of non-Western folkways, this is a more sophisticated form of relativism very different from "anything goes" relativism since cultural norms impose moral standards that may be quite stringent. Nevertheless, this version of relativism is disturbing to absolutists because it implies that the same moral standards do not apply to everyone, allegedly leaving us with no criteria by which to criticize actions we find abhorrent. The relativist is in the uncomfortable position of being unable to mount objections to judgments that conform to dangerous or pernicious social norms since social norms are the only court of appeal.

The thought that drives this version of relativism is that judgments can be correct only if they conform to a standard. If we lack objective, universal principles to guide moral judgment, the only standards available are the principles and norms accepted in the societies and groups in which a person participates. The claim that all moral judgments are relative to culture seems to follow inevitably from the denial that there are objective moral truths. But this inevitability is a myth that I want to contest, for it falsely assumes that we must either perpetuate the burlesque of consecrating our motives as universal or belly up to the communal feeding trough to receive our daily ration of moral substance. Neither image is inspiring, but, since correct judgments need not conform to standards or norms, we need grab neither horn of this false dilemma.

As a first step in demonstrating the mistake here, it is important to keep in mind the substantial evidence weighing against the idea that moral judgment is relative to culture. Social norms exert substantial pressure on our decisions and judgments but they hardly determine the limits of moral response. The lives of Gandhi, nineteenth century southern abolitionists, and anti-Semitic rescuers of Jews during the Holocaust are just a few of the historical examples that demonstrate the human ability to transcend the limits of cultural norms.

Neither do judgments that violate or transcend social norms inherently lack justification. Practical justification is a matter of sustaining in one's imagination a vision of how life can be lived in hope and security while continually testing that vision against the congealed thickness and resistance of reality. Our judgments along with their authority emerge from this tension between the impetus for change and the inertia of habit and circumstance. Any side of this equation can produce good reasons depending on the fecundity of our imaginations and the responsiveness of emotion and intellect to the realities we confront. Society and culture condition our judgments but do not determine them, because hope and fear can drive out any allegiance.

Thus, the peculiar authority that moral judgments acquire ultimately rests on the capacity of these judgments to block vulnerabilities or engender promise. In the final analysis, our hopes and fears supply the moral police with their writs and armaments; society's rules and regulations merely reflect and codify our passions. Independent judgments are rare because of the costs imposed on those who make them, not because our judgments are logically connected to social norms. Moral judgments are not relative to anything aside from one's ability to peer through the fog of fate and circumstance in order to maintain connections to that about which one cares and the wider world in which we act.

In our complex circumstances, given the limits of our understanding, we are justified in hesitating to jump to conclusions regarding those who are differently situated. But there is little reason to think differences mark an absolute boundary beyond which judgment can never penetrate. Thus, skepticism regarding the objectivity of moral beliefs should not lead us to believe that some sort of self-limiting relativism follows.

If the assumptions of relativism seem misguided, so are the assumptions of absolutism (the claim that there are objective moral truths), for those very same factors that explain the authority of moral judgment independently of social norms make the authority of moral absolutes irrelevant as well. Both relativism and absolutism assume that there must be some fixed framework that carries with it special authority to which our judgments are logically related. The relativist argues the framework is society's norms or cultural constraints; the absolutist thinks it is the eternal truths of reason or God's laws. But logical frameworks are not necessary in cementing adherence to a moral point of view. The call of conscience is not an instrument of logic, law, habit, or convention, but emerges from deep within the caverns of the psyche where apparitions of the future and intimations of life's meaning conspire with the weight of human need to impel us to respond.

Moral absolutists demand a moral authority more imperious and peremptory than the contingent, psychological authority imposed by our fragile, fluctuating hopes and fears. If moral beliefs are to enjoy absolute allegiance, they must be supported by an authority that permits no contradiction or dissension—God's laws or the dictates of a rigorously logical system of moral principles. Only the certainty produced by having no alternatives will provide an adequate defense of our way of life for the moral absolutist. Unfortunately, paeans to certainty will never root out the idiosyncratic, continually fluctuating, personal point of view from our moral judgments. The constellation of motives and reasons, however dimly understood, that constitute our idiosyncratic perspectives, will always seem more compelling and authoritative than abstract worries about whether our judgments are written in stone. Moral judgments are traceable to the same sphere of intimacy that generates one's love of jazz or attachments to friends.

Moral judgments help us solve problems in living when we feel the gravity of human need pulling us apart. If, after due consideration of all the messy details, a particular judgment solves a problem better than its rivals can, it is justified. If it does not, it is not justified. The idea that for the judgment to do its work it requires additional certification by demonstrating its logical connection to a fixed and independent system of principles is an intellectual fantasy akin to the view that one can't enjoy a novel without a theory of how novels are to be enjoyed.

Properly formulated, then, "relativism," as it is mistakenly called, is the observation that up to now no one has been particularly successful in demonstrating objective, universal standards for moral judgments that are sensitive enough to real life to make a difference. It is not the self-refuting view that all judgments are equally suspect, nor is it the self-limiting view that judgments outside those of one's social group have no warrant.

Formulated in this way, the real issue is an empirical question. Given that human beings face a variety of similar problems that must be solved, are there universally accepted norms of conduct, embedded perhaps in cultural traditions, which our fragmented, negligent, complacent, and bewildered culture is failing to acknowledge at our peril? In other words, do the exigencies of the human condition itself produce the kind of moral responses in human beings that are best understood as moral absolutes? There are reasons to be skeptical of such a claim. Cultural anthropologists have made their living pointing out the strange and sometimes repugnant practices of people across the globe and throughout history. Should we wish to confine our examples to modernity, subcultures such as the Nazis, the mafia, or radical Islam would suffice as examples of people with strict codes of behavior utterly inimical to our own.

By itself, such diversity does not demonstrate the absence of a universal moral code, for it might be that amidst all this superficial diversity there are common principles at a deeper level that all successful communities accept. Any community to avoid implosion must have norms that provide security, preserve the truthfulness of communication, sustain care of the young, etc., and some individuals in any community must possess virtues such as courage, honesty, and kindness. Nazis and the mafia then would be examples of failed communities that failed precisely because they did not adhere to these fundamental principles.

But this is not a defense of a substantive and meaningful universal code that could lay claim to objectivity. Though all successful cultures might adhere to a few basic principles, these principles are so general and vacuous that they take a variety of mutually incompatible forms. For example, respect for women in traditional Islamic societies means something much different from respect for women in Western societies. Even within a culture, substantial agreement in principle does not produce agreement in practice.

Consider, for instance, the abortion issue in this country. Both sides agree on the basic principle that an individual human life is sacred. Yet, that agreement does not help us decide what is to count as an individual human life. General principles will severely underdetermine their interpretation because the exigencies of life will win out over the logical pressure exerted by principles. We fight over interpretations as readily as about principles and with no less intransigence. Furthermore, qualities of personal character are similarly underdetermined. What counts as courage for some is foolish peril for others; honesty in one culture is effrontery in another. There is little reason to think that if we look hard enough we will find that despite all our disagreements there are universal agreements lurking in the brush. The evidence suggests that human beings left to their own devices will generate radically different conceptions of what is meaningful and important. Moral absolutism thus is not only irrelevant, as an empirical matter, it is false.

At this point in the argument, the standard philosophical move is to argue that ethics is not about what people in fact do. It is about what we ought to do. The fact that we lack agreement on standards of conduct does not entail the absence of universal standards, for many people may simply be wrong in their moral perspective. The aim of moral reflection, on this view, is to discover the moral requirements that our nature, our reason, or God imposes on us—the ideals to which we often imperfectly conform. This philosophical task is both inspirational and insightful, but will succeed in providing the foundation for moral absolutes, only if philosophers agree on which principles are moral requirements. Unfortunately, the only people who disagree more vehemently than the public on moral standards are philosophers, and this after 2,500 years of the most rigorous analysis of this question.

Moreover, this inquiry into what actions we ought to perform is very peculiar. It usually takes the form of asking what an ideally rational human being would do under the circumstances if her interests and desires were suspended or viewed impartially. The outcome of this allegedly objective procedure is to provide the content of a universal moral code since it is shorn of the biases and prejudices that make our judgments parochial. But with this suggestion we are drifting toward Plato's spirit world once again, attempting to transcend our human condition. Moral judgment is meaningful only when it is accompanied by all our cares and attachments and the prejudices that inevitably come with them, for it is these cares and attachments that give rise to the moral problems we wish to solve. To suggest that someone struggling with a dilemma of fidelity or friendship adopt an impartial attitude toward her desires is to suggest she should somehow decide what to do if she didn't have the desires she has. This is a curious, indeed irrational gambit, for if she didn't have the particular desires she has, there would be no dilemma in the first place and no motive for deciding. Thus, as a conceptual inquiry into what it means to adopt a moral point of view, the philosophical search for an objective standpoint from which to generate unconditional moral principles is not very promising.

Our current cultural debate over values is often framed as a disagreement between those who prefer clear, unambiguous answers to moral questions, anchored in firm, unchanging moral principles, and those who think what is right just depends on where you were raised. I have been arguing that neither side of this debate can support its position, and thus they contribute little but noise to our attempts to live and act well. Perhaps the deeper issue is whether either of these unsupportable positions causes any real harm. Does it make any practical difference whether one is a relativist or an absolutist? As I noted above, the exigencies of life force relativists, against their inclinations, to make reasonably consistent moral judgments. Aside from a tendency toward misplaced tolerance, which though incurring the liabilities of naiveté nevertheless enjoys the benefits of trust, there are few consequences to being a relativist. Unfortunately, the search for moral absolutes is not so benign. In fact, moral absolutism is positively pernicious. Far from providing a moral anchor, the fruitless search for evaporating absolutes encourages the abdication of moral responsibility.

The baleful effects of this long search for absolutes underlie one of our most persistent popular moral attitudes—the idea that if an action is legal it is right. Recent accounting scandals attest to the ubiquity of the belief that the perfume of legal casuistry masks the stench of corruption. Yet, a legal code is an unwieldy instrument for dealing with moral questions. It is inefficient and insensitive at best, coercive and tyrannical at worst, and ceding moral authority to government officials is inimical to American ideals. Ironically, the search for universality and objectivity, with its unrealistic demands, encourages this transfer of moral liability, for it eviscerates the only moral resources available to individuals in our current situation.

Contemporary society places increasingly abstract moral demands on us, as we try to cope with the unfamiliar, the unexpected, and the unintended. We routinely interact with others whose lives seem opaque; we use technology that promises to utterly transform human existence in ways that even our most prescient prognosticators cannot foresee; and each of us occupies multiple, incompatible social roles with conflicting norms and expectations. There is seldom a straightforward answer to the question of what moral burdens an individual must accept. Yet, in these circumstances, the task of sustaining a moral point of view, nevertheless, falls by default squarely on the shoulders of individuals who must use their own critical judgment while bootstrapping moral feelings by cobbling together communities of interest or accident and sustaining relationships across time and distance.

It is not surprising, in this atmosphere of ambiguity and uncertainty, that many struggle unsuccessfully to hone their basic moral impulses. We acquire the capacity for compassion and the disposition toward honesty, loyalty, and justice in face-to-face meetings where issues of dependence and support have palpable consequences and emotional weight. Unfortunately, in the face of increasingly abstract demands, where consequences are less obvious and relationships less secure, our moral feelings become confused and attenuated—less compulsive, and ultimately less trustworthy. Though we look for moral authorities to replace these impulses, there are too many and they are in conflict. Only the law with its explicit sanctions and reasonably sure consequences provides guidance. Thus, we cede moral authority to the lawmakers and their lawyers.

Does our moral tradition with its insistence on moral absolutes and universal norms offer a solution to this diffusion of responsibility? The history of Western ideas has produced a variety of images and metaphors in terms of which we have been encouraged to think of ourselves: Plato's disembodied souls, Augustine's citizens of the City of God, Kant's legislators in a kingdom of ends, the rational choosers and welfare maximizers of modern liberalism, and agents of a distant utopia in Hegel and Marx. These disparate images have at least one demand in common. They demand that we see our moral selves as having severed our attachments to the people and things that make up the substance of ordinary life in favor of allegiance to monumental figures such as the kingdom of ends, the realm of the Forms, or the common good, all in the name of a commitment to objectivity.

There is little in this tradition to encourage individuals to accept the weight of responsibility, because as abstract agents who neither feel attachments that nurture moral feelings nor see themselves embedded in particular roles with normative content there is nothing of flesh and blood to command responsibility. Although this approach to ethics encourages us to see ourselves as bearing the weight of the world on our shoulders, it is a nebulous world populated by sprites and angels.

Given that we cannot realistically adopt the position of universal moral legislators, the demand that morality nevertheless be universal, absolute, and transparent encourages us to cede moral authority to those megalomaniacs who claim to have the God's eye view—experts, bureaucrats, religious leaders, and tyrants in whose decisions we simply acquiesce. Yet, the cacophony of authorities claiming hegemony ought to convince us that no seamless and consistent moral point of view or genuine foresight is possible in a world of such opacity.

Hence, the ambivalence our students, and much of the rest of culture, feel toward ethics. This ambivalence arises not from the lack of moral authority but from the presence of too many moral authorities and an unachievable, arid ideal of objectivity that cannot be met, which thus encourages the ceding of responsibility to any half-baked authority that promises stability. Contemporary citizens hesitate to judge, not because they lack civilizing contact with tradition or because they stupidly think all judgments are equivalent, but because our traditions don't help much in seeing through the fog of our present circumstances.

Plato's vision has sustained its power because this quest for universal, objective moral truths is responding to a fundamental human longing to have divisions healed and conflict settled through reason rather than force, offering the hope that sectarian differences are not absolute. Perhaps more fundamentally, it responds to our fears that without moral absolutes to which all humans are antecedently committed, the precious commodity of human freedom will produce chaos. But as understandable as this longing and this fear are, they are nevertheless symptoms of immaturity.

After centuries of horror, we should now know that what keeps us on the rails is neither regulations nor theories but simply the sense that others call upon us to respond. Moral conscience has never had to wait for the word magic of philosophers or social scientists—it arises unbidden and often incoherent. Yet, as imperfect as it is, moral conscience is all we have, though it is too dynamic and idiosyncratic to rest on moral absolutes, since it flourishes only in caves where spirits fear to tread.

Since Plato's attempt to upgrade our living quarters, 2,500 years of hard philosophical labor and oracular pronouncements by moralists have failed to produce the absolute truths that so many argue must exist if human beings are to flourish. This long history should convince us that this quest will not lead us out of our uncertain, anxious existence.

Most importantly, in the face of reason's limitations, we should resist the temptation to make common cause with the German philosopher Heidegger, who culminated his defense of German blood and soil with the remark "only a God can save us now." Ironically, the upshot of any attempt to ground moral absolutes in God is a malignant relativism in which moral disagreements are anchored in even less tractable doctrinal disputes regarding whose God and which interpretation of the word. The moral absolutist of both the secular and religious varieties provides us with one of humanity's most enduring and persistent images—the righteous zealot who spouts chapter and verse while bombing the infidel into bloody scraps. Redemption does not lie at the end of this road.

Our longing for absolutes encourages two metaphors that drive the contemporary debate over a moral crisis in Western Civilization. Some lament our fall from grace, imagining that we were made of firmer moral fiber in a mythological past. Others hope for the Promised Land, reveling in the healing power of an edited future in which antagonism has been censored to comfort the children. We should give up both of these metaphors because they prevent us from achieving the maturity that will help us muddle through. We may face a moral crisis, but not because we have fallen off the wagon or have failed to reach our destiny. For morality can never be anything but a crisis and the most rigorous of truths merely flickering shadows on the walls of a cave.

STUDY QUESTIONS

1. Why do some critics of contemporary society think that relativism has negative effects on society, according to Furrow?
2. On Furrow's view, why are most people unable to take seriously the view that all claims about what is morally right are equally valid? Do you agree? Explain.
3. Why is the view that the justification of moral judgments is relative to a person's cultural background troubling?
4. What reasons do we have for doubting that moral judgments are relative to a person's cultural background?
5. On Furrow's view, why is the choice between relativism and moral absolutism a false dilemma?
6. What does Furrow mean when he claims that the idiosyncratic, first person point of view cannot be eliminated from moral judgments? Do you agree? Explain.
7. Why does the fact that there are some moral principles that any successful culture must accept in order to survive fail to establish a meaningful account of the objectivity of moral truths, according to Furrow?
8. Briefly explain why Furrow thinks that moral absolutism is a part of the cause of our moral uncertainty.
9. Furrow argues that moral responsibility is not encouraged by moral absolutes or other moral authorities but by the demands that people with their vulnerabilities, hopes and fears place on us. Do you agree or disagree? Why?

INTERVENTIONS: AUTONOMY AND OBJECTIVITY

Moral relativism is the view that moral judgments are relative to cultures or social groups. Moral relativism, therefore, is incompatible with moral autonomy or moral freedom, which requires that our judgments cannot depend solely on the authority of any social group. In either of the versions of autonomy we are investigating here, an autonomous person must be capable of establishing some independence from his or her social context. This is especially true of autonomy understood as self-sufficiency.

But what about the idea of objective moral truth? Is that compatible with autonomy? As I noted in on p. 191, many philosophers have claimed that genuine autonomy is achievable only when objective moral requirements, arrived at through our own rational deliberations, guide our actions. Only then, it is argued, can we be free of emotions, desires, inclinations, and external authorities and achieve genuine self-control.

However, there are strong objections to this view. When we strive for objectivity, we strive to transcend our subjective points of view. An objective moral judgment is a judgment that is impartial because anyone can recognize its correctness independently of her point of view or circumstances. By contrast, an autonomous person is able to make her subjective point of view count in her life and establish a degree of independence from the beliefs and desires of others. Our subjective points of view are unique and particular to each of us, and the high value we place on autonomy is a recognition that this uniqueness and particularity ought to play a significant role in our thoughts and actions. The independence and freedom from interference that constitute the idea of autonomy express the fact that there are substantial and important differences between us. With respect to a particular judgment, to demand that we be impartial is to demand that our subjectivity not count in that instance—a renunciation of autonomy at least with regard to the judgment in question. Autonomy and objectivity seem to be pulling in opposing directions.

Of course, though each of us is unique, human beings share a nature and a condition as well. Can it not be argued that certain objective values arise out of the fact that we all face mortality and must cooperate in order to survive, find ways of raising children, consume the required number of calories, etc.? Since such basic goods are the object of desires that presumably all of us have, there is no necessary conflict between objective moral values based on such goods and autonomy.

The difficulty is in how we move logically from empirical claims about what human beings in fact need to normative claims about what our moral obligations are. The dominant view throughout the history of philosophy has been that we discover our moral obligations only by assessing our circumstances impartially. However, as I noted above, impartial judgments deny the importance of our subjective points of view, thus introducing conflicts with autonomy.

Philosopher Alasdair MacIntyre, in his influential book *After Virtue*, argued that the route to moral truth is not through impartial judgments but rather through a deep and thorough engagement with one's own moral tradition. Confrontations between many moral traditions, in the struggle to survive, will weed out inadequate rivals and ultimately produce moral truth. Christina Hoff Sommers, in chapter 17, seems to rely on such a view when she argues that contemporary students' lack of grounding in our moral traditions inhibits their capacity for judgment.

Such a view seems to fit well with the self-direction model of autonomy, which permits the conventions and practices of a tradition to have some degree of authority and influence. However, critics of this approach to morality argue that only a sustained and comprehensive critique of our tradition will free us from the racism, sexism, homophobia, and imperialism embedded in our tradition. According to critics of traditional beliefs, a way of life can become deeply bound up with prejudices and superstitions that undermine the ability of those who hold traditional beliefs to see their implications or assess them honestly, without self-deception. Only significant efforts to escape the confines of one's own tradition will suffice to make our judgments genuinely autonomous. On this view, traditions have no tendency to lead us toward moral truth.

The difficulty with this critique of tradition, however, is that it appears to reintroduce the idea of impartiality that I argued above is incompatible with autonomy. To escape the influence of traditions is to strive for a position that is not situated within human experience. I doubt that we can ever thoroughly escape the influence of traditions, and to attempt to do so is to discount significant elements of our personal point of view that autonomy protects. It is no wonder that angry debates between relativists and absolutists persist inconclusively. The idea of autonomy does not fit well with either relativism or the idea of objective moral truths.

Summation

The sections entitled "Interventions" have traced the arguments for and against two views on how we should conceptualize autonomy. We can see a pattern emerging from these discussions. Self-sufficiency attempts to disable a variety of external influences on our decision-making capacities. But this leaves us with little content to our identities and few strong attachments on which to build a conception of value that can guide our decisions. Self-direction seeks to leave our sources of value in place though insisting that we adopt a critical perspective on those sources of value in order to achieve autonomy. But this approach fails to recognize that those sources of value can inhibit our ability to rationally assess our situation. Furthermore, by focusing primarily on the psychological conditions of autonomy, self-direction pays too little attention to how social and political conditions inhibit autonomy.

Each approach articulates an important dimension of autonomy, but it appears impossible to unify them into a single theory. The difficulty is that autonomy refers to our capacity to live life from the inside. As such, it is the uniqueness and distinctiveness of our individual points of view that we value in ourselves and respect in others and that we want to protect from interference. However, our subjective points of view are fraught with entanglements that make up our subjectivities and constitute their value. Our individual points of view are what they are because of the external influences that shape us, thus making self-sufficiency implausible. The various avenues of escaping these entanglements threaten to sacrifice precisely what autonomy seeks to preserve. Yet, preserving these entanglements, as self-direction aspires to do, seems to interfere with the independence characteristic of autonomy.

Fortunately, we can overcome these difficulties. In the following part, I will suggest a potential solution.

VIII

RENEWALS

The preceding chapters provide competing diagnoses of our moral condition by focusing on specific issues of controversy. The aim of this part is to offer a more general, comprehensive vision of how our moral condition might be improved, and to resolve the questions regarding autonomy that arose in preceding parts. The question that ties these essays together is the question of what enables human beings, under current cultural conditions, to be moral agents.

19

Ecological Humanism: A Moral Image for Our Emotive Culture

Steven Fesmire

Steven Fesmire teaches philosophy at Green Mountain College in Vermont. He is the author of *John Dewey and the Moral Imagination: Pragmatism in Ethics* (2003). Fesmire argues that the root of social conflict and moral failure is a mistaken way of seeing our connection to the world. We see ourselves as isolated individuals who recognize that our self-interest requires that we cooperate and thus submit to moral rules or moral authorities as long as others agree to do the same. But this picture fails to acknowledge a deeper interconnectedness to the persons and things we live with and thus fails to sustain an understanding of why our social and natural ecology is important to our flourishing. Fesmire advocates that we adopt metaphors that more accurately reflect our interdependence and clarify why we must be more responsive to our surroundings.

In a December 1999 news broadcast, a man in his thirties was interviewed as he sifted through some of the thousands of "Dear Santa" letters that the Chicago post office receives annually.

Each year, he explained, he takes gifts to a few impoverished children who write letters. Asked about his motives, this obviously caring person replied, "Because it makes me feel good inside, so it's like a gift to myself."

Should we take his remarks at face value? Is he motivated exclusively, or even primarily, by a selfish thirst for pleasure? Perhaps he was responding not solely to his yearning for subjective delight but to a larger situation in which others' lives are interwoven with his own. In that case, our individualistic language doesn't provide him the means to tell the whole story.

From *The Humanist*, January 2001. Reprinted by permission.

We think and act as though we're separate from our surroundings, like sacks of skin or disembodied minds. The irony of this individualism is that it is a cultural phenomenon—one that takes an especially extreme form in the United States. We think we exist separately because we have been socialized to believe this. To be free in the United States is to be left alone, not imposed upon by external authority. There is a facile and perverse assumption that we can happily "go it alone" so long as we are free from restrictive political measures and free from demands placed on us by others' lives.

A friend of mine who taught English in Japan relates the opposite extreme. The first time she asked a student, "What do you think?" she expected the reply, "I think. . . ." It surprised her when the student turned to consult classmates and then reported their collective findings: "We think. . . ."

It's crucial to guard individual creativity from being thwarted by an over-organized social environment, like Star Trek's "Borg" collective. But it's equally pressing to construct new conceptions of individuality and freedom in touch with the complexity and interconnectedness of contemporary life. Consider that the world's human population was 1.7 billion in 1900. Today it is 6 billion. By 2050, the United Nations estimates it could skyrocket as high as 11.2 billion! Family planning aside, we urgently need greater cooperation. Genuine freedom lies neither in throwing off the yoke of social life nor in stoic resignation to it. Ironic as it may seem, we are most free when we welcome shared experience as something desirable and set ourselves to imaginatively tap its potential.

Our cultivation of obtuse egos has become appallingly destructive. John Dewey lamented over eighty years ago that such individualism leads to aloofness and indifference. It often makes an individual so insensitive in his relations to others as to develop an illusion of being really able to stand and act alone—an unnamed form of insanity which is responsible for a large part of the remediable suffering of the world.

There is, in John Steinbeck's words, "a failure here that topples all our success." It is a failure to cultivate habits of interworking, of coordinated development, of acting in concert.

OUR EMOTIVE CULTURE

When asked in an interview what inescapable question faces us in the twenty-first century, sociologist Robert Bellah replied:

> The most critical question is how can we give interdependence—which is so obvious in connection with everything we do—a moral meaning? . . . We don't like the fact that we depend on a lot of other people, or that what people do in other parts of the world can have effects on our lives.

One of the most interesting studies of individualism is *Habits of the Heart* by Bellah and his colleagues. The authors found that people in the United States tend to have little sense of the "whys" of conduct: why they live their lives as they do, make the choices they make, and hold a specific set of values to be worthwhile. For example, probed for a justification of his recent shift in priorities from career to family, one person replied, "I just find that I get more personal satisfaction from choosing course B over course A. It makes me feel better about myself."

Our extreme individualism bears much responsibility for this. Since our interrelations with each other (and with nature) are concealed, it's not surprising that we have a hard time making sense of moral commitments. Our "habits of the heart"—inherited ways of thinking about ourselves and our relationships—are out of harmony with the demands of associated life.

Similar insights led philosopher Alasdair MacIntyre to lament that we live in an "emotivist culture" where value judgments are boiled down to "nothing but expressions of preference, expressions of attitude or feeling." The long and short of this is that many of us carry an implicit assumption—betrayed in behaviors if not paraded in professed beliefs—that moral choices are fundamentally arbitrary and subjective. If so, moral outlooks are simply one person's opinion against another's. Most religious justifications are on no better footing, since they terminate in unexaminable faith commitments that make further discussion pointless in the face of competing advocacies.

MORAL IMAGES

There's a prevailing myth in the ethics industry that the only way to avoid this chaos is to identify a supreme moral principle. But the quest for an all-encompassing governing principle is misguided. Much philosophical ethics is as intellectualized as medieval scholasticism, criticized by Francis Bacon for its "cobwebs of learning." Like spiders spinning intricate webs from their own innards, ethicists spin out minutely detailed rules from within a system. Better to emulate a honey bee, says Bacon, turning to life experience for the raw materials of a more fruitful, transformative labor. The absence of respect for ordinary experience is a reason most share Henry David Thoreau's perception of philosophers as builders of conceptual castles that nowhere touch the Earth.

When we turn to life experiences, we discover that moral decision making at its best has little to do with ready-made rules singling out the right thing to do. Principles are helpful summaries of past moral experiments, but letting them dictate behavior saps our ability to respond intelligently to unique situations that cannot fit prefabricated rules. And all situations are unique: just as you can't put your foot in the same river twice, you can't apply a rule to the same situation twice. Deliberation is more a matter of imaginatively scoping out what would happen if we acted on this or that alternative. In other words, moral rules cannot substitute for moral imagination.

We need to get refocused on this sort of engaged intelligence, but extreme individualism (along with much that passes for ethical theory) hampers us. What's required is a better "moral image of the world," to borrow a phrase from philosopher Hilary Putnam. That is, we need a more apt and trustworthy metaphor—or, better yet, myriad complementary metaphors—for organizing our moral lives.

In this spirit, let me highlight some alternatives to individualistic moral images. Bear in mind there's no single "right" metaphor for the self/world relation. Still, as linguist George Lakoff and philosopher Mark Johnson point out: metaphors are more than rhetorical flourishes; different metaphors open up different possibilities and connections.

Perhaps what is called for is a sort of moral artistry, more analogous to an improvising musician than to a calculating accountant (Utilitarianism's preferred metaphor). At our moral best, we skillfully extemporize in response to each other with the aim of harmonizing interests. But coordinated impromptu thinking is difficult. Jazz pianist Bill Evans discusses the challenge of group improvisation on new material, saying of his collaboration with Miles Davis: "Aside from the weighty technical problem of collective coherent thinking, there is the very human, even social, need for sympathy from all members to bend for the common result." An improvisational musician takes up the part of others by catching a cadence from the group's signals while anticipating the group's response to her or his own signals.

This is creative intelligence at its best and most free. Just as improvising musicians cannot simply impose rhythms or tones on the rest of the group, in our moral behavior we must be richly responsive to each other. Jazz musician and poet Michael Harper sums it up nicely: "It's a matter of waiting for an opening rather than just rushing into what's happening." And in jazz, as in morality, the tradition of the art form structures group improvisation while being remade through innovation. As philosopher and classicist Martha Nussbaum says, the jazz player "should be more responsible than the score reader, and not less, to the unfolding continuities and structures of the work."

A complementary moral image can be drawn from the ecological sciences. Ecology (from the Greek *oiko*, meaning "household") is the study of our home in the broadest sense. An ecological or "ecosystemic" approach highlights that we function only as integral parts of larger natural, cultural, and interpersonal systems. Individual organisms—whether rainbow trout, spotted owl, or human—may initially appear to be self-sufficing, but study reveals they are situated in webs of interdependence. In a nutshell: the "moral" of this is that we must learn how to manage our household better.

ECOLOGICAL HUMANISM

Ecosystemic thinking is best accommodated and developed within the context of naturalistic humanism. Supernatural religions, in contrast, are poor resources for constructing socially responsible, experimentally plausible, and ecologically sensitive moral images. "Be in the world," Christianity commands, "not of it." Coupled with its theological apparatus, this offers a powerful moral image. An emotional balm for hundreds of millions, it has rallied flagging consciences back to the well of consecrated values. But it's a problematic image. To begin with, it is wrapped up with faith in a nonnatural spring for values, external to terrestrial life, and peculiarly revealed. Homage to this has diverted energy away from improving worldly life and channeled it into rationalization of priestly doctrines. Values pretending to be "not of this world" are quarantined from critical scrutiny and our moral imaginations are left to atrophy.

The Christian command also slights the fact that we are already in, of, and about the world. It conceives of us as items in containers (souls in bodies in a material world). Philosopher John McDermott observes: "Traditionally, we think of ourselves as 'in the world,' as a button is in a box, a marble in a hole, a coin in a pocket, a spoon in a drawer." The marble or coin may be in its container while of and about extraneous things. A coin is of and about economic transactions and isn't integrally related to the pocket containing it. The coin is "in the pocket but not of it."

Likewise, to be in the world but not of it means our lives are properly oriented toward a spiritual realm more weighty and real than mere Earthly happenings. Like the coin, in a Christian view, we ultimately have our being and value independent of where we temporarily happen to be sheltered. John Calvin took this to its logical extreme when he said, "If Heaven is our country, what is the Earth but a place of exile?" On the other hand, to say we are of and about the world implies there is no transcendent basis for the soul and substance of life. To err is human; to forgive, equally human. Our moral deliberations lose their efficacy if we ignore this.

McDermott contrasts the standard container metaphor with a richer image that complements those already discussed:

> Let us consider ourselves as being in a uterine situation, which binds us to nutrition in a distinctively organic way. . . . We are floating, gestating organisms, transacting with our environment, eating all the while. The crucial ingredient in all uterine situations is the nutritional quality of the environment. If our immediate surroundings are foul, soiled, polluted harbors of disease and grime, ridden with alien organisms, then we falter and perish.

Just as gestating organisms must be nourished to survive, a nurturing natural and social environment is required for human well-being. If substances are nutritious, a healthy transaction ensues—no universal mind or metaphysical monarch is required. In a virulent environment, it is as difficult to avoid starvation or poisoning (physical or moral) as it is for a crack baby to avoid her or his mother's toxins.

A mythical individual is contained by, but not organically unified with, the world. The person must concede that his or her body is connected with the environment. But underneath all that she or he is, the person believes there is a rational ego, mind, or soul—a nugget existing autonomously. Since other egos inevitably bump up against the person, he or she may make strategic sacrifices for a social contract securing both his or her person and property from intrusions. The person may also advocate rigid moral rules to govern humanity because of a supposition that humans are so insulated from each other that caring commitments aren't par-for-the-course. But identity isn't wrapped up with environment any more than a jelly bean is related to its jar.

Admittedly, self-in-inert-container metaphors don't necessarily preclude cooperation. For example, as "shipmates on the life raft Earth" it makes no sense to say when discovering a leak that "it's on your side." Still, this is compatible with self-interested egos which are obliged by their shared peril to cooperate. Beyond the peril, the passengers aren't connected to each other or to their raft any more than a coin to a pocket.

The gestation metaphor is richer. Since a self-aware gestating organism is unified with its environment, it would be incoherent for it to ignore that environment. Furthermore—to tweak the metaphor a bit—the organism is part of the environment in which others are gestating and therefore is depended on as well as dependent upon. The organism identifies itself with the welfare of its natural and social environments not because it makes it feel good inside or because a deity wills it but because, lacking this, interactions are noxious.

ON NATURE

There's no metaphysical caste system in which humans have a superior status. Human beings, consciousness and all, are out-croppings of nature. Benedict Spinoza wasn't too wide of the mark: we're simultaneously nature naturing and nature natured. Nature (from the Latin nasci, meaning "to be born") is more a womb in which we gestate than a divine creation to be subdued, more a home to be sustained than a resource to be exploited.

These insights need not lead us to yet another supreme moral principle, such as that of Aldo Leopold, who in *A Sand County Almanac* compellingly argued: "A thing is right when it tends to preserve the integrity, stability, and beauty of the biotic community. It is wrong when it tends otherwise." Nor do these simple insights finally resolve heated debates in environmental philosophy about whether "value" is human centered. But minimally we must re-examine the anti-ecological thinking reflected in many of our metaphors for nature, such as those noted by George Lakoff in *Moral Politics*: a resource for immediate consumption, a foe to be conquered, property to be owned and sold, or a wild animal to be tamed into submission.

Ecological humanism forgoes metaphysical faith leaps like James Love-lock's "Gaia hypothesis," which views nature as a superorganism to be revered. The doctrine that nature is (non-metaphorically) a living organism with an all-enveloping purpose is experimentally suspect. Still, Gaia theorists and other mystically inclined folks do share a pivotal insight with ecological humanism: nature isn't an alien and hostile adversary set over and against us.

"Man did not weave the web of life," runs a popular poem inspired by Chief Seattle. "He is merely a strand in it. Whatever he does to the web, he does to himself." Compare this to remarks by the chief engineer of an inter-state highway recently completed through the Appalachians: "Those moun-tains have stood in the way of progress for far too long!"

STUDY QUESTIONS

1. Fesmire suggests there is something missing from the postal worker's explanation for why he gives gifts at Christmas time to impoverished children. What is missing from the postal worker's explanation?
2. On Fesmire's view, why doesn't the postal worker have a vocabulary in which to express his motives? Do you agree?
3. Why is extreme individualism an inappropriate way of relating to the world, according to Fesmire. Do you agree? Explain.
4. Why, according to Fesmire, will a search for fundamental moral princi-ples fail to help us more appropriately relate to the world?
5. Fesmire suggests two metaphors to help us rethink our relationship to the world. Briefly explain how thinking in terms of these metaphors would revise human activities and practices.
6. Critically assess these metaphors. Can you think of ways in which these metaphors might be inappropriate in describing our relationship to the world?
7. Explain why Fesmire thinks supernatural religions such as Christianity fail to provide the appropriate conception of how human inter-relatedness.

20

American National Pride

Richard Rorty

Richard Rorty is Professor of Comparative Literature and Philosophy at Stanford University. He is the author of many books including *Philosophy and Social Hope* (1999), *Truth and Progress: Philosophical Papers, Vol. 3,* and *Achieving Our Country* (1998) from which the following excerpt is taken. Rorty views the ills of American society as primarily a product of the age-old human afflictions of greed and a penchant for cruelty. However, our inability to cope with greed and cruelty is exacerbated by social criticisms that fail to emphasize pride in American ideals or that express the need for a transcendental moral authority in which to anchor our hopes. Such criticisms lack practical import because they inhibit the social solidarity and social hope required to achieve justice and freedom.

National pride is to countries what self-respect is to individuals: a necessary condition for self-improvement. Too much national pride can produce bellicosity and imperialism, just as excessive self-respect can produce arrogance. But just as too little self-respect makes it difficult for a person to display moral courage, so insufficient national pride makes energetic and effective debate about national policy unlikely. Emotional involvement with one's country—feelings of intense shame or of glowing pride aroused by various parts of its history, and by various present-day national policies—is necessary if political deliberation is to be imaginative and productive. Such deliberation will probably not occur unless pride outweighs shame.

The need for this sort of involvement remains even for those who, like my-self, hope that the United States of America will someday yield up sover-eignty to what Alfred, Lord Tennyson called "the Parliament of Man, the Fed-eration of the World." For such a federation will never come into existence unless the governments of the individual nation-states cooperate in setting it up, and unless the citizens of those nation-states take a certain amount of pride (even rueful and hesitant pride) in their governments' efforts to do so.

Those who hope to persuade a nation to exert itself need to remind their country of what it can take pride in as well as what it should be ashamed of. They must tell inspiring stories abut episodes and figures in the nation's past—episodes and figures to which the country should remain true. Nations rely on artists and intellectuals to create images of, and to tell stories about, the national past. Competition for political leadership is in part a competition between differing stories about a nation's self-identity, and between differ-ing symbols of its greatness.

In America, at the end of the twentieth century, few inspiring images and stories are being proffered. The only version of national pride encouraged by American popular culture is a simpleminded militaristic chauvinism. But such chauvinism is overshadowed by a widespread sense that national pride is no longer appropriate. In both popular and elite culture, most descriptions of what America will be like in the twenty-first century are written in tones either of self-mockery or of self-disgust.

Consider two recent novels: Neal Stephenson's *Snow Crash*, a bestseller, and Leslie Marmon Silko's *Almanac of the Dead*, a critical triumph which was not as widely read. Both are powerful novels. Readers of either may well think it absurd for Americans to continue to take pride in their country.

Snow Crash tells of a twenty-first-century America in which the needs of the entrepreneurs have won out over hopes of a free and egalitarian society. The country has been divided into small franchised enclaves, within each of which a single corporation—IBM, the Mafia, GenTech—holds the rights of high and low justice. The U.S. government has gone into business for itself and is one more corporate entity, running its own little enclaves. But the gov-ernment is not even first among equals. There is no overall political entity, much less any sense of citizenship, that binds the eastern and western states together, or that links even the various districts of the big cities.

In *Snow Crash*, the relation of the United States to the rest of the world is symbolized by Stephenson's most frightening creation—what he calls the "Raft." This is an enormous agglomeration of floating hulks, drifting end-lessly round and round the Pacific Rim, inhabited by millions of Asians who hope to jump ship and swim to North America. The Raft is a sort of vast in-ternational slum ruled by cruel and anarchic criminal gangs; it is quite dif-ferent from the orderly franchises run by profitable business enterprises, re-specting each others' boundaries and rights, in what used to be the United

States of America. Pride in being an American citizen has been replaced by relief at being safer and better-fed than those on the Raft. Abraham Lincoln and Martin Luther King are no more present to the imagination of Stephenson's Americans than were Cromwell or Churchill to the imagination of the British whom Orwell described in his book *1984*.

Snow Crash capitalizes on the widespread belief that giant corporations, and a shadowy behind-the-scenes government acting as an agent for the corporations, now make all the important decisions. This belief finds expression in popular thrillers like Richard Condon's *Manchurian Candidate* and *Winter Kills*, as well as in more ambitious works like Thomas Pynchon's *Vineland* and Norman Mailer's *Harlot's Ghost*. The view that the visible government is just a false front is a plausible extrapolation from the fact that we are living in a Second Gilded Age: even Mark Twain might have been startled by the shamelessness with which our politicians now sell themselves.[1]

Novels like Stephenson's, Condon's, and Pynchon's are novels not of social protest but rather of rueful acquiescence in the end of American hopes. Silko's *Almanac of the Dead* also assumes that democratic government has become a farce, but her novel is dominated by self-disgust rather than self-mockery. Its focus is on the relation of European-Americans to Native Americans and to the descendants of the slaves brought from Africa. Silko's novel ends with a vision in which the descendants of the European conquerors and immigrants are forced back to Europe, thereby fulfilling Native American prophecies that the whites would be a temporary disaster, a plague that would last no more than five hundred years. Silko portrays the American government collapsing amid riots and food shortages, as the descendants of the Maya and the Aztecs stream into California, Arizona, and Texas.

One does not need to know whether Silko has read Foucault or Heidegger to see her novel as offering a vision of recent history similar to the one which readers of those two philosophers often acquire. In this vision, the two-hundred-year history of the United States—indeed, the history of the European and American peoples since the Enlightenment—has been pervaded by hypocrisy and self-deception. Readers of Foucault often come away believing that no shackles have been broken in the past two hundred years: the harsh old chains have merely been replaced with slightly more comfortable ones. Heidegger describes America's success in blanketing the world with modern technology as the spread of a wasteland. Those who find Foucault and Heidegger convincing often view the United States of America as Silko does: as something we must hope will be replaced, as soon as possible, by something utterly different.

Such people find pride in American citizenship impossible, and vigorous participation in electoral politics pointless. They associate American patriotism with an endorsement of atrocities: the importation of African slaves, the slaughter of Native Americans, the rape of ancient forests, and the Vietnam

War. Many of them think of national pride as appropriate only for chauvinists: for the sort of American who rejoices that America can still orchestrate something like the Gulf War, can still bring deadly force to bear whenever and wherever it chooses. When young intellectuals watch John Wayne war movies after reading Heidegger, Foucault, Stephenson, or Silko, they often become convinced that they live in a violent, inhuman, corrupt country. They begin to think of themselves as a saving remnant—as the happy few who have the insight to see through nationalist rhetoric to the ghastly reality of contemporary America. But this insight does not move them to formulate a legislative program, to join a political movement, or to share in a national hope.

The contrast between national hope and national self-mockery and self-disgust becomes vivid when one compares novels like *Snow Crash* and *Almanac of the Dead* with socialist novels of the first half of the century—books like *The Jungle*, *An American Tragedy*, and *The Grapes of Wrath*. The latter were written in the belief that the tone of the Gettysburg Address was absolutely right, but that our country would have to transform itself in order to fulfill Lincoln's hopes. Transformation would be needed because the rise of industrial capitalism had made the individualist rhetoric of America's first century obsolete.

The authors of these novels thought that this rhetoric should be replaced by one in which America is destined to become the first cooperative commonwealth, the first classless society. This America would be one in which income and wealth are equitably distributed, and in which the government ensures equality of opportunity as well as individual liberty. This new, quasi-communitarian rhetoric was at the heart of the Progressive Movement and the New Deal. It set the tone for the American Left during the first six decades of the twentieth century. Walt Whitman and John Dewey, as we shall see, did a great deal to shape this rhetoric.

The difference between early twentieth-century leftist intellectuals and the majority of their contemporary counterparts is the difference between agents and spectators. In the early decades of this century, when an intellectual stepped back from his or her country's history and looked at it through skeptical eyes, the chances were that he or she was about to propose a new political initiative. Henry Adams was, of course, the great exception—the great abstainer from politics. But William James thought that Adams's diagnosis of the First Gilded Age as a symptom of irreversible moral and political decline was merely perverse. James's pragmatist theory of truth was in part a reaction against the sort of detached spectatorship which Adams affected.

For James, disgust with American hypocrisy and self-deception was pointless unless accompanied by an effort to give America reason to be proud of itself in the future. The kind of proto-Heideggerian cultural pessimism which Adams cultivated seemed, to James, decadent and cowardly. "Democracy"

James wrote, "is a kind of religion, and we are bound not to admit its failure. Faiths and utopias are the noblest exercise of human reason, and no one with a spark of reason in him will sit down fatalistically before the croaker's picture."[2]

> In 1909, at the beginning of his book *The Promise of American Life*, Herbert Croly echoed James: The faith of Americans in their own country is religious, if not in its intensity, at any rate in its almost absolute and universal authority. . . . As children we hear it asserted or implied in the conversation of our elders. Every new stage of our educational training provides some additional testimony on its behalf. . . . We may distrust and dislike much that is done in the name of our country by our fellow-country-men; but our country itself, its democratic system, and its prosperous future are above suspicion.[3]

If anybody attributed this sort of civic religion to Americans today, it would be assumed that he was speaking only of the chauvinists—of the Americans who think of John Wayne rather than of Abraham Lincoln as our representative man, and of America as invincible rather than as kind. Novels like Silko's, Stephenson's, Mailer's, and Pynchon's are our equivalent of Adams's resigned pessimism.

It rarely occurs to present-day American leftists to quote either Lincoln or Whitman. It is no longer the case that, in Herbert Croly's words, "every new stage of our educational training provides some additional testimony" on behalf of Americans' faith in their country. On the contrary, a contemporary American student may well emerge from college less convinced that her country has a future than when she entered. She may also be less inclined to think that political initiatives can create such a future. The spirit of detached spectatorship, and the inability to think of American citizenship as an opportunity for action, may already have entered such a student's soul.

In this first lecture I shall try to describe the role of Whitman and Dewey in creating the image of America which was ubiquitous on the American Left prior to the Vietnam War. I say "image" rather than "myth" or "ideology" because I do not think that there is a nonmythological, nonideological way of telling a country's story. Calling a story "mythical" or "ideological" would be meaningful only if such stories could be contrasted with an "objective" story. But though objectivity is a useful goal when one is trying to calculate means to ends by predicting the consequences of action, it is of little relevance when one is trying to decide what sort of person or nation to be. Nobody knows what it would be like to try to be objective when attempting to decide what one's country really is, what its history really means, any more than when answering the question of who one really is oneself, what one's individual past really adds up to. We raise questions about our individual or national identity as part of the process of deciding what we will do next, what we will try to become.

As an example of such a process of decision, consider James Baldwin's book *The Fire Next Time*. Early in that book Baldwin says, "This is the crime of which I accuse my country and my countrymen, and for which neither I nor time nor history will ever forgive them, that they have destroyed and are destroying hundreds of thousands of lives and do not know it and do not want to know it."[4] This lack of forgiveness can easily take the form it does in the theology of the Nation of Islam—with whose prophet, Elijah Muhammad, Baldwin describes an encounter. The Black Muslims say that white people started out as homunculi created by a diabolical scientist. This hypothesis seems to them the best explanation for the inhuman cruelty of the slave auctions and the lynchings.

Those who accept Elijah Muhammad's story use it to convey the whole-hearted, gut-wrenching disgust for white America which is manifest in Silko's novel. But as Baldwin's narrative of self-creation unfolds, we watch him combining a continued unwillingness to forgive with a continuing identification with the country that brought over his ancestors in chains. "I am not," he writes, "a ward of America; I am one of the first Americans to arrive on these shores."[5]

In another passage Baldwin says, "In short, we, the black and the white, deeply need each other here if we are really to become a nation—if we are really, that is, to achieve our identity, our maturity, as men and women."[6] He ends his book with a sentence which has been quoted over and over again: "If we—and now I mean the relatively conscious whites and the relatively conscious blacks, who must, like lovers, insist on, or create, the consciousness of the others—do not falter in our duty now, we may be able, handful that we are, to end the racial nightmare, and achieve our country, and change the history of the world." The difference between Elijah Muhammad's decision about how to think of America and the one reached by Baldwin is the difference between deciding to be a spectator and to leave the fate of the United States to the operation of nonhuman forces, and deciding to be an agent.

I do not think there is any point in arguing that Elijah Muhammad made the right decision and Baldwin the wrong one, or vice versa. Neither forgave, but one turned away from the project of achieving the country and the other did not. Both decisions are intelligible. Either can be made plausible. But there are no neutral, objective criteria which dictate one rather than the other.

For the same reasons that I think there is no point in asking whether Baldwin made the right decision, I think there is no point in asking whether Lincoln or Whitman or Dewey got America right. Stories about what a nation has been and should try to be are not attempts at accurate representation, but rather attempts to forge a moral identity. The argument between Left and Right about which episodes in our history we Americans should pride ourselves on will never be a contest between a true and a false account of our country's history and its identity. It is better described as an argument about which hopes to allow ourselves and which to forgo.

As long as our country has a politically active Right and a politically active Left, this argument will continue. It is at the heart of the nation's political life, but the Left is responsible for keeping it going. For the Right never thinks that anything much needs to be changed: it thinks the country is basically in good shape, and may well have been in better shape in the past. It sees the Left's struggle for social justice as mere troublemaking, as utopian foolishness. The Left, by definition, is the party of hope. It insists that our nation remains unachieved. As the historian Nelson Lichtenstein has said, "All of America's great reform movements, from the crusade against slavery to the labor upsurge in the 1930's, defined themselves as champions of a moral and patriotic nationalism, which they counterposed to the parochial and selfish elites which stood athwart their vision of a virtuous society."[7]

Insofar as a Left becomes spectatorial and retrospective, it ceases to be a Left. I shall be claiming in these lectures that the American Left, once the old alliance between the intellectuals and the unions broke down in the course of the sixties, began to sink into an attitude like Henry Adams's. Leftists in the academy have permitted cultural politics to supplant real politics, and have collaborated with the Right in making cultural issues central to public debate. They are spending energy which should be directed at proposing new laws, on discussing topics as remote from the country's needs as were Adams's musings on the Virgin and the Dynamo. The academic Left has no projects to propose to America, no vision of a country to be achieved by building a consensus on the need for specific reforms. Its members no longer feel the force of James's and Croly's rhetoric. The American civic religion seems to them narrow-minded and obsolete nationalism.

Whitman and Dewey were among the prophets of this civic religion. They offered a new account of what America was, in the hope of mobilizing Americans as political agents. The most striking feature of their redescription of our country is its thoroughgoing secularism.[8] In the past, most of the stories that have incited nations to projects of self-improvement have been stories about their obligations to one or more gods. For much of European and American history, nations have asked themselves how they appear in the eyes of the Christian God. American exceptionalism has usually been a belief in special divine favor, as in the writings of Joseph Smith and Billy Graham. By contrast, Elijah Muhammad and Leslie Marmon Silko are examples of inverted exceptionalism: in their visions, white America will be the object of special divine wrath.

Dewey and Whitman wanted Americans to continue to think of themselves as exceptional, but both wanted to drop any reference to divine favor or wrath. They hoped to separate the fraternity and loving kindness urged by the Christian scriptures from the ideas of supernatural parentage, immortality, providence, and—most important—sin. They wanted Americans to take pride in what America might, all by itself and by its own lights, make of itself, rather than in America's obedience to any authority—even the authority of God. Thus Whitman wrote:

> And I call to mankind, Be not curious about God, For I who am curious about each am not curious about God.[9]

Whitman thought there was no need to be curious about God because there is no standard, not even a divine one, against which the decisions of a free people can be measured. Americans, he hoped, would spend the energy that past human societies had spent on discovering God's desires on discovering one another's desires. Americans will be curious about every other American, but not about anything which claims authority over America.

Kenneth Rexroth claims that Whitman invented the idea of "the realization of the American Dream as an apocalypse, an eschatological event which would give the life of man its ultimate significance." He goes on to say:

> Other religions have been founded on the promise of the Community of Love, the Abode of Peace, the Kingdom of God. Whitman identified with his own nationstate. We excuse such ideas only when they began 3,000 years ago in the Levantine desert. In our own time we suspect them of dangerous malevolence. Yet Whitman's vision exposes and explodes all the frauds that pass for the American Way of Life. It is the last and greatest vision of the American potential.[10]

Everything Rexroth says in this passage seems to me correct, except for the phrase "last and greatest." Whitman had successful imitators in his attempt to tie up the history of our nation-state with the meaning of human life. Perhaps because I am a philosophy professor, and have a special interest in philosophical restatements of moral ideals, I think that John Dewey was the most successful and most useful of these imitators.

Whitman explicitly said that he would "use the words America and democracy as convertible terms."[11] Dewey was less explicit, but when he uses "truly democratic" as a supreme honorific, he is obviously envisaging an achieved America. Both Dewey and Whitman viewed the United States as an opportunity to see ultimate significance in a finite, human, historical project, rather than in something eternal and nonhuman. They both hoped that America would be the place where a religion of love would finally replace a religion of fear. They dreamed that Americans would break the traditional link between the religious impulse, the impulse to stand in awe of something greater than oneself, and the infantile need for security, the childish hope of escaping from time and chance. They wanted to preserve the former and discard the latter. They wanted to put hope for a casteless and classless America in the place traditionally occupied by knowledge of the will of God. They wanted that utopian America to replace God as the unconditional object of desire. They wanted the struggle for social justice to be the country's animating principle, the nation's soul.

"Democracy," Dewey said, "is neither a form of government nor a social expediency, but a metaphysic of the relation of man and his experience in nature."[12] For both Whitman and Dewey, the terms "America" and "democracy" are shorthand for a new conception of what it is to be human—a conception which has no room for obedience to a nonhuman authority, and in which nothing save freely achieved consensus among human beings has any authority at all. Steven Rockefeller is right to say that "[Dewey's] goal was to integrate fully the religious life with the American democratic life."[13] But the sort of integration Dewey hoped for is not a matter of blending the worship of an eternal Being with hope for the temporal realization, in America, of this Being's will. It is a matter of forgetting about eternity. More generally, it is a matter of replacing shared knowledge of what is already real with social hope for what might become real. The word "democracy," Whitman said, "is a great word, whose history . . . remains unwritten, because that history has yet to be enacted."[14]

STUDY QUESTIONS

1. Why is national pride important, according to Rorty?
2. According to Rorty, why do critics of America think it is impossible to continue to take pride in America?
3. What is the difference between early twentieth century critics of America and contemporary critics? What sort of hopes did the earlier critics express?
4. How does Rorty's contrast between agent and spectator help to clarify the difference between early twentieth century critics and contemporary critics?
5. Why does Rorty claim that attempts to achieve an objective description of U.S. history or an objective account of national identity are futile?
6. What are debates about the moral significance of episodes in American history really about, according to Rorty?
7. What kinds of nationalism does Rorty oppose? Why does he oppose them?
8. Is Rorty critical enough of American society? Explain your view.
9. How is Rorty's call for national pride related to Fesmire's call for ecological humanism? Discuss similarities and differences.

NOTES

1. One particularly good example of such purchase is the Senate's vote for an ad hoc change in the law so as to hinder the Teamsters Union from organizing the Federal Express Company. See the debate on this matter initiated by Senator Edward Kennedy's speech (Congressional Record, October 1, 1996, pp. S12097ff.), especially Senator Paul Simon's remarks: "I think we have to honestly ask ourselves, why is Federal Express being given preferential treatment in this body now? I think the honest answer is Federal Express has been very generous in their campaign contributions" (p. S12106). After the Senate had voted in the company's favor, a spokesman for Federal Express was quoted as saying, "We played political hardball, and we won."

2. William James, "The Social Value of the College-Bred," in James, *Essays, Comments, and Reviews* (Cambridge, Mass.: Harvard University Press, 1987), p. 109.

3. Herbert Croly, *The Promise of American Life* (New York: Capricorn Books, 1964; orig. pub. 1909), p. 1.

4. James Baldwin, *The Fire Next Time* (New York: Dell, 1988; orig. pub. 1963), p. 5.

5. *The Fire Next Time*, p. 98.

6. *The Fire Next Time*, p. 97.

7. Nelson Lichtenstein, *The Most Dangerous Man in Detroit: Walter Reuther and the Fate of American Labor* (New York: Basic Books, 1994), p. 383.

8. I use "secularism" in the sense of "anticlericalism" rather than of "atheism." Dewey's dislike of "aggressive atheism" is made clear in *A Common Faith*. I have argued elsewhere that Dewey, like James, wanted pragmatism to be compatible with religious belief—but only with a privatized religious belief, not with the sort of religious belief that produces churches, especially churches which take political positions. See Rorty, "Religious Faith, Intellectual Responsibility, and Romance," in Ruth-Anna Putnam, ed., *The Cambridge Companion to William James* (Cambridge: Cambridge University Press, 1997); idem, "Pragmatism as Romantic Polytheism," in Morris Dickstein, ed., *The New Pragmatism* (Durham, N.C.: Duke University Press, 1998); idem, "Religion as Conversation-Stopper," *Common Knowledge* 3 (Spring 1994): 1–6. This last is a reply to Stephen Carter's argument that religious voices should be heard in the public square.

9. *Leaves of Grass*, p. 85. All references to both *Leaves of Grass* and *Democratic Vistas* are to Walt Whitman, *Complete Poetry and Selected Prose* (New York: Library of America, 1982).

10. Kenneth Rexroth, "Walt Whitman," *Saturday Review* 3 (September 1966), reprinted in Graham Clarke, ed., *Walt Whitman: Critical Assessments*, vol. 3 (New York: Routledge, 1994), p. 241.

11. Whitman, *Democratic Vistas*, p. 930.

12. John Dewey, "Maeterlinck's Philosophy of Life," in *The Middle Works of John Dewey*, vol. 6 (Carbondale: Southern Illinois University Press, 1978), p. 135. Dewey says that Emerson, Whitman, and Maeterlinck are the only three to have grasped this fact about democracy. Dewey's term "metaphysic" is a bit unfortunate. He might have expressed his meaning better by saying that, Nietzsche to the contrary, democracy is the principal means by which a more evolved form of humanity will come into existence. Kenneth Burke once wrote (*A Grammar of Motives*, p. 504) that "characters possess degrees of being in proportion to the variety of perspectives from which they

can with justice be perceived. Thus we could say that plants have 'less being' than animals, because each higher order admits and requires a new dimension of terms not literally relevant to the lower orders." Democratic humanity, Dewey and Burke might have agreed, has "more being" than predemocratic humanity. The citizens of a democratic, Whitmanesque society are able to create new, hitherto unimagined roles and goals for themselves. So a greater variety of perspectives, and of descriptive terms, becomes available to them, and can with justice be used to account for them.

13. Steven Rockefeller, *John Dewey: Religious Faith and Democratic Humanism* (New York: Columbia University Press, 1991), p. 4.

14. Whitman, *Democratic Vistas*, p. 960.

21

Society in the Postmodern Era

Albert Borgmann

Albert Borgmann is Regents Professor of Philosophy at the University of
Montana. His most recent book is *Holding on to Reality: The Nature of Information at the Turn of the Millennium* (1999). Borgmann argues that
modern technology, by eliminating many of the hardships that earlier generations had to confront, eliminates the resistance of reality that demanded
of human beings that they develop moral character and pursue moral excellence. However, despite the ease with which we live, reality still maintains a splendor that, in the postmodern world, we must make an extra effort to realize if morality is to be meaningful. Survival no longer demands
that we test our physical, mental, and communal skills, but reality still offers the resistance to test our mettle if we have the will to do so.

Why did we like the Marlboro Man in spite of ourselves? He had character.
He wore the imprint of his world and his work on his face and clothing. He
was tanned not because he'd been to a tanning salon but because he'd endured the sun of the plains and the high country. His face was heavily
lined. He squinted, not from staring at a computer screen too long, worry-
ing over derivatives, but because he moved in the cloudless outdoors of
the prairie. He wore faded jeans, not at Tommy Hilfiger's dictate but because jeans were the toughest pants around and they showed the wear and
tear of his riding and roping. He wore a sheepskin jacket, not because it
was cool but because it was bitter cold in January and his neighbor ran
sheep and sold their skins. He wore a slicker, not because it made him look

Albert Borgmann, "Society in the Postmodern Era," *The Washington Quarterly* 23:1 (Winter,
2000), pp. 189–200, by the Center for Strategic and International Studies (CSIS) and the Massa-
chusetts Institute of Technology.

tall and imposing but because it was the only way to keep reasonably dry on a horse in a rainstorm. And at Christmas time, the Marlboro Man didn't go to the corner lot for a manicured Scotch pine at $10 a foot. No, he rode into the hills behind the home place, looked for a young, handsome Douglas fir, cut it, roped it to his saddle horn, and slowly dragged it home in the failing winter light.

What so impressed us about the Marlboro Man was not the mere fact that his world was inscribed on his appearance. That is true of the homeless as well. It was the kind of reality that impressed us as it left its imprint on him— the vastness of the plains, the ruggedness of the mountains, the violence of the weather, the orneriness of cattle, and the grace of his horse. Our affection for the Marlboro Man was troubled, however, by doubts. It was hard to ignore the ubiquitous cigarette or to separate the rancher's wholesomeness from his addiction, hard to forget that his purpose was to get us (or keep us) addicted too. It was hard seeing that Marlboro country was actually a cemetery. And it was disconcerting to learn that those rugged clothes were available to all from the mail-order Marlboro store whose address was given on the very advertisement. Most unsettling, perhaps, were the rumors that many a Marlboro man was an actor who didn't know a cinch from a stirrup.

The corruption of the best is worst, the Romans said. At the heart of what we would like to believe is genuine and wholesome we find fakery and exploitation. We might think that the world of ranching is still out there and can be captured in its purity and vigor by writers, photographers, or documentary filmmakers, and to be sure, such recordings and celebrations can be done. But melancholy shadows such accounts, and closer reflection reveals that the reality that underlies ranching life is brittle, fractured, and falling apart.

The economic base of ranching is thin and crumbling. The price of beef and a reasonable return on labor and investments are beyond the diligence and prudence of ranchers. Prices are determined by faraway forces such as beef production in South America and Australia, exchange rates, the welfare of Asian economies, and the preferences of consumers.

Beyond ranching, other industries we have considered basic, in which men wrest resources from nature—mining, logging, agriculture—are losing their fundamental status as well. Raw materials are being eclipsed in the knowledge economy, and sophisticated machineries and methods now come between humans and reality. These methods lessen and obviate direct engagement with reality. Along with cowboys and ranchers, the miners and loggers of old are being replaced by operators of powerful and intricate machines.

On Montana's ranches, the entering wedge of these developments is the personal computer. About half of the ranchers (often the women) use computers regularly for financial and cattle production records, and they are significantly more satisfied with their performance of these chores than their paper-and-pencil neighbors.[1] Still, there is skepticism about the spreading of cyberspace under the big sky. "The first four ranchers that I know of that started using computers," said one rancher, "all went broke within five years."[2] But when tax accountants, breeders' associations, suppliers, and county agents all computerize, ranches cannot afford to remain islands of traditional information. Some ranchers look forward to cyberherding. "When scanners can read top [identification of cattle]," said one, "and use a scale under a working chute, then we will gather the info. Data gathering needs to be automated."[3] This meek request will quickly be met by the agricultural information industry. Information technology is eager to deliver "precision agriculture," where everything under the sun will be measured, monitored, and controlled. As in business generally, whether increased productivity will justify the investment in computers is an open question though not one the individual ranchers are at liberty to answer. In any event, what is likely to get lost in the equation is the symmetry of rugged reality and human competence reflected in this observation: "My husband knows his cattle personally by working with them and has a memory for traits, problems, and style. His father had that trait and . . . our son seems to have it also."[4]

A similar loss is taking place in the wilderness of Montana. Smoke Elser, Missoula's revered outfitter, knows the Bob Marshall Wilderness as well as anyone and can tell his clients any time just where they are on their trip. But he has been shown up, at least in ease and accuracy, by a know-nothing dude carrying a global-positioning system (GPS) receiver that tells him within fifty or so feet where he is. The device can also track his progress, tell him how far he has traveled from the trailhead, and how long it will take to reach camp. And if he likes the trip, he can store all this information and re-trace his steps exactly a few years hence, stopping at all of Smoke's favorite campsites and fishing spots. In time, ranchers will be replaced by agricultural technicians and outfitters by recreation specialists.

These changes are merely the local manifestation of a global phenomenon. Information technology is rendering the entire earth ever more transparent and controllable. Remote sensing by way of satellites is delivering immense streams of data not only about the topographical particulars of every acre on earth but also about the weather, the vegetation, the soils, water, and more. All of this is being computerized and integrated with demographic and economic data through geographical information systems.

Control will always lag behind transparency. We know more than we can manipulate. But knowledge is the basis of control and allows us to adapt or avoid what we cannot subdue. In any case, there is something like an irreversible lightness to postmodern reality. The world has lost much of its darkness and heaviness. It is as though the laws of gravity and density have been, if not abrogated, at least loosened and softened.

We can see the charms and perils of lightness in the fate of the Montana ranches. The original homesteads in Montana were places where men and women removed a quarter section, as Locke would have it, "out of that state that nature hath provided and left it in," and mixed their labor with it and made it theirs.[5] The hardness of reality was overwhelming then, and old-timers will show you many a log cabin where someone in the dead of winter committed suicide. Those who survived began to expand and prosper and became the rugged and quietly self-confident individuals who have a legitimate claim on our admiration.

One lawful relation, however, has not been affected by these epochal upheavals. It is the symmetry between reality and humanity, the one that seemed so grandly instantiated by the Marlboro Man: a majestic world reflected in a remarkable man. How then does the postmodern lightness of being affect postmodern people? In a liberating way, it seems at first. Lesser density allows us to unfold more fully, lesser gravity to move more expansively. But there is the real danger that at length the growth will come to bloat and mobility to aimlessness.

Postmodern affluence, however, comes to people who produce information or entertainment rather than cattle or wheat, people who cast desirous glances at ranches ringed by rocky mountains and snowy peaks. They can acquire and own those ranches without mixing their sweat with the soil. Nor are they tied to the daily chores that get you up at five and won't let you get away for a vacation. Postmodern ranches have lost their gravity. They have become trophies and toys, and the country around them has been reduced to distant wallpaper. Often they are abandoned as quickly as they were acquired, leaving no trace on their transient owners.

The lightness of being is in many ways a blessing we should be grateful for. It has greatly diminished the threat of a nuclear holocaust and the specter of an environmental cataclysm. It has given us an economy that is improbably vigorous and stable. There are of course perils that lurk in the recesses of ignorance and unpredictability. More important, there are people in this country and entire peoples around the globe who are excluded from the blessings of the moment. Our insensitivity to their plight, however, may be a consequence of the very favors most of us in this country enjoy.

Peace and prosperity seem to exercise an enervating force on our moral tone. Adversity energizes. People on the left used to draw moral vigor from their opposition to nuclear arms and environmental exploitation. People on the right gained strength from their fight against the evil empire of communism. Without those enemies, our ethical vigor seems to atrophy. No hardship, no character—that appears to be our predicament.

For illustration, consider the plight of 18-year-olds who were required to give an account of themselves for admission to prestigious universities. As the *New York Times* sympathetically put it: "In her desperation, 17-year-old

Jane Doe found herself wishing that somebody—anybody—in her family had died. 'Because then I could write about it,' she said. 'It's horrible and I hated myself for it. But I just wished I had something tragic happen to me.'"[6]

It makes one long for the ancient pain of sticks and stones, and some have been privileged to feel it, for instance, John Smith, a white Newton North senior who grew up in Africa and "actually did have a big thing happen."

> I wrote about racism toward myself. When I was about 11 or so, a group of kids threw stones at me, and that stuck in my head. That was just a big, big experience for me, and I guess I'm really lucky to have that because I know kids that are writing about, like, concerts they went to and stuff like that.[7]

On a larger scale, rigor has drained from everyday life and left novelists little to write about. Sven Birkerts traces this vacuity to a fundamental transformation of reality.

> Fifty years ago the human environment was still more or less the natural environment. We had central heating and labor-saving devices and high-speed travel, but these were still only partial modifications of the natural given. It is the natural given that is now gone. Now, for better or for worse, we move almost entirely within a regulated and mediated environment. Our primary relation to the world has been altered.[8]

Birkerts then treats us to a sketch of a day in the life "of the average American business man" and asks how does one give this sort of life "a meaningful, never mind dramatic, contour?"[9]

We are beginning to miss the hungry years. But obviously it would be childish and irresponsible willfully to bring about starvation, deprivation, or war to tone up our society's moral fiber. What is needed, one might think, are new horizons and new challenges. Since the frontiers of the material world have been closed, many have looked to the immaterial realm of cyberspace as the brave new world in which to define and affirm ourselves. Certainly, claims that have been made inspire hope that a new proving ground for human excellence has been found.

John Perry Barlow, cofounder of the Electronic Freedom Foundation, has said that the advent of cyberspace is "the most transforming technological event since the capture of fire," and Louis Rossetto, cofounder of the magazine *Wired*, has called it "a revolution that makes political revolution seem like a game."[10]

In reality, the pervasiveness of change is more subtle and difficult to discern. Imagine Rip van Winkle had gone to sleep thirty-five years ago and awoke just now. The world would look much the same to him as it did in the late fifties and early sixties, though further developed along lines visible at the time. All of our characteristic structures and devices were then already in place—automobiles, high-rises, jet airplanes, interstate highways, shopping malls, televisions, stereo sets, microwave ovens. Under the surface of their appearance and use, these devices are of course quite different today. Computers have insinuated themselves in the machineries of our utilities and appliances. Invisibly they monitor and regulate our thermostats, cars, financial instruments, insurance policies, and in fact every technological object and arrangement of any complexity.

The one appliance that would be unfamiliar to Rip van Winkle is the computer, a television screen cum keyboard as it would look to him. With great advances in user-friendliness, the functions of a computer are now more easily explained than they would have been twenty years ago. To a lay person, its evidently novel function is communication, and the distinctive instantiation of communication is e-mail, instantaneous typing at a distance, as Rip might call it. Computers have transformed telephony too, and the near-term goal of that transformation will be reached when everyone carries a light and slender cell phone and can easily call anyone anywhere from any place at any time.

Most astounding perhaps is the ease and scope of information retrieval that cyberspace has made possible. If one should come across the Latin version of the proverb I quoted earlier, *corruptio optimi pessima*, and wonder whether one has guessed its genre and meaning correctly, a query on, say, Alta Vista will produce thirty-six hits, most of them occurrences of the phrase in some text. One, however, lists it under the heading of *"Proverbi Latini"* and furnishes an Italian translation. If you do not read Italian, you can have a machine translation into English: "That that was optimal, once corrupt, is *pessimo.*"[11]

These instances of how computers have invaded our lives, though far from exhaustive, represent something of the effect cyberspace has had on identity and character. That effect is a strange coincidence of control and withdrawal. *Prima facie*, computers have extended and strengthened our grasp of reality. We seem more firmly in control of our means and ends. We can drive more safely and effortlessly, we can reach people more easily, and we can call up information about the world more quickly.

Yet considered more closely, computers distance us from our world. When they control fuel injection in the engine, we lose touch with the notion that internal combustion requires a mixture of fuel and air, a fact our mechanics used to remind us of when they had to clean or rebuild the carburetor. When computers control the speed the vehicle is cruising at, we no longer need attend to the grade of the road and the force of the wind.

As for our relations to other people, having them call us at any time, regardless of what we are doing, can be annoying. Hence for a while we will shunt all the incoming calls to our voice mail so that we can respond (or not) when it is convenient. Or we will have the calls identified by number or name so we can decide whom to talk to and whom to ignore. E-mail, of course, is the means of communication that provides both ease and control. In a democracy, however, control is usually a two-way affair. The control you assume over others' access to you is reflected in your loss of access to them. As you take control of people, you must yield control over yourself. Through this increasing mutual control, we can create greater distance from one another.

Information constitutes the singular concern and triumph of the computer. In fact we speak as often of the information revolution and information age as we refer to computers to characterize our era. Hence one should expect that when it comes to information, computers, with their links and peripherals, have truly opened a new world for us to explore, a world in which we can nourish and unfold ourselves. In one sense this is particularly so. Computers have made the retrieval of information easier and quicker by orders of magnitude. Where identifying the genre and meaning of an unknown phrase would have taken an hour before the era of computers, it takes only a minute in cyberspace.

Though information is much more readily at hand in cyberspace, the social, physical, and conceptual architecture of information gets lost from view. At the time when our Rip fell asleep—in the early 1960s, say—determining the origin and meaning of *corruptio optimi pessima* would have taken you out of your office. You would have encountered your students and colleagues—indeed, sky and tree and the rhythm of your own stride—on your walk to the library. You would have encountered the reference librarian. If she were unable to translate the phrase she might have guessed that it was a Latin saying, discoverable either in a thesaurus of Latin or in a book of quotations. The thesaurus being forbidding both in language and in size, you would have tried the books of quotations first, shelved elsewhere in the reference library. There, confronted by roughly a dozen collections of saws and quotations, you would have found different principles of organization, varying degrees of inclusiveness, some misses, and a hit or two. Among the hits there may have been sayings of different analogies and like intent. In short, the information, when finally obtained, would have had its place in the social organization of the campus, in the physical arrangement of reference works, and in some conceptual scheme of collection and selection.

When you retrieve information in cyberspace using a search engine, most of these contextual structures are submerged. The computer conjures up the item in question and a few dozen more or less related ones from a vast ocean of information. The item rises to the surface as from nowhere and, unless tied down by a bookmark, disappears again without being traceable in real space and often, therefore, without leaving much of a trace in your mind either.

Computer technology has come between people and reality, between one person and another, and between human beings and the architecture of information and knowledge. It has established an invisible zone of distance and disposability between us and our world. In allowing this zone to arise and by helping to establish it, we are deprived. We have deprived ourselves of the real resistance a person needs to acquire character.

Although this condition generally inspires disengagement and disorientation, it has also inspired a number of hyperactive and highly focused people. The pleasures of comfort and control are too insubstantial to engage their ambition. It is, rather, the undergirding structure of comfort and control that provokes their ingenuity and industry. They are the elite who understand and improve the machineries of research and development, of industry and commerce, of finance and law, of medicine and education. The people engaged in these endeavors truly constitute a vanguard. They are bright, ambitious, and highly educated. They work long hours and are well remunerated. Most important to our discussion, they meet and overcome severe challenges. The underlying machinery of the technological society is the zone where the comfort of consumption connects with the recalcitrance of reality, and where ease and safety are wrested from resistance and risks.

Does this struggle with reality leave an imprint on the warriors? Does it confer character? On some it surely does. They get old and severe before their time. More generally, we recognize something like an ideal type of the elite person, however infrequently it may be fully realized. Such a person is sure of himself or herself without being vain, listens well but does not waste time, shows politeness without flattery, is forthright but does not disclose more than is required, and absorbs abuse without holding grudges. In short, women and men of this cast have something of Aristotle's high-minded man about them.[12]

Yet a contradiction haunts the efforts and triumphs that lend the elite character. The endeavors that challenge and provoke their greatness result in challenges eradicated and greatness leveled. To bring digital, high-definition television to a technically satisfactory solution requires great ingenuity and perseverance. But as soon as success is at hand, ingenuity of construction will yield to banality of consumption. The greatness of the elite devours the greatness of the masses.

But should one insist on greatness? It has, after all, honorable alternatives. Decency is one, and by and large ours is certainly a country of decent people. Is it not blue-nosed to demand more? The question at the least reveals that the forum of social and moral criticism has changed fundamentally of late or, more precisely, has come to the conclusion of a radical, even though gradual, transformation. The era of clarion calls is over because so are the causes that used to warrant ringing appeals—civil rights, gender equity, nuclear disarmament, anticommunism, environmental protection. Of course, none of these challenges has been fully met. But their legitimacy is widely granted and their urgency has been blunted. Attempts to rally the troops once more under the banner of these causes now strike us as shrill and politically all too correct.

If there is to be a vital moral conversation any longer, it must proceed in the realm of what philosophers call supererogatory norms, standards that go beyond what is required as a matter of law and decency. There is of course a well-established school of liberal democratic theory that holds that the state and society have no business taking sides on questions of moral perfection and should restrict their concern to advancing the means rather than the ends of the good society. Conservative theorists have keenly felt the need for virtues that surpass the moral minimalism of the liberals, but their arguments often converge at a deeper level with liberalism. Civic virtues are frequently defended as the glue that holds society together; virtues turn out to be but one of the means of a basically open-ended society.

The reply to the liberals is that state and society are inevitably involved in shaping and constraining the moral choices individuals make. To the conservatives one must say that moral perfection is not a means but an end, and more important, an end that today is implicated in a new constellation of moral and material conditions.

These are involved and contentious issues. They come into relief, however, in the typical evening of U.S. citizens. At around ten, he and she rise from the couch, having spent two or three hours snacking and watching television. They have done this during their leisure time, the period that is entirely theirs to do with as they please. Is it a sin or crime, what they have just done? No, but on reflection, they feel empty and dissatisfied. Life is slipping by. They have nothing to show for the last two or three hours. They vaguely realize that mentally they have become more slack and physically they have become more shapeless. They are losing definition of mind and body.[13]

Whenever social scientists inquire into the ways Americans shape their leisure, television is the looming phenomenon, and a vague uneasiness looms above the television culture. The moral misery today is no longer focused sharply on this commission and that omission. It surfaces in the vague apprehension that we are wasting our time and in time our lives, that we have become unfaithful to things out there, to people, and to our best talents. We watch on television what and where we would like to be, outside somewhere, bravely and skillfully facing real challenges, but we never get around to doing and being what we watch. Thus the moral concern that the typical human condition inspires today is not outrage or indignation but the sort of searing regret one feels when something beautiful is being defaced by neglect.

The moral life under premodern conditions was simpler though no easier. Presumably people found it as difficult as they now find it to be good. But then the call to goodness rose more clearly from the tangible circumstances of life. At a time when the family was the economic fundament of life, the basic welfare of children could not be assured outside of, or prior to, the establishment of a family. And since reliable contraception and safe abortions were not to be had, the reasons for sexual discipline were palpable. When leaving one's spouse meant grave economic jeopardy for the remaining spouse and children and servitude the only route to survival for the depart-ing spouse, marital fidelity was strongly advised by material circumstances. At a time of scarce food and expensive liquor, lack of moderation in eating was the cause of someone else's starvation and intemperance of drinking meant abject poverty. Nor did it require courageous resolve to confront re-ality out there, to keep in touch with the neighbors, or to exercise one's body. Walking was then the primary means of traveling, not to work with one's hands was the privilege of nobility, and interaction with one's neigh-bors was the very fabric of survival.[14]

Much of premodern morality was the response to tangible demands, and the primary question was not whether but how well one would meet those demands. Today technological devices have disburdened and distanced us from the material exigencies of chastity, fidelity, temperance, courage, charity, and vigor. The reasons of those virtues being remote, we no longer see them but only hear their faint voices. On those occasions, however, when someone prevails on us to answer those voices, the presence and power of those virtues is restored to us. When someone begs us to turn off the television and go to a concert or for a walk in the park, the real pres-ence of others, of music, of lawns and trees floods us with grace and re-stores our vigor. And similarly, when we submit to the discipline of fasting, or at least to abstinence between meals, the life-sustaining force of food comes home to us.

There has been an inversion of the material and moral forces of things. In premodern times, the material presence and force of things issued in moral demands. In the postmodern era, the moral demands of things call us back to the material splendor of reality. It is then mere semblance to see post-modern reality as soft, yielding, and elusive, and it is a mistake to think that, there being no resistance, the normal postmodern condition is to be without character or that masks must take the place of faces.

The postmodern world has a hardness that can restore character to our minds and definition to our bodies. It is a hardness that first meets us as the duress of heeding the call of people and things and of having to cross the threshold of comfort and withdrawal. Hyperactive overachievers, by the way, have to cross the same threshold although from a different angle. For them, the duress lies in letting go of the adrenaline rush, of the blandishments of competition and control, and of the seductions of unambiguous goals and successes. The reality of nature, urbanity, athletics, art, or religion seems as boring to the hyperactive as it seems forbidding to the sullen. In any case, once the threshold of duress is crossed, the hardness of postmodern reality engages us as the firmness of those things that claim and test the fullness of our bodily, spiritual, and communal skills.

But why do we so regularly fail to answer those claims? Broadly put, it is the implicitness and individualism of our moral lives. The official discourse in this society about the ways we order our fundamental material and social relations carefully and inevitably stops short of the ultimate and actual ways we inhabit those relations. We have much to say about Sam Walton and Wal-Mart, but we rarely discuss just how all of the stuff Wal-Mart sells ends up in our homes and informs the moral complexion of our households.

In practice, of course, we must somehow answer these questions. But the answers remain implicit and hence unexamined. We assume, moreover, that however the answers are arrived at, they spring from our individual decisions as consumers. This assumption overlooks the fact that it was not the individual consumer who invented television, refrigeration, automobiles, suburbs, the separation of work and home, etc. These devices and arrangements have been put in place cooperatively and so as to imply a default decision for the evening of a weekday—enter the house, turn on the TV, open the refrigerator.

To regain character and definition, we need to put the final enactment of daily life on the public agenda. We must collectively and cooperatively make sure that interaction with one another and the common devotion to the great things of the city and of the country are the normal response to the way we have laid out our world. Having become more thoughtful of mind and more vigorous of demeanor, we will be able to say goodbye to the Marlboro Man.

STUDY QUESTIONS

1. The eclipse of the Marlboro Man as icon and the importance of new technologies in industries such as farming, ranching, and mining indicate a phenomenon which Borgmann refers to as the "lightness of postmodern reality." What does Borgmann mean by this?
2. How does the "lightness of postmodern reality" affect the possibility of building moral character?
3. How have computers affected our relationship to reality, according to Borgmann?
4. What aspects of reality are lost from view when we make use of the easy accessibility of information through computers?
5. Borgmann is claiming that strong moral character as traditionally defined is no longer necessary as a means of survival. Is he correct? Explain.
6. What reasons do we still have to seek moral perfection, according to Borgmann?
7. Why does Borgmann think it is difficult for people in contemporary society to rediscover the importance of moral improvement? Do you agree? Why?

NOTES

1. Lee Tangedahl and Jackie Manley, "Computer Cowboys," Montana Business Quarterly 34 (Autumn 1996): 11–12.

2. "Computer Cowboys," 14.

3. "Computer Cowboys," 14

4. "Computer Cowboys," 13.

5. John Locke, *Treatise on Civil Government and a Letter Concerning Toleration*, Charles L. Sherman, ed. (New York: Appleton-Century-Crofts, 1965), 19.

6. Carey Goldberg, "Admissions Essay Ordeal: The Young Life Examined," *New York Times*, December 31, 1997, p. A1.

7. "Admissions Essay Ordeal"

8. Sven Birkerts, *The Gutenberg Elegies* (New York: Fawcett, 1994), 205–6.

9. *The Gutenberg Elegies*

10. John Perry Barlow's remark in "What Are We Doing On-Line?" *Harper's*, August 1995, p. 36; D. T. Max, "The End of the Book?" *Atlantic*, September 1994, p. 62, quoting Louis Rossetto.

11. Available at info2.ing.univaq.it/ordine/auleinf/filippo/latino.htm on August 3, 1998.

12. Aristotle, *Nicomachean Ethics*, book 4, chapter 3.

13. Robert Kubey and Mihaly Csikszentmihalyi, *Television and the Quality of Life* (Hillsdale, N.J.: Erlbaum, 1990); John P. Robinson and Geoffrey Godbye, *Time for Life* (University Park: Pennsylvania State University Press, 1997).

14. Peter Laslett, *The World We Have Lost*, 3rd ed. (New York: Scribner, 1984).

INTERVENTIONS: HOW TO RECONCILE MORAL FREEDOM AND MORAL RESPONSIVENESS

Throughout much of this book, I have focused on a central problem with accounts of autonomy. How can agents preserve autonomy while remaining embedded in socialization processes, and deeply committed to traditions and relationships they do not choose, cannot fully control, and from which they can seldom fully escape? Many philosophers have argued that the solution to the dilemmas of autonomy is to construe autonomy and moral freedom relationally. The relational approach to autonomy views persons as social beings who develop the capacity for autonomy through social interaction. Relationships enable autonomy in two ways. First, relationships with parents, teachers, friends, and others enable us to acquire the ability to act independently as we develop into adults, and help us to sustain autonomy throughout our lives. Second, the social contexts in which we live constitute our self-conceptions as autonomous persons. How we see ourselves is as much a product of feedback from others as it is a self-generated perception. This is especially the case given that the words and concepts we use to describe ourselves, the significance of our goals and projects, our very habits and inclinations are thoroughly penetrated by social understandings. We understand our characteristics, goals, and inclinations, in part, as others in our society or culture view them.

However, there is a third and deeper sense in which relationships enable autonomy. We have viewed autonomy as the capacity to live life from the inside. Each of us has a unique, subjective point of view, and autonomy is valuable because we want our decisions and actions to express this point of view. However, our subjective points of view are fraught with involvements with people (as well as things, practices, activities, etc.) in terms of which we value our subjectivity. Our personal points of view are filled with and guided by what we care about, and the value of that personal point of view is dependent in part on the things in our world that provoke our caring responses. People and things that we care about are not merely external objects but are also elements of our subjective experience. Without attachments to people, activities, and things we care about, there is no subjectivity to preserve. Autonomy has value only to the extent autonomous choices are directed toward something of value. We value autonomy because it protects this capacity to connect with things of value.

However, this inherent relatedness of autonomy to the things we care about cannot be all there is to autonomy, since our caring can be the product of coercion, manipulation, or other factors outside our control. In addition, autonomy requires that our relationships reflect the distinct point of view that each of us brings to experience. My subjective experience consists of beliefs, values, patterns of cognition, and emotions, etc., situated within a point of view that is shared by no one. Each of my experiences attaches to a unique spatial and temporal location and each is situated within a flow of further experiences that are uniquely my own. Acts of choosing flow from this background of unique experience and, when something is valued, it is valued because of how it fits within my particular narrative. Although acts of choosing do not have value independent of what is chosen, to the extent they reflect our distinct points of view our acts of choosing add value to what is chosen.

For our purposes, it is useful to think of subjective experience as made up of two dimensions. One dimension is my relatedness to something other than me—the fact that my acts of conferring value have an object. The second dimension is the distinctive, particular way I relate to the object of experience. We suffer a loss of meaning when either dimension is compromised. For instance, when a person is humiliated because of her ethnicity she suffers a loss of meaning—that which she deeply cares about is diminished. However, when a person's ethnic identity imposes norms on her that inhibit her ability to express her sense of uniqueness and particularity through her choices, she suffers an equally egregious loss. In other words, I may value something deeply but be unable to intelligibly situate that valued thing within my life. In such a case I suffer a loss of autonomy that can be regained only by finding ways of engaging more productively with that which I value. To reject that which I value is to deepen the loss. To lead life from the inside is to lead a life that protects both dimensions of one's subjectivity—the value things have and the particular way we value them.

We are now in a position to see how this relational view of autonomy helps resolve the inadequacies of self-sufficiency and self-direction. Self-sufficiency advocates an independent form of life in which we must be prepared to sacrifice much of what we care about in order to preserve autonomy. This conception of autonomy protects the distinctiveness of one's point of view, but does not preserve the richness of value that makes up that point of view. In diminishing the goods available to us, self-sufficiency makes our lives less than what they can be.

By contrast, self-direction builds a conception of autonomy that is compatible with a form of life that is dependent on traditions or relationships of obligation as long as we maintain a critical perspective on these attachments. However, this view does not build in sufficient critical resources to guarantee autonomy, given that sources of value can often inhibit our ability to be critical. This view preserves the richness of what we care about but fails to protect the distinctiveness and particularity of our points of view. The problem with traditions, conventional ways of doing things, habits of thought and emotions that become entrenched in our psychologies, and moral authorities that go unchallenged is that their prescriptions may be routinized, stereotypical responses that fail to conform to our distinctive points of view and the complexities of situations in which we must make decisions.

An adequate account of self-direction would involve the capacity to find within the constellation of things we care about our own way of caring—one that is sensitive to both the quality of what we care about and the uniqueness of our own mode of caring. The achievement of autonomy, then, involves cultivating increasingly perceptive and imaginative modes of relatedness with others. This is the sense of renewal that Fesmire, Rorty, and Borgmann (as well as West with his ethic of love in chapter 4) articulate in very different ways.

This view of autonomy as requiring both relatedness and particularity is suggested in Borgmann's critique of what he calls the "implicitness and individualism" of postmodern life. In a world where modern conveniences obscure the hardships and dependencies that build character, character survives by greater attentiveness to the quality of our interactions with things and people.

I am not suggesting that we should discard independence as one of the conditions that enables autonomy. We gain control over our lives by dislodging beliefs or extinguishing desires and attachments with which we can no longer identify. I am suggesting that such independence can be achieved only through more imaginative, engaged attention to our unique, distinctive modes of caring. Such engagement is not easily achieved. Rejecting old ways of thinking and adopting new ones is not like changing clothes before going out to dinner. It takes a great deal of experience to understand the difference between responsible intervention and meddling, between tough love and abandonment, between thoughtful acquiescence and submission. Having the skill to navigate the entanglements that can enable or disable self-direction requires knowing all their twists and turns, points of weakness and strength, and most importantly, the areas of elasticity and adaptability that enable us to preserve relationships while transforming them in ways that enhance self-direction. Disengagement from adverse situations may ultimately be appropriate, but we seldom gain autonomy by leaping out of our attachments without further engagement that yields a deeper understanding of the nuances of our circumstances. To adapt one of Fesmire's organic metaphors, genuine independence is more like finding a niche than it is like discovering new lands.

Furthermore, as Rorty emphasizes in his criticism of a spectator's view of politics, our critical capacities function well only when they aim at something that matters so much that we are willing to act to bring it about. Thus, the aim of living life from the inside is not directly or primarily independence or criticism, but engagement with what matters.

Moral Standards and Moral Freedom

Self-direction, when properly understood, is compatible with the ideal of moral freedom, because self-direction does not subvert our individual capacity for judgment or replace it with a moral authority. Our individual conceptions of what is worth caring about drive our judgments. Yet, the contours of our situation and the demands of others constrain and influence our deliberation since, as I argued above, these constitute the very terms in which we understand our personal points of view. Fesmire's metaphors of organic attachment nicely capture the sense in which self-direction requires fine attunement to the particulars of one's situation without the presence of a moral authority. Even when we seek control over our individual lives, from within the standpoint of our individuated personal points of view, we must sustain the connections that nurture that subjectivity in a way that promotes mutual flourishing.

A similar theme is implicit in Rorty's chapter "American National Pride." Rorty argues that despite the fact that individuals may feel alienated from despicable episodes in America's past and present, opting out of political engagement or attempting to criticize our tradition from a point of view outside liberal democratic institutions is fruitless and ineffectual. Disenchantment with America must rest on some insight or other, and it is likely that, for Americans, those insights as well as the disenchantment are enabled by the liberal, democratic tradition of thought being criticized. For those of us socialized in that tradition, escape from it seems unlikely and undesirable. The wholesale rejection of liberal, democratic ideals is an attempt at a radical form of moral freedom that fails to acknowledge the importance of social solidarity.

As Rorty argues, a better approach would be to acknowledge our dependence on the ideals of justice and freedom expressed in that tradition and the fellow citizens who admire them, and engage in practical attempts to reshape institutions to better conform to those ideals.

Advocates of the view that we face a moral crisis often argue that moral commitments and values have become matters of individual choice—moral freedom has become our moral philosophy. Consequently, there are no standards for what we should choose except what each of us desires, nothing to encourage us to lose our harmful desires, nothing on which to build moral character. The foregoing discussions suggest a response to this criticism.

From the claim that individuals are the ultimate authority in judging what counts as right, wrong, good, or bad it does not follow that there are no constraints on that judgment. In fact, if we pay close attention to the constraints on our actions, a robust picture of morality emerges. Our engagements with people and things impose moral demands on us that we must honor if we are to sustain those engagements. Of course, we can fail to comply with these demands, but in doing so we are weakening the very relationships that constitute our subjectivity. Or we can fail to take an interest in our lives and thereby succumb to a kind of pathology requiring therapy rather than philosophy. But in neither case would we be pursuing moral freedom.

The point of moral freedom is to enable that which we value to conform to our distinctive points of view. Thus, agents who take an interest in their moral freedom cannot do so without engaging more fully and firmly, with perceptiveness and imagination, the circumstances of their lives. One cannot engage fully in family life without acquiring the ability to trust and be trusted, to give and receive affection, and to meet standards of loyalty. One cannot engage fully in business without instilling trust in one's customers and suppliers, caring and being curious about their needs, and acting to strengthen the community on which one depends. To be a teacher one requires a level of concern for students, a grasp of their individual needs but also a sense of fairness toward all, patience, and enthusiasm for one's subject. To be a member of a community is to be aware of the complex interrelatedness of its elements, its particular needs, how it supports one's activities, and the ways in which one's activities can contribute. Traditions, moral exemplars, social institutions, and relationships of obligation sustain these activities and enable us to learn what we need to know in order to participate successfully.

However, if we are to sustain moral freedom, it remains up to each individual to determine whether she can weave these prescriptions into the particular narrative that is each individual's point of view. If when accepting the demands that others place on us, we are able to find in these demands the expression of our distinctive way of caring, we are expressing the content of our personal point of view, living life from the inside. There is something like moral authority here in that others make demands on us that compel us to respond, but only with our active complicity and encouragement. This is moral freedom, though not the kind of moral freedom that understands itself as self-sufficiency. It is the kind of freedom through which we shape our lives as we see fit, in full recognition that our vision of fitness is inherently relational.

Throughout the comments on autonomy in this text, I have been building an account of what it means to be self-directed. This account included the awareness and endorsement of beliefs and desires and the process through which we acquire them, a critical evaluation of the coherence between our desires and deepest values, and the capacity to imagine alternative selves. In this chapter, I am suggesting that autonomy depends upon the presence of deep and abiding relationships, and respect for the particularities of our connections to people and things.

It should be apparent that many desires we have are likely to be incompatible with these conditions and should be discarded. Moral freedom is not the freedom to act on any desire we happen to have. Some desires will distract us from engaging more fully with that which is most important to us. Others will be the product of self-deception that prevents us from knowing our genuine interests. Lack of attention to one's distinctive point of view or lack of discipline in holding on to what we care about can lead us astray. The concept of moral freedom, when understood in its complexity, deepens rather than inhibits our moral response because it is directed toward deeper engagement with the circumstances of life. Genuine moral freedom is incompatible with thoughtless obedience, mindless conformity, fixed ideas, and tired traditions that are no longer responsive to modern life. If there is a moral crisis it is a crisis caused by the distractions of modern life, many of which are seductive and rightly so, but must be placed in the appropriate relation to what one most cares about if they are to be of genuine value.

However, moral freedom is not without its drawbacks. I have been insisting that accounts of morality that are compatible with autonomy as a basic value must take both our relatedness to others and our personal point of view seriously. But problems of accounting for social justice persist. If I look at matters from my personal point of view, even when that personal point of view is constituted by what I most deeply care about, in what sense must I care about those with whom I am only distantly related, on whom I do not depend, whose lives in the ordinary course of events seldom reach the level of recognition? The problem of social justice raised by Thomas Pogge in his essay, "The Demands of Global Justice," may be the most persistent crisis for the new century. For if Alan Wolfe is right that moral freedom has become the moral philosophy of Americans, we may lack the conceptual resources to respond to this demand.

Suggestions for Further Reading

READINGS ON THE ISSUE OF A MORAL CRISIS

Bennett, William. *The Death of Outrage: Bill Clinton and the Assault on American Ideals*. New York: Free Press. 1998.

Bloome, Alan. *The Closing of the American Mind: How Higher Education Has Failed Democracy and Impoverished the Soul of Today's Students*. New York: Simon & Schuster, 1987.

D' Souza, Dinesh. *The Virtues of Prosperity: Finding Values in an Age of Techno-Affluence*. New York: Free Press, 2000.

Etzioni, Amatai. *The New Golden Rule: Community and Morality in a Democratic Society*, New York: Basic Books, 1996.

Fevre, R.W. *The Demoralization of Western Culture: Social Theory and the Dilemmas of Modern Living*, New York: Continuum, 2000.

Himmelfarb, Gertrude. *One Nation, Two Cultures: A Searching Examination of American Society in the Aftermath of Our Cultural Revolution*. New York: Vintage Press, 2001.

Putnam, Robert. *Bowling Alone: The Collapse and Revival of American Community*. New York: Simon & Schuster, 2000.

Turiel, Elliot. *The Culture of Morality: Social Development, Context, and Conflict*, Cambridge, England: Cambridge University Press, 2002.

Wolfe, Alan. *Moral Freedom: The Search for Virtue in a World of Choice*. New York W.W. Norton & Company, 2001.

PHILOSOPHICAL READINGS ON AUTONOMY

Christman, John, "Liberalism, Autonomy, and Self-Transformation," in *Social Theory and Practice*, April 2001.

Dworkin, Gerald. *The Theory and Practice of Autonomy*, Cambridge, England: Cambridge University Press, 1988.

Frankfurt, Harry, "Freedom of the Will and the Concept of a Person," in *Journal of Philosophy* 68, January 1971.

Haworth, Lawrence. *Autonomy: An Essay in Philosophical Psychology and Ethics*. New Haven: Yale University, 1986.

Kymlicka, Will. *Liberalism, Community, and Culture*. Oxford: Clarendon Press, 1989.

Meyers, Diana Tietjens, "Intersectional Identity and the Authentic Self?: Opposites Attract!" in *Relational Autonomy: Feminist Perspectives on Autonomy, Agency, and the Social Self*, ed. Catriona Mackenzie and Natalie Stoljar. New York: Oxford University Press, 2000.

Mackenzie, Catriona, and Natalie Stoljar, eds. *Relational Autonomy: Feminist Perspectives on Autonomy, Agency, and the Social Self*. New York: Oxford University Press, 2000.

Wolff, Robert Paul. *The Autonomy of Reason*. New York: Harper & Row, 1973.

Index

African Americans: and racial
discrimination, 51–58; and threat of
nihilism, 51–58
Aristotle, 27, 156, 157, 158, 160, 168,
232, 280, 284
atheism, 171, 186, 187, 188, 189, 270
Augustine, Saint, 244
Austen, Jane, 232
autonomy, xvi–xxiv, 251, 285–91; and
capitalism, 1, 5, 8, 16, 26, 31, 47–48,
174; and civil rights, 123; definitions
of, xvii, xix–xxii, 24, 26, 35, 47, 48,
94, 107, 130–34, 174, 191, 193,
221–24, 247, 248, 249, 285–90; and
equality, 49–50, 65, 80–81, 88, 94;
and family structure, 100, 107, 108,
110, 112, 17, 122, 129, 131–33; and
future generations, 137, 142, 143,
166; and genetic self-knowledge, 141;
government constraints on, 31; and
government interference, 65; limits
of, 21, 24, 151, 160, 290; in
marginalized groups, 51, 53, 57;
moral, 191 (see also moral freedom);
and moral obligations, 94, 248, 287,
289; and objectivity, 191, 247–49; and
personal and social identity, 221–24;
and personal identity, 47–48, 221–24;

political, xvii; as precondition of
morality, 26, 27; and property rights,
59; as relational, 174, 285–91; and
religious belief, 188, 191–93; and
technology, 155, 173–74, 273–83; as a
universal value, 222. See also self-
sufficiency; self-direction; tradition

Bacon, Francis, 156, 159, 160, 168, 169,
170, 171, 172, 255
Baldwin, James, 266, 270
Barlow, John Perry, 277, 284
Baudrillard, Jean, 44
Bell, Daniel, 7
Bellah, Robert, 104, 254, 255
Bennett, William, 177
Berlin, Isaiah, 150
Bible, 227, 232
biotechnology, 135–71
Birkerts, Sven, 277, 284
Bosworth, David, 3
Bourdieu, Pierre, 44
Buddhism, 189
Burke, Edmund, 27
Bush, Geoge W., 189, 201, 206

Calder, Lendol, 41
Calvin, John, 16, 17, 39, 178, 257